THE NETHERLANDS AND THE GOLD STANDARD, 1931-1936

NEHA-SERIES III

1. P.M.M. Klep e.a. (red.), Wonen in het verleden 17e-20e eeuw; economie, politiek, volkshuisvesting, cultuur en bibliografie. Amsterdam 1987. ISBN 90-71617-02-5
2. R.T. Griffiths (ed.), The Netherlands and the gold standard 1931-1936; a study in policy formation and policy. Amsterdam 1987. ISBN 90-71617-04-1

International distributors:
Kluwer Academic Publishers

United States of America and Canada
101 Philip Drive, Assini PPC Park, Norwell, MA 02061, USA

UK and Ireland
Falcon House, Queen Square, Lancaster.,la1 1rn, UK

All other countries except for sales within the Netherlands
P.O. Box 322, 3300 AH Dordrecht, The Netherlands

Sales within the Netherlands
NEHA, Herengracht 218-220, 1016 BT Amsterdam

CIP-GEGEVENS KONINKLIJKE BIBLIOTHEEK, DEN HAAG

Netherlands

The Netherlands and the gold standard 1931-1936 : a study in policy formation and policy / ed. by R.T. Griffiths. - Amsterdam : Nederlandsch Economisch-Historisch Archief. - Ill. - (NEHA-series III van het Nederlandsch Economisch-Historisch Archief ; 2)
Met bibliogr.
ISBN-13: 978-90-71617-04-1 **e-ISBN-13: 978-94-009-4067-3**
DOI: 10.1007/978-94-009-4067-3
SISO 345.1 UDC 336.743(492)"1931/1936"
Trefw.: geldwezen ; Nederland ; geschiedenis ; 1931-1936.

THE NETHERLANDS AND THE GOLD STANDARD, 1931-1936

A Study in policy formation and policy

Editor

Richard T. Griffiths

AMSTERDAM
NEHA
1987

Preface

On 26 September 1936, deep in the night, the Dutch cabinet took the decision to cut the guilder's link with gold and to devalue its currency. It was the last of the increasingly isolated and beleaguered 'gold bloc' countries to do so, having outlasted Switzerland by less than a day; the last country in Europe in which holders of a currency could exchange it for gold at the rate which had prevailed before the First World War; the last country to leave the gold standard. The reason why the 'Gold Bloc', which in September 1936 comprised only France, Switzerland and the Netherlands, should have hung on so long is something of a puzzle to historians since it has become virtually axiomatic that their recoveries would have begun sooner and proceeded more strongly had they cut the link with gold and devalued their currencies much earlier. The fact that the decision not to do so has been seen as perverse, combined with the fact that in order to cope with the consequences of that decision governments chose to adopt deflationary policies to 'correct' the economy, has led historians for a long time to dismiss a whole generation of politicians and their 'advisors' as stubborn, conservative and short-sighted. The Keynesian revolution and the long post-war economic boom had consigned them and their ilk to the dustbin of history for ever.

Fifty years after the devaluation of the guilder it appears that that judgement may well have been a little precipitous. Now, just as then, politicians and economists were unprepared and overwhelmed by the speed of events which overtook them. Now, just as then, they were confronted with a faltering economy, soaring unemployment and yawning budget deficits. Now, just as then, there was a belief that the maladjustment of the economy could be corrected by paying due attention to fiscal and monetary variables and the 'real' economy would somehow respond by itself. In the five years between 1981 and 1986 governments have struggled to reduce the size of the budget deficit, civil service salaries and social security benefits have been cut in both nominal and real terms, informal pressure has been directed at reducing private sector pay settlements to make the economy more competetive and a strong currency has been seen as a valuable asset in achieving policy goals. Not, it was argued, that they had much choice on this last point: the guilder was tied into the European Monetary System and natural gas revenues helped generate balance of payments surpluses which made currency depreciation an impossible policy option.

Those self same policies, that self same rationalisation were the hall-marks of the years 1931-1936 with which this book is concerned. Who are we to condemn that generation as 'conservative'? Admittedly there are large differences between then and now. But then, at least, people had alternatives – alternatives in a Keynesian work-creation policy, alternatives in a restructuring of responsibility for running the economy at the level of business, alternatives in the form of exchange role manipulation. Where, amid today's numbing concensus, are today's alternatives? Compare the two, which is the more conservative in economic terms? Today's policies seem to have worked, you answer? Well, in 1936 too, the Dutch cabinet could console itself that the dawn was in sight. In 1936 too, the international recovery was beginning to pull the Dutch economy in its wake and would continue to do so until the down-turn in 1937. But right in the middle of that recovery the guilder was devalued, the recovery intensified (nationally and internationally) and, in historical terms, the fate of the reputation of the 'untarnished guilder' policy was sealed. A historical lesson to be drawn from this? Perhaps one – internationally induced booms and slumps can play havoc with a politician's place in history.

With hindsight it is possible to argue that an earlier abandonment of the gold standard would have been beneficial for the Dutch economy but that is not the central question with which this book is concerned. What it does try to answer is whether the decision not to devalue was, if not justifyable, at least understandable. When we set up the research project early in 1984, we worked from the premise that governments make and change decisions as a result of external information and external pressure, It was logical, therefore, that the study should embrace the internal policy-making process of the government itself as well as that of the political parties, since it was there, ultimately, that political responsibility rested. However, the political parties themselves could be expected to respond, in part at least, to the interests of their support groups and so we extended the research backwards, so to speak, to include the national organisations representing employers, farmers and workers. In each case we attempted to answer the following questions:

- was a standpoint arrived at and, if so, what was it?
- if a standpoint was arrived at, how was it translated into pressure?
- if no standpoint was arrived at, why not?

Difficulties in access to historical sources and gaps in the sources themselves meant that the analysis was not always as deep as might have been desired, but it will hopefully not spoil the book to reveal that one of the reasons why the government did not bend to pressure to devalue the guilder was that, from the side of the established national interest groups at least, there was no such pressure. This makes all the more interesting the role of the single-issue pressure groups specially set up around the devaluation issue – one for, one against. Finally, we decided to round off the study with a brief examination of developments in the other 'gold bloc' countries – Belgium, France and Switzerland.

Was the decision not to devalue earlier understandable? That question we leave for the reader to decide. The devaluation debate has raged within the corridors of the *Vrije Universiteit* for well over a year, leaving us probably as deeply divided as it did the original protagonists. Certainly the issue is more complex than it is often portrayed, involving not only theoretical arguments and statistical debate, but conflicting economic interests and different group perceptions of their own roles within the body politic. Indeed, in the course of our research we came to learn almost as much about Dutch organised society in the 1930's as we did about the gold standard question itself.

No book of this kind can be written without the help and cooperation of the staff of the archives and libraries used in the course of the research. On behalf of the authors I would like to express my gratitude to them for their efforts on our behalf. We are also indebted to A.F. Bronsing, D.A.Delprat and Professor S. Postuma for sharing their recollections in the form of interviews. A word of thanks is also due to the students at the Free University and the University of Leiden who contributed to seminar courses centred on these problems. Successive versions of the text were typed by Miss Judith Ellington on the somewhat archaic word-processor we managed to hire for the purpose.

There have been too many people who have helped us to be able to mention them all by name but an exception must be made in one case. I would like to express my gratitude to Professor Johan de Vries for sharing his information with me and for the sympathy and support he has shown this venture from its inception. The final publication of this book was made possible by the generosity of the Stichting Fonds voor de Geld- en Effectenhandel, de Staal-Stichting en het Unger van Brerofonds.

VRIJE UNIVERSITEIT, AMSTERDAM, 1986 RTG

Contents

List of Tables

List of Figures

Abbreviations

ABTB	Algemeene Boeren- en Tuindersbond General Farmers' Association
ARKWV	Algemeene Roomsch-Katholieke Werkgevers Vereeniging General Roman Catholic Employers' Association
ARP	Anti-Revolutionaire Partij Anti Revolutionary Party
CBTB	Christelijke Boeren- en Tuindersbond Protestant Farmers' Association
CDU	Christelijk Democratische Unie Christian Democratic Union
CHU	Christelijk-Historische Unie Christian Historical Union
CNV	Christelijk Nationaal Vakverbond Christian National Trade Union
CWV	Christelijke Werkgeversvereeniging Christian Employers' Association
KNBTB	Katholieke Nederlandsche Boeren- en Tuindersbond Catholic Dutch Farmers' Association
KNLC	Koninklijk Nederlandsch Landbouw Comité Royal Dutch Agricultural Committee
LSP	Liberale Staats Partij Liberal State Party
NAS	Nationaal Arbeids Secretariaat National Workers' Secretariat
NMHN	Nederlandsche Maatschappij voor Nijverheid en Handel Dutch Society for Industry and Trade
NSB	Nationaal-Socialistische Beweging National Socialist Movement
NVC	Nederlandsch Vakbond Comité Dutch Trade Union Committee
NVWG	Nederlandsche Vereeniging voor Waardevast Geld Dutch Association for Value Stable Money
RKSP	Rooms-Katholieke Staats Partij Roman Catholic State Party

RKVWV	Roomsch-Katholiek Verbond van Werkgeversvereenigingen Roman Catholic Union of Employers' Associations
RKWV	Rooms-Katholiek Werklieden Verbond Roman Catholic Workers' Union
SDAP	Sociaal-Democratische Arbeiders Partij Social Democratic Labour Party
SGP	Staatkundig Gereformeerde Partij Reformed Political Party
VDB	Vrijzinnig Democratische Bond Free-Democratic Union
VNW	Verbond van Nederlandsche Werkgevers Union of Dutch Employers

CHAPTER ONE

Economy and Politics

The object of this chapter is briefly to sketch the economic and political background to the events described in the rest of the book. It is intended to be neither exhaustive nor particularly innovatory and, for those students of the period, parts of it may be superfluous.

What this chapter sets out to do is to trace some of the main features of the Great Depression and to describe the response of Dutch governments to these events. This will be followed by a short account of the viewpoints opposing various aspects of Dutch policy, dealing in somewhat more detail with the implications of the 'devaluation option'. This last section could easily be skipped by those with a background in economics. It then goes on to give a basic outline of the concept of 'Pillarisation', a social structure peculiar to the Dutch and some comprehension of which will help to explain the reactions to the devaluation question. Finally, the chapter ends with a short reference to the major sources which we used to identify those for or against devaluation but which have not always been included in the footnotes.

THE DUTCH ECONOMY IN DEPRESSION

The onset of the World economic depression is generally associated with the Wall Street crash in October 1929, though indices of industrial production in both Germany and the United States had peaked before then, the signs of a crisis in agriculture had already become increasingly acute and an international debt problem had hung continuously like a dark cloud over World financial markets. Nonetheless, whatever the trigger, the World was rapidly plunged into a deep depression from which it was to achieve what turned out to be a fragile recovery by 1936. The depression affected different sectors of the economy in different ways. In terms of output, foodstuffs production remained relatively stable, whilst production of raw materials and industrial goods both fell sharply before recovering. The League of Nations attempted at the time to compile global figures on the basis of the available national statistics – which ranged in quality from the highly dubious to the downright awful. The results of the exercise are presented in Table 1.1. It cannot be stressed too strongly that these figures should only be used as a rough indicator of broad trends.

TABLE 1.1
WORLD AND EUROPEAN INDICES OF ECONOMIC ACTIVITY (Index 1929 = 100)

	1929	1930	1931	1932	1933	1934	1935	1936
World Primary Production	100	99	95	92	95	97	99	104
of which Foodstuffs	100	102	100	100	102	101	101	103
Raw Materials	100	94	85	75	81	87	95	106
World Industrial Activity *	100	86	74	63	71	77	86	96
European Primary Production*	100	97	96	96	98	101	102	104
of which Foodstuffs	100	99	102	104	106	107	107	106
Raw Materials	100	76	80	73	77	80	88	90
European Industrial Activity*	100	91	80	70	76	85	93	101

* Excluding USSR.
Source: Calculated from League of Nations, *World Production and Prices.*

The apparent stability in foodstuffs production did not mean that it was isolated from the recession. On the contrary, the failure to adjust production and marketing of agriculture, and to a lesser extent raw materials, downwards to cope with the reduced international demand, exposed them to a precipitous drop in prices both in absolute terms and relative to the price of industrial goods. Indeed, the course of international prices generally followed that of production, falling until 1932/33 and then recovering. So, too, did the pattern of World unemployment. Again on the basis of suspect statistics, the International Labour Office estimated that World unemployment rose from 5.4 per cent in 1929 to a staggering 21.1 per cent in 1932 before settling back to 10.1 per cent in 1937.(1)

The World's governments attempted to cope with the crisis, which none of them saw as being particularly their own fault, by trying to isolate their economies from the deflationary forces emanating from abroad. This began in agriculture, which was the earliest and most acutely affected sector. As tumbling prices undermined the very existence of domestic farmers they resorted first usually to tariffs and, when this appeared ineffective, to physical controls to limit the flow of cheap imports and to allow domestic price support schemes to be introduced. Similar measures were soon to be introduced across the whole range of industrial products as well. This naturally invited retaliation from those whose trade had thereby been adversely affected and by 1931 the World had already been plunged into a full-blooded trade war. It was at this point that two further weapons for insulating the domestic economy came into their own. In the summer of 1931 a banking crisis had reverberated across central Europe, with the countries concerned facing massive speculation against their currencies. They responded by imposing what is called 'exchange controls' which effectively rationed access to the available reserves of foreign currency. Although this was initially intended as a purely financial measure, it did not take long for governments to realise that, ultimately, without foreign currency you cannot buy foreign goods. Intended or not, exchange control was to become a highly

TABLE 1.2
REAL VALUE OF WORLD TRADE (Index, 1929 = 100)

	1929	1930	1931	1932	1933	1934	1935	1936
World Trade	100	93	85	75	75	78	82	86
of which Foodstuffs	100	–	–	89	83	82	85	85
Raw Materials	100	–	–	81	87	88	91	95
Manufacturers	100	–	–	59	60	66	69	75

Source: Calculated from League of Nations, *World Production and Prices.*

sophisticated weapon for restricting and redirecting trade. The United Kingdom responded to similar speculation in September 1931 by allowing the pound to depreciate and it was to be followed in its example before the end of the year by almost forty other countries, including all of the commonwealth, the Scandinavian economies and Japan. The effect of devaluation or depreciation, which will be discussed more fully below (see pp 10-12), is to raise the price of foreign goods expressed in terms of your own currency thereby making them less attractive. Those countries which had neither imposed exchange controls nor allowed their currencies to depreciate responded by increasing the level and range of the more traditional trade restrictive arsenal. At the same time, more and more bilateral trade deals were struck designed to direct whatever trade did occur into preconceived channels. The result was, that although levels of World activity improved, the recovery of World Trade lagged far behind (see Table 1.2).

How did the Dutch economy fare whilst all this was going on? Before answering this question it is important to make two points. Firstly, it would be wrong to directly compare the statistical information provided here with that for any other country or group of countries. Sometimes the Dutch data is better than elsewhere, more often than not it is worse, but there is one thing it is never and that is internationally comparable.(2) Secondly, it has to be said that we now know considerably more about what was going on then than did the politicians and economic analysts who were actually caught up in the events we are about to describe. Up to 1936 there were no national income statistics, no industrial production statistics and no adequate wholesale price index. The balance of payments data was a mess once one tried moving beyond the balance of trade, and the government had so muddied the definitions within its own ordinary budget, that it is doubtful whether even it knew what was happening. It is true that governments usually have the statistics they deserve, but that cannot detract from the fact that policy and policy analysis, and the latter is especially important for this book, was made in something of a vacuum.

The best indicator for assessing the overall health of the economy would have been the data for real national income, but although the nominal series appears reasonably trustworthy the price series used to convert it into constant prices is

TABLE 1.3
DUTCH AGRICULTURAL AND INDUSTRIAL ACTIVITY (Index, 1929 = 100)

	1929	1930	1931	1932	1933	1934	1935	1936
Arable and Animal Farming [1]	100	102	106	107	105	105	101	104
Market Gardening [2]	100	106	102	101	97	103	104	100
Total Manufacturing Output [3]	100	100	94	83	88	92	92	97
of which Consumer Goods	100	103	100	91	96	99	99	104
Producer Goods	100	93	77	61	66	72	70	77

Sources:
[1] *Verslagen en Mededelingen Directie van den Landbouw*, 1949 p.428.
[2] Centraal Bureau voor de Statistiek, *Nationale inkomen van Nederland 1921-1939*, Utrecht, 1948.
[3] Calculated from Archive of the Centraal Bureau voor de Statistiek E8/739.

not and therefore we will refrain from using it.(3) That leaves us with the data for agriculture and industry, which would suggest for the former a pattern of output broadly similar with the rest of Europe. For industry the pattern would seem to suggest a milder, though longer, recession than Europe as a whole, but perhaps even this statement is going too far (see Table 1.3).

These tentative observations should not lead to a too optimistic picture being drawn for the economy as a whole. As in the rest of the world agricultural output might have been maintained but the fall in prices seriously eroded farmers' incomes, and continued to do so until 1933/34. Only in 1936/37 was a really marked improvement discernable.(4) Moreover, shipping and foreign investment earnings, which both constituted important elements in the economy, were severely hurt by the recession. A more visible and potentially more worrying indicator that all was not well with the economy was provided by the growing ranks of the unemployed. Again, direct comparison is not possible, but whilst the World trend had turned downwards from 1932/33 in the Netherlands it still proceeded remorselessly upwards (see Table 1.4).

Just as today, this unemployment was not purely a cyclical phenomenon – the previous high birth rate was serving to churn numbers onto the labour

TABLE 1.4
UNEMPLOYMENT IN THE NETHERLANDS

	1929	1930	1931	1932	1933	1934	1935	1936
Total (thousand man years)	80	100	190	310	350	380	430	480
Ibid., as percentage of employed and unemployed	2.8	3.4	6.6	11.3	12.8	13.8	15.6	17.4

Source:
Unemployment: P. de Rooy, *Werklozenzorg en werkloosheidsbestrijding 1917-1940*, Amsterdam, 1978, 262.
Employment: Centraal Bureau voor de Statistiek, *Het nationale inkomen van Nederland 1921-1939*, Utrecht, 1948.

TABLE 1.5
REAL VALUE OF DUTCH EXPORTS (Index, 1929 = 100)

	1929	1930	1931	1932	1933	1934	1935	1936
Total	100	95	88	73	69	70	70	75
of which Industrial Products	100	92	86	69	68	69	72	73
Agricultural Products	100	105	102	91	75	77	68	76

Source: *Statistische en Economische Onderzoekingen*, Vol. 6 no.2 (1951) 112-119

market at a rate unmatched in Western Europe, whilst the rise in industrial productivity served to mute the impact on employment of whatever recovery there was. However, it was perceived at the time primarily as a problem which could only be aleviated by a cyclical improvement in the economy.

Finally, with, in 1929, approximately 30 per cent of national income going in exports,(5) and with foreign trade one of the more lastingly damaged victims of the depression, it is necessary to pause at the Dutch export performance. Here again, the impression which can be reinforced from other sources(6) is that until 1931 the Dutch economy fared better than the World economy as a whole, but thereafter somewhat worse (see Table 1.5).

The initial reaction of the Dutch government to the crumbling of the international economy was to hope that it would all go away. It remained fervently loyal to all the international efforts, under the auspices of the League of Nations, to achieve World economic disarmament until the debacle of the World Economic Conference in the Spring of 1933 – signing international tariff truces and setting up the Ouchy Convention with Belgium and Luxembourg in June 1932.(7) Nonetheless, the government could not afford to stand idly by whilst large and important sectors of the economy went to the wall. Towards the end of 1930 it bowed to pressure from the nascent 'green front' of agricultural pressure groups and introduced legislation to limit wheat imports. This was the thin end of the wedge and by the spring of 1933 a virtual avalanche of 'crisis' laws and decrees had been passed by parliament covering the entire range of agricultural output. Industry was not far behind, although it was never to enjoy the same level of protection. In September 1931 parliament accepted a 'fiscal' increase in all tariffs of 25 per cent and the following month the 'crisis import law', giving the government powers to impose import quotas, began its passage through parliament. Although originally intended as an agricultural measure its provisions were soon extended to industry and already by the end of 1932 9 per cent of the industrial labour force worked in industries enjoying quota protection.(8)

In 1931 a new strand was introduced into the government's strategy – *aanpassing*, the nearest English equivalent would be 'adaptation'. Until 1930 the state of central government finances had prompted little cause for concern, though at the end of that year it had been necessary to introduce fiscal measures

Colijn defends his policy of 'adaptation' in parliament (1935). Photo: Historisch Documentatiecentrum voor het Nederlands Protestantisme.

to cover a small anticipated deficit. However, it soon transpired that the situation was out of control and, year-in year-out, the government was faced with the need to prune expenditure and increase taxation in a vain effort to restore equilibrium. However, the concept of *aanpassing* went even further than merely 'adapting' the government's role in the economy to the more straitened circumstances – and even beyond the idea that a balanced budget was the best way of avoiding inflation. It was also intended to contribute to the 'adaptation' of national cost levels to the new competitive environment. Cuts in civil servants' salaries and in the levels of unemployment benefits were intended to lead the way for a general reduction in labour costs. Similarily, the granting of help to industry was often made contingent upon wage-cutting measures having already been taken.

Thus, by the beginning of 1933 one could characterise government policy in the following terms: a misplaced belief in an 'international solution', a whole-hearted commitment to agricultural protection, a half-hearted commitment to protectionism elsewhere and a strategy of *aanpassing*. 1933 was marked by two important events: the US dollar abandoned the gold standard and the Netherlands got a new government under the leadership of Hendrik Colijn. Colijn had been a fervent internationalist. He was chairman of the economic committee at the World Economic Conference in London and had witnessed first hand its

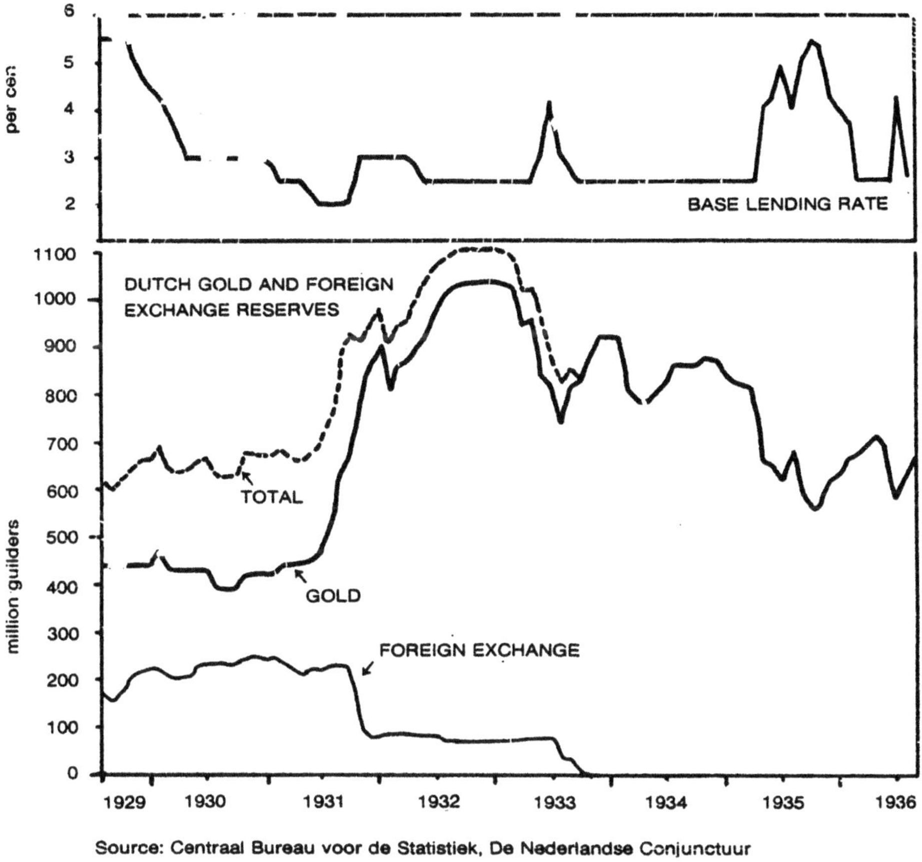

Figure 1.1. Dutch Gold and Foreign Exchange Reserves and Bank Rate, 1929-1936.

collapse when the US government refused to commit itself to a stabilisation of the dollar. As a result, he accomplished a transition to the more protectionist camp with alarming alacrity. The government's powers of initiative in agricultural measures were sharply increased, the numbers working in industries enjoying quota protection were doubled and new measures were introduced giving Dutch exports preferential access to colonial markets. Meanwhile, the faith in *aanpassing* remained unshaken. There was one other 'new' element in this period – the battle for the guilder (see Figure 1.1).

The decision by the government not to devalue, combined with a deterioration in the balance of payments (as far as that can be ascertained), implied an acceptance of the fact that the guilder would be continually vulnerable to attack by speculators. It is noticeable, however, that until the devaluation of the Belgian franc in March 1935, this decision never really jeopardized the 'cheap money policy' pursued by the Netherlands Bank. Although gold reserves had fallen by virtually a quarter from a peak in the last months of 1932 until Spring 1935, the base lending rate fluctuated between 2.5 and 3 per cent. It is a good reflection of the turbulance which characterised the following eighteen months that the Netherlands Bank adjusted its base lending rate on no less than twenty-two occasions.(9) On the other hand, the guilder was never in any danger of being forced off gold – in the sense of it falling beneath the minimum gold cover for the currency of 40 per cent – not that is until September 1936.

The government's policy came under attack from a number of quarters and, along with the criticism, alternatives were offered. The first alternative came from what we could term the orthodox liberal camp. They pointed out that even on the basis of its own figures, the government was failing to balance the budget and that the problem was even worse if the effects of 'camouflaging' were taken into account. This camouflaging could take place because although the 'ordinary budget' was supposed to cover all items of current expenditure the true situation was masked by milking reserve funds, by pushing expenditure into self-liquidating funds which never seemed to self-liquidate and by sluicing current items into the capital account. An attempt to quantify this is made in Table 1.6.

Secondly, they argued that the government's twin policies of *aanpassing* and protectionism were self defeating, that behind protectionist barriers prices could be maintained and that the protection of agriculture in particular, which was based on the consumer-pays principle, was serving to keep the cost of living unnecessarily high. By the end of 1935 it was estimated that the various support measures in agriculture had added between 7 and 8 per cent to the cost of living.(10) Their solution was radically simple: the government should stick with doing what it should be doing and balance the budget and nothing else; 'natural' *aanpassing* under market forces would take care of the rest.

The painfully slow reduction in the cost of living also prompted concern from another source. Both catholics and socialists criticised the way in which government policy rested too one-sidedly on wages and ignored other components in industrial costs and, therefore, the cost of living (see Table 1.7). The catholics in

TABLE 1.6
REPORTED AND ESTIMATED RESULTS OF DUTCH ORDINARY BUDGETS

	1931	1932	1933	1934	1935	1936
Reported Results (million guilders) [1]	– 3	+ 2	– 22	– 1	– 1	–
Estimated Results (million guilders) [2]	– 85	– 121	– 114	– 145	– 114	– 201
Estimated Results as a percentage[3] of nominal national income	1.5	2.5	2.4	3.1	2.4	4.2

Sources:

[1] F.A.G. Keesing, *De conjuncturele ontwikkeling van Nederland,*Utrecht, 1948, 129, 195.

[2] Annual budget statements, *Handelingen der Tweede Kamer der Staten Generaal*, Various years. Recalculated on the basis of *Ibidem*, 1937, 126-129, 146-147.

[3] Estimated results divided by national income data in Centraal Bureau voor de Statistiek, *Het Nationale inkomen van Nederland 1921-1939*, Utrecht, 1948.

TABLE 1.7
MOVEMENT OF WAGES AND COST-OF-LIVING INDICES IN THE NETHERLANDS
(Index, 1931 = 100)

	1929	1930	1931	1932	1933	1934	1935	1936
Industrial Wage *	100	100.8	100	95.4	91.1	87.7	84.2	82
Cost-of-living, workers families, Amsterdam	111.1	106.6	100	93.2	92.3	92.8	90.2	87.3
Real Wage	90.0	94.6	100	102.4	98.7	94.5	93.3	93.9

* Industry in this context includes mining, utilities and construction
Source: Calculated from Centraal Bureau voor de Statistiek, *Jaarcijfers voor Nederland*, various years.

particular focused on fixed charges, *vaste lasten*, which had been fixed by contract at a time when the prevailing price level had been much higher and whose burden had increased as prices and incomes had fallen. These included interest and mortgage payments, rents, and some even went so far as to include the original nominal sum of the debt itself. Their demand was for 'consistent' deflation in the form of legislation to reduce these *vaste lasten*. Indeed, the government was eventually to introduce such legislation but was forced to withdraw it in the face of parliamentary opposition.

Another source of criticism was that the government was too fixated with the budget deficit and that this was preventing it from taking effective measures to stimulate the economy. It is true that aside from agriculture and those industries protected by quotas (which cost nothing) the expenditure involved in subsidising the rest of industry and shipping was paltry. Their alternatives included increased expenditure on work-creation schemes and, a catholic hobby-horse, special industrial finance banks. But the most coherent alternative came from the ranks of the social democrats in the form of the *Plan van den Arbeid* (labour Plan) published in 1935. It suggested that the government should borrow Dfl. 200 million a year for three years for the execution of a comprehensive public works scheme. This injection of purchasing power into the economy together with the expected 'multiplier effect' was anticipated to create 120,000 new jobs in the first year alone, whilst various other measures (shorter working hours, compulsory retirement, raising the school leaving age) would remove a further 80,000 from the unemployment registers. In this way the Plan's authors hoped to lift the economy out of its current crisis but, in order to keep it from slipping into a new one, they also proposed changes in the structure of the economy along more socialist lines. Colijn's reply, incidentally, was coolly cynical: "What is useable in the Plan, the government is doing already."(11)

Finally, without trying to be exhaustive, there were those who argued that it was politically impossible for the government to succeed in reducing the nominal price level within the Netherlands to a point at which the economy's competitiveness would be restored. Moreover, the painful reductions which the Dutch had managed to achieve between 1931 and 1934 (provoking in the last year

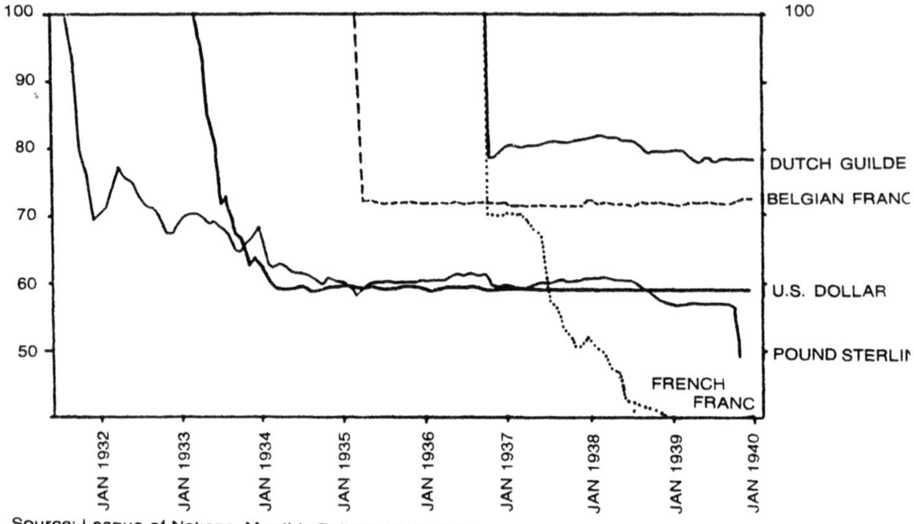

Source: League of Nations, Monthly Bulletin of Statistics

Fig. 1.2. Exchange Rates Expressed as a percentage of their 1929 Parities, 1931-1939.

bloody riots in the working class Jordaan district of Amsterdam) had been more than wiped out by the further depreciation in the currencies of major competitors (see Figure 1.2). What they advocated was that the government should restore competitiveness not by pushing down the domestic price level but by reducing the value of the guilder in terms of foreign currencies; in other words, by devaluation. It is their efforts and arguments and those of their opponents with which this book is primarily concerned.

THE DEVALUATION ISSUE MADE SIMPLE

There is no mystique about what a devaluation involves – it is simply a matter of definition. If a country devalues its currency, it alters its exchange rate in such a way that one unit of its own currency will purchase fewer units of everyone else's. Put the opposite way, everyone else will have to offer fewer units than before of their own currency to buy one unit of the currency which had just devalued. Let us illustrate this with a simple example. Throughout 1935 one pound sterling could purchase approximately 7.25 guilders and one guilder could purchase approximately 0.14 pounds (about two shillings and tenpence in those good old days before decimalisation). Suppose the guilder was devalued by 20 per cent, one pound would then be able to buy 8.70 guilders and one guilder could purchase approximately 0.11 pounds (about two shillings and tuppence). If the change in the currency's value is achieved in one stroke and the new parity is irrevokably fixed (until the next time!) we talk about a devaluation, but if no new official parity is established we talk about a depreciation. However, to keep matters simple we have used the term 'devaluation' throughout the text, even though strictly speaking the guilder depreciated after September 1936. After a devaluation all other currencies are more expensive in terms of the devalued currency and, therefore, so too are all goods and services purchased abroad (i.e. to purchase £0.14 will cost Dfl. 1.20 after devaluation compared with Dfl. 1.00 before) and *vice versa* (i.e. Dfl. 1 will cost £0.11 after devaluation compared with £0.14 before).

This last point explains why devaluation was seen by its proponents as a means for aleviating the depression – if the guilder was cheaper for foreigners, so too would be goods and services priced in guilders, foreigners would hopefully buy more and employment and business activity would increase. In the same way, foreign currency and foreign goods and services would become more expensive expressed in guilders and so Dutchmen would switch to home-produced goods in preference to the more expensive foreign product with the same beneficial result for the economy. If it were that simple, it is difficult to imagine any rational opposition being possible. Let us take the export side first. If his product has sold for £0.14 before the devaluation, our exporter might decide to leave the price at £0.14 and pocket the extra £0.03 as profit, which he may or may not choose to invest in the Netherlands. In this case the increased export demand would not materialise. Why should he do that? Possibly because he is involved in some market sharing cartel, possibly because he would rather have the extra profit and possibly because he fears that if he does begin to make inroads into foreign markets, foreign governments will step in with protectionist measures designed to keep his products out. Thus at one extreme the devaluation may not effect an increase in demand or employment at all, but it will then have an effect on profitability. Let us now suppose that our Dutch exporter does decide to lower the price for his product to £0.11, it might still only have a marginal impact on sales volume. This could occur because the foreign government does indeed take repraisal measures designed to wipe out the newly acquired price advantage (a far from remote possibility in the 1930's) or equally because domestic producers or other exporters to that market respond with a similar price reduction. But even if neither of these things occur exports might still not rise because of what economists call 'inelastic demand' – the demand for some goods is not particularly sensitive to changes in price. Still, for the individual producer any increase in demand will be welcome since he can spread his fixed costs over a larger volume of production and so average profits will rise. For the balance of payments, however, a 20 per cent reduction in price expressed in pounds will have to be matched by a rise of more than 20 per cent in volume if the total foreign currency earnings are not to decline.

So far in our examples we have assumed that the full 20 per cent devaluation could be used either to raise profits or to lower prices but, in fact, the margins are likely to be less. This is because every £0.14 of imports will cost Dfl. 1.20 instead of Dfl. 1.00. Thus, the extent to which an exporter, or a domestic producer for that matter, uses imported raw materials and other inputs will determine by how much his costs will rise. Thus part of the original price advantage could be eroded by rising costs. Moreover, the price of imported foodstuffs and consumer goods would also rise, fuelling in turn a demand for wage increases which could again erode the initial price advantage. Pro-devaluationists argued with some purpose that the government could compensate this to some extent by reducing taxes and levies on internal consumption (if a levy was placed on domestic consumption of pork to subsidise exports, if the price-gap was reduced by devaluation, so too would be the need for such a high levy) and, somewhat less convincingly, that consumer resistance would prevent retailers from passing on the full price increase (lucky old retailers!). Thus, the cost of living increase could be muted. Moreover, it was argued that the wages pressure might not materialise at all because of the high prevailing level of unemployment, but in that case the workers would face a cut in their standard of living. Nobody, however, denied that part at least of the original advantage would be lost.

Many of these same considerations applied to the position of domestic industries which were expected to roll back foreign competition: it all depended on the existence of cartel agreements, the price response of foreign competitors, the ability to expand or create production facilities to make use of any new opportunities and the extent to which the initial price advantage was eroded by subsequent raw material and labour cost increases. Moreover, it was equally possible that competing industries would use the opportunity to raise their prices rather than expand their markets. This would increase their profitability but the impact on the 'real' economy would depend on how the profits were used.

This treatment is not intended to be comprehensive in its coverage but to illustrate what is actually known about the impact of a devaluation on an economy. What should be apparent is that it is relatively easy to make statements about the direction of a change, but very difficult to say anything with any certainty about the magnitude of that change. This is true of controversies in economics today. How much more so then in the 1930's when the quality of analysis and the quality of statistical data was much, much lower? Exports might increase, imports might fall; but would they do so enough to make much difference to the levels of employment and economic activity, enough to stop the balance of payments deteriorating? Domestic price levels would rise; but would it be by a lot or a little, would it wipe out the competitive advantage or not? The level of profitability would increase; but by how much and for how long? It was upon the answers to these questions, among others, that the battle lines were drawn..... but there were no answers. On the basis of the same information the most optimistic pro-devaluationists could project the Dutch economy into an export boom accompanied by import substitution with virtually no increase in domestic prices, whilst the most pessimistic anti-devaluationists could plunge it into the middle of a new trade war with rampant domestic inflation and the currency in an unstoppable downward spiral. And we haven't really touched upon the psychological effects....

PILLARISATION

In order to be able to understand the reactions within Dutch society to the devaluation question it is necessary to say something by way of introduction over a peculiarly Dutch phenomenon – *verzuiling*, which translates somewhat awkwardly into English as 'pillarisation'. This concept implies that Dutch society can best be understood in terms of a number of vertical columns or pillars (*zuilen*) which cut right across the more traditional horizontal classification into social classes. The unity in the *zuil* is seen as lying in religion or ideology and an important characteristic was the existence of its own organisations, which covered virtually all aspects of social life. In this way one arrives at a definition of a *zuil* as a population group united in a complex of social organisation based on a common philosophy of life.(12)

Perhaps not surprisingly, there is no agreement in the literature over the number of *zuilen* which can be identified in the Netherlands. Most authors concur that in the 1930's one can speak of a roman catholic *zuil* and an (orthodox-)protestant *zuil*, but after that the problems really start. Lijphart, whose book, published towards the end of the 1960's,(13) dominated the discussion for over a decade, argues in favour of a 'general' *zuil* which he distinguishes from the two confessional *zuilen*. However, he then muddies the waters by subdividing it into a socialist and a liberal, or neutral, *zuil* – on which point he has justifiably been criticised for ambiguity. Blom chooses unequivocally for both a socialist and a neutral/liberal *zuil*; and as a result ends up with four.(14) This position has recently been attacked by Stuurman. On the basis of a number of criteria which he considers have to be satisfied to speak of a *zuil* – including the contention that it has to embrace all strata in society and that the unifying ideology has to have a religious basis(15) – he denies the separate existence of a social-democratic and a liberal *zuil*. Without going into the advantages and disadvantages of the various concepts, we have plumped for four, for the pragmatic reason that it offers the most points of contact for our practical goal: that of obtaining an insight into the reaction of Dutch society towards the devaluation question. In making this choice we in no way wish to underplay the differences between the various population groups pointed out by Stuurman and others.

Within the roman catholic *zuil* the catholic church formed the central organisation. Its cohesion and homogeneity can be explained to a large extent by the strongly hierarchical structure of the church and its dominant position. In this respect, due to the large number of denominations, the degree of unity among the orthodox-protestants was much less. Though it is possible to point to a common religious philosophy in the form of a protestantism which still adhered to tenets of faith established in the 16th and 17th century. Even so, the contrasts were often sharp, for example between the two largest denominations within the *zuil* – the *Gereformeerde Kerken* and the orthodox part of the *Nederlandse Hervormde Kerk*. This religious divide largely coincided with a political split –

with the ARP, *Anti-Revolutionaire Partij*, being supported mainly by the former and the CHU, *Christelijk-Historische Unie*, by the latter. Alongside a basically similar religious outlook, the unity of the orthodox-protestant *zuil* can also be demonstrated by a large number of unsegregated orthodox-protestant organisations covering various fields of society.

The unity of ideology and the great number of organisations were also characteristics of the social-democratic movement, but in other respects the situation was completely different. There were no specific church ties (though some social-democrats adhered to the more liberal protestant denominations) and the ideology was specifically non-religious. The position of the social democrats differed from that of the others in another way also. Lijphart stresses in particular the element of 'pacification' in the system of pillarisation.(16) By this he means the willingness of the *zuil* elites to compromise in matters of every-day politics, regardless of differences in ideologies. This spirit of compromise was necessary since no *zuil* could muster an absolute political majority and without practical compromises between them the country would have been ungovernable. However, in many fields the social-democrats had yet to be accepted into this system of pacification in the 1930's.(17) This was especially so in the field of national government from which they were excluded until 1939.

Another important difference between the religious groups and the social-democrats was the social structure of the *zuil*. Among the catholics and orthodox-protestants one could find people from all social classes, whereas the social-democratic *zuil* was mainly working class with few representatives from the middle classes and hardly any from the upper classes. Its complement was the neutral/liberal *zuil* with its prominent upper and middle class membership and the virtual absence of working-class support. All of this had obvious consequences for the organisations represented within each. While the unions were very important within the labour movement, there were scarcely any organisations for other social groups. By contrast, the trade union element was very weak within the liberal *zuil*, though there were plenty of employer, farmer and other middle class organisations.

The neutral/liberal *zuil* had also another specific characteristic of its own. The three others could be seen as the result of the emancipation struggle against liberal domination by orthodox-protestants, catholics and socialists alike. Their organisations still carried the stamp of this struggle of the last quarter of the 19th and the beginning of the 20th century. Liberal organisations, on the other hand, had not been created with this motive in mind. Often they were older, more general organisations whose liberal character was strengthened when others – like the catholics – deserted them. A good example is the 19th century KNLC, *Koninklijk Nederlandsch Landbouw Comité* (Royal Dutch Agricultural Committee), which represented all farming interests until separate catholic and orthodox-protestant agricultural organisations were created in the 20th century. A typical characteristic of the neutral/liberal *zuil* was the reluctance to create (aside from politics) any organisational substructure at all. However, the action

TABLE 1.8
MAIN ZUIL ORGANISATIONS AND POLITICAL PARTIES IN THE NETHERLANDS

	Catholic zuil	Orthodox-protestant zuil	Socialist zuil	Neutral/ liberal zuil
Employers' organisations	ARKWV	CWV	–	VNW
Employees' organisations	RKVW	CNV	NVV	NVC+
Agricultural organisations	RKBTB	CBTB	–	KNLC
Political parties	RKSP	ARP/CHU	SDAP	LSP, VDB

ARKWV: Algemeene Roomsch-Katholieke Werkgevers Vereeniging
ARP: Anti-Revolutionaire Partij
CBTB: Christelijke Boeren- en Tuindersbond
CHU: Christelijk-Historische Unie
CNV: Christelijk Nationaal Vakverbond
CWV: Christelijke Werkgeversvereeniging
KNLC: Koninklijk Nederlandsch Landbouw Comité
LSP: Liberale Staats Partij
NVC: Nederlandse Vakcentrale
NVV: Nederlandsch Verbond van Vakvereenigingen
RKBTB: Roomsch-Katholieke Nederlandse Boeren- en Tuindersbond
RKSP: Roomsch-Katholieke Staats Partij
RKWV: Roomsch-Katholiek Werklieden Verbond
SDAP: Sociaal-Democratische Arbeiders Partij
VDB: Vrijzinnig-Democratische Bond
VNW: Verbond van Nederlandsche Werkgevers

of others left behind a complex of more of less liberal organisations almost by default. Paradoxically, Blom views as essential for understanding the liberal *zuil* the intention not to be a *zuil*.(18) The formal links between the various liberal organisations were much looser than those of the other *zuilen*, or were even missing altogether. However, there were more than enough informal links among the liberal elite of Dutch society to suggest that in practice it made little difference.

The Table 1.8 lists the national organisations (employers', farmers', workers' organisations and political parties) commonly associated with the various *zuilen*.

Since pillarisation is considered such an important aspect of Dutch society in the 1930's, why was it not used to determine the structure of this book? Why are the views of the different *zuilen* not presented and analysed one after another? There are two answers. It became clear in the early stages of research that few organisations within the *zuilen* had been able to reach a concensus on the devaluation issue. It could therefore be assumed that the institutional channels within the *zuilen* had not been used to agree on a common position and to put pressure on the government accordingly. This assumption was reinforced by the activities of the two single issue pressure groups and especially of the NVWG, *Nederlandsche Vereeniging voor Waardevast Geld* (Dutch Association for Value Stable

Money). Precisely because no clear pro-devaluation opinion was to be heard from any of the *zuilen*, the NVWG was brought into being, its leading figures and its members being drawn from all four of the *zuilen*, although the orthodox-protestants were weakly represented. The anti-devaluationist group, founded by prof. H.W.C. Bordewijk, was an immediate reaction and its members and supporters also came from all the four *zuilen*.

There is another reason why pillarisation has not dictated the structure of the book. *Zuilen* have been described as groups of people with a common philosophy of life. In matters of philosophical outlook, therefore, a strong unity within the *zuil* was to be expected. One example of this is the system of state subsidies for confessional education for which the catholic and the orthodox-protestant *zuilen* had always struggled together. Another example is national disarmament which was supported almost unanimously by the social-democrats until the second half of the 1930's. The devaluation issue was of a different nature; matters of religion or ideology were considered to be of little or no importance. Only within the ARP did we find some elements of an appeal to basic religious principles. So, instead of a treatment per *zuil* we have opted for a consecutive analysis of the different organisations. Naturally within this structure the *zuil* concept rears its head and, indeed, one of the intriguing questions which arose in the research was the extent to which the differences between the various organisations on the devaluation issue could be explained by reference to the *zuil*.

PRO- AND ANTI-DEVALUATIONISTS

Throughout the text we have been able to determine individuals' standpoints in the devaluation debate by their writings and statements but also on the basis of their membership or support of one or other of the single issue pressure groups devoted to this issue. These groups are examined at length in Chapter 7 but individual members surface in the earlier chapters. When they have done so, we have referred in the text to the source but we have refrained from citing it in the footnotes. For this reason we will now mention the major sources used.

Our knowledge of pro-devaluationists is the most complete partly because they organised themselves much earlier and partly because they publicly advertised for adherents whereas the anti-devaluationists did not. The first 'pro-devaluation' petition was sent to the government in July 1933 and contained 29 signatories. We have always used inverted commas when referring to it because it did not come out unambiguously in favour of devaluation but left open the option of more rigorous deflation.(19) In January 1934 a second petition was sent, with no ambiguity this time, with 25 signatures. When it was decided to set up the NVWG, in September 1934, the group did so by publishing a manifesto signed by 50 prominent citizens.(20) By 1936 the group had gone public and in the course of the year two short petitions were sent. The first, sent in May 1936, contained 232 signatures (21) and the second, in July, 612.(22)

The anti-devaluationist group was determined to remain small and recruited new members and adherents through its network of personal contacts. In total 37 people were members at one time or another, a fact we can determine since we have had access to a complete set of the group's minutes.(23) In February 1935 the anti-devaluationists too, sent a petition to the government containing 63 signatures including those of the 26 members at the time.(24)

In the Index of Historical Persons we have alphabet coded those individuals whose names appeared in any of these sources.

Notes

1. International Labour Office, *Yearbook of Labour Statistics*, Geneva, various years.
2. In fairness it should be stated that some comment could be made for every country in the inter-war period.
3. Centraal Bureau voor de Statistiek, *Het nationale inkomen van Nederland 1921-1939*, Utrecht, 1948.
4. *Verslagen en Mededeelingen van de Directie van den Landbouw*, various years.
5. Calculated from *Het Nationale inkomen van Nederland* and Centraal Bureau voor de Statistiek, *Tachtig jaren statistiek in tijdreeksen*, 's-Gravenhage, 1979.
6. See, for example, the share of the Netherlands in the total imports of its major trading partners in League of Nations, *International Trade Statistics*, various years.
7. This was an 'open agreement', which could be joined by other countries, committing the adherents not to impose net quotas on each others' trade and to reduce mutual tariffs by 10 per cent a year for 5 years. It collapsed when the United Kingdom insisted on its right to be party to any bilateral tariff reductions.
8. Calculated from *De gevoerde contingenteeringspolitiek en hare gevolgen. Verslagen en mededelingen van de Directie van Handel and Nijverheid van het Departement van Economische Zaken*, 1939, No.1, 30, 38-40.
9. F. de Roos and W.J. Wieringa, *Een halve eeuw rente in Nederland*,Schiedam, 1953, 254.
10. Cited in P.A. Blaisse, *De Nederlandse handels politiek*, Utrecht, 1948, 198.
11. Cited in P. de Rooy, *Werklozenzorg en werkloosheidsbestrijding. Landelijk en Amsterdams beleid*, Amsterdam, 1979, 146.
12. J.C.H. Blom, *De muiterij op De Zeven Provinciën. Reacties en gevolgen in Nederland*, Bussum, 1975, 18.
13. A. Lijphart, *The Politics of Accommodation. Pluralism and Democracy in the Netherlands*, Berkely (Calf.), 1968.
14. Blom, *Muiterij*, 18. In a later publication Blom stated with regard to the desired research that he did not want to give a tight description of what was to be understood by of zuil and further refrained from stating how many zuilen there were. J.C.H. Blom, *Verzuiling in Nederland in het bijzonder op lokaal niveau*, 1850-1925, Amsterdam, 1981, 21-24.
15. S. Stuurman, *Verzuiling, kapitalisme en patriarchaat. Aspecten van de ontwikkeling van de moderne staat in Nederland*, Nijmegen, 1983, 71.
16. The great value that Lijphart saw in *pacificatie* appears from the fact that the definition comes into the title of the Dutch version of the book mentioned in note 13: A. Lijphart, *Verzuiling, pacificatie en kentering in de Nederlandse politiek*, Amsterdam, 1968.
17. Blom, *Muiterij*, 22.
18. *Ibid.*, 19.
19. Algemeen Rijksarchief (ARA), Ministerie van Financiën (MF), Generale Thesaurie (GT) (199) – Nederlandse Monetaire Politiek. Devaluatie. Address to the Minister van Koloniën, Voorzitter van den Ministerraad, 19.7.1933.

20. ARA, Ministerraad, ingekomen stukken, 307, 13d. Address to Minister van Staat, Voorzitter van den Raad van Ministers, 5.1.1934.
21. *Ibid.*, 318, No.188, *Petitie voor muntcorrectie*, 23.5.1936.
22. *Ibid.*, 324, No.9d, *Petitie voor muntcorrectie* 10.7.1936.
23. Archive of De Nederlandsche Bank, Dossier Notulen vergaderingen Groep van Anti-devaluïsten.
24. ARA, MF, GT (199) Nederlandse Monetaire Politiek, Devaluatie,Address of the Anti-devaluationists, 9.2.1935.

CHAPTER TWO

The Economists' Debate

The four decades before the First World War constituted the heyday of the gold standard. A sufficiently large number of countries adhered to it so as to be able to speak of a true standard, and economic development was gradual enough not to necessitate abrupt adjustments of exchange rates or price levels. Neither of these conditions were fulfilled in the twenties and thirties when the system experienced a short-lived revival.

The essence of any form of gold standard – with or without gold coins circulating – is a fixed gold price, implying stable exchange rates. The nice thing about a gold standard is that, if it works, two objectives of economic policy are promoted with one instrument: a certain degree of price stability and balance of payments equilibrium. (In general, economists are happy if two instruments will help to realise even part of a single goal). Today, many people are convinced that a belief in a world with fixed exchange rates is utopian, let alone the idea of a re-established gold standard. Nevertheless, there are a number of economists who still believe that a well observed gold standard could work again.

In the following pages we shall briefly examine three questions: the theory behind a well observed gold standard; the re-established gold standard of the twenties and thirties; and the issues in the debate among Dutch economists.

A WELL OBSERVED GOLD STANDARD

Let us start from the wrong end, so to speak, and take the example of a system of floating exchange rates. Suppose there are two countries, Holland and Germany, which only trade with each other and no-one else: there is a Dutch demand for Volkswagen cars and a German demand for summer holidays in Scheveningen. Ultimately, the VW's have to be paid for in Duitschmarks (DM), and the services of the Scheveningers in Dutch guilders (Dfl.). When we start from an equilibrium situation, the rate of the guilder to the mark is stable. But when the Dutch demand for VW's rises, the equilibrium in the respective demand for Dfl. and DM is disturbed. The increased demand for the German product induces an increased offer of guilders to meet the same amount of marks in the exchange market. This will push up the DM in relation to the Dfl. until a new equilibrium in the trade of goods and services between the two countries is established.

How would this example work out under a gold standard? Now both the guilder and the DM are in a fixed ratio to gold their (relative) rates cannot vary. In this system an increased demand for German products (meaning an increased offer of guilders) will also provoke a tendency for the DM to rise. But then very soon it will be more advantageous for the Dutch to pay in gold rather than in guilders. Thus, the gold circulation in Holland will shrink and this deflationary development (in the monetary sense) will have a depressing effect on the Dutch price level. The opposite will happen in Germany. A new equilibrium is reached when Dutch home-produced substitutes for imported goods have become cheap enough to compete effectively and stem the demand for imports. This theoretical system is called 'the price-specie flow mechanism'.

But not even in the most successful period of the gold standard was this completely effective. Gold movements did not balance international payments; in practice other international liquidities were preferred. And rigid prices – generally there is a downward rigidity and only an upward flexibility of prices – hampered a sufficiently fast adjustment of national price levels. Foreman-Peck contrasts the one per cent average (gold value) growth of exports for 'gold countries' during twenty years at the end of the 19th century with the export performance of countries with a silver standard in the same period: "The average silver country's exports grew at more than 4 per cent per annum in gold values, and there is no evidence that any silver country experienced a decline in the gold value of its exports."(1)

If the success of the gold standard before 1914 may have been modest, its vulnerability without an international authority to enforce its observance came to light even more clearly in the interwar years. It will suffice here to name but a few of the most apparent weaknesses. Firstly, the problem of German war reparations had not been settled in a satisfactory way when Britain returned to gold in 1925. Secondly, the adoption and abolition of the gold standard at various moments by different countries made it difficult to speak of a true standard. Finally, the real and financial disturbances of 1929 and subsequent years would probably have been too much for any world monetary order without a supranational policeman. So we can agree with Foreman-Peck: "The gold standard offered no remedy for an overvalued exchange rate than price or wage deflation or persistent unemployment."(2) Both these ills would plague the Dutch economy in the thirties.

THE GOLD STANDARD AFTER 1925

The gold standard can operate with or without gold coins in circulation. If a fixed gold price is maintained, one can always convert (paper) money into gold. We speak of full convertability if central banks guarantee this exchange. Even before 1914 many countries already operated in practice a gold exchange standard, keeping most of their reserves in the form of foreign currencies that were convertable or linked to gold (only in England, the Netherlands and the U.S. were there free markets in gold).

Not unexpectedly, the real and monetary distortions of the First World War severely shocked the exchange system. Once the British government had stopped supporting the pound against the dollar – at a cost of over $2000 million – it fell from almost $5.00 to less than $3.50 in 1920. Much more spectacular was the complete collapse of the German mark, a phenomenon not to be dealt with here. Taken as a whole, there were good psychological as well as economic reasons for pegging currencies at fixed rates again. Britain returned to gold in 1925, after two years of strong pressure from the Dominions to do so. The parity was fixed at the pre-war rate, which soon proved to have been too high as gold started to flow out of the country. The opposite happened in France from 1926 onwards, when the exchange rate of the franc was fixed to gold at a level which caused gold to flow into the country.

Foreman-Peck notes that during the slump of the early twenties, the great downward flexibility of prices was one of the helpful factors in the subsequent recovery.(3) This was no longer the case in 1929, at least not for the many products traded through cartels. This may seem paradoxical since in 1920-22 exchange rates were floating and adjustment of rates rather than price levels was to be expected, whereas in 1929 most exchange rates were pegged to gold so adjustment of price levels would have been a logical solution. The slump, which started in 1929, accentuated the process by which gold flowed into the U.S.A. and France. By September 1931, the pressure exerted on the pound by this gold flow and by the German currency controls, which effectively 'froze' the availability of sterling investments, caused the U.K. to suspend the gold standard, incidentally causing a considerable loss to the Dutch central bank. The next target for speculative gold movements became the dollar. As the depression lasted there were no forces to counter this development (increased exports would have induced an increased demand for the dollar which might have balanced the offering of gold for dollars, but trade fell almost continuously). In April 1933 the United States went off gold and the dollar, like the pound almost two years earlier, fell to about two thirds of its former gold value.

This left a gold bloc of France, Switzerland, Belgium and the Netherlands – countries which were destined to experience a later recovery from the depression than almost any other.

DUTCH ECONOMISTS AND THE GOLD STANDARD

As could be expected, much economic literature in the Netherlands was devoted to the gold standard in the three and a half years between the dollar devaluation and the final breaking up of the gold bloc in 1936 – Belgium had already defected in 1935. In the early thirties, monetary economics could scarcely be said to have existed as a separate subject. Universities (in which we include the *Hogescholen* of Rotterdam and Tilburg) made only a rough distinction between professors of general economics and those of business economics. It is true that Pierson's classic Dutch textbook, first published in the late 19th century, included a considerable section on money and prices, but the much used comprehensive textbook of C.A.Verrijn Stuart, published in 1920, hardly dwelt upon the subject at all.

The rapid development of monetary economics as a subject in the twenties was noted by J.G. Koopmans in a thesis draft written in 1931/2 (but only published half a century later). In his opinion many propositions considered path-breaking in 1920 were looked upon as banalities only a decade later: "One can be glad that this rapid evolution is not confined to professional theorists. Among the leading members of the world of international finance as well the conviction has grown that the return to pre-war traditions – notably the return to the gold standard now realised in almost all civilised countries – must not be considered as the last but, in the most favourable case, as one of the first steps on the road to a rationally ordered monetary system both nationally and internationally."(4) The gist of his argument on the concept of 'neutral money' was contained in his monumental essay *Zum Problem des Neutralen Geldes* in a German reader on monetary theory, edited by F.A. Hayek in 1933.

This example of German (Austrian) orientation coincides in with the conclusion of M.H.J. Dullaart in his recent thesis on Dutch economic thought in the interwar period: "Academic economics in the Netherlands after Pierson was Austrian economics" (i.e. in the years 1910 and 1920)(5). As a possible explanation he offers "the fact that, while Marshall was primarily interested in the supply side of the market, the Austrians were concentrating on the demand side". In the thirties, the Anglo-American (and sometimes also the French) perspective was re-established. Koopmans saw the necessity of Dutch scholars acquiring an orientation in foreign schools and in different tongues as an advantage since it served to avoid any national bias: "England in particular still preserves its 'splendid isolation' in this respect".(6)

When trying to make a rough division in 'parties' or 'schools' in the Dutch economists' debate, it is tempting to draw the lines between 'supply siders', 'Keynesians' and 'monetarists'. J. Tinbergen had already tried to do this in 1933 with regard to the employment problem. Comparing right and left wing views on the economic crisis, he saw the right interpreting the situation as a cyclical phenomenon and the left as a process of structural change. But this had little impact on perspectives on employment itself. Neither group differed much: "Because of the rationalisation and the shift of production to colonial areas after the war, high unemployment figures are generally expected for a longer period."(7)

In monetary matters it is quite impossible to distinguish any clear lines of approach running parallel to other criteria. Many professors taking part in the public debate were not monetary specialists at all, including the like of N.J.Polak (Rotterdam), H.A. Kaag (Tilburg), T.Limperg (Amsterdam) and H.W.C. Bordewijk (Groningen). Many of them were even primarily business economists. Another factor muddying a clear divide was what we might call the 'Dutch Twist', if we may thus label the preoccupation with moral and ethical questions in economic affairs. This pervaded the 'great debate' of the period concerning the problem 'regulation or freedom?' but it was also present in the gold standard discussion. The (protestant) defenders of the gold standard especially voiced the argument that its maintenance was a matter of good faith. Thus ethical beliefs and value judgements tended often to supersede pure economic analysis.

In 1929, the annual meeting of the Dutch Association of Economics and Statistics was devoted to 'The Essence of Price Stabilisation', and discussion papers were written by miss E.C. van Dorp and professor G.M. Verrijn Stuart (the son of C.A. Verrijn Stuart). Miss van Dorp did not altogether exclude the possibility of complete abolition of monetary uses of gold; but she advocated some kind of gold standard on two grounds. Firstly, she considered that gold always had a 'value in use' of its own – apart from any nominal value attributed to it by monetary authorities. Secondly, she preferred fixed rates of exchange to fixed price levels and saw gold as the best pivot. But she conceded the necessity to economise on the stock of gold kept by the central banks. In her opinion, the fact that 2,250 million pounds were lying in vaults without yeilding any interest would be something for posterity to ridicule. We quote her conclusion: "The gold standard must be maintained, and the League of Nations must undertake a stabilisation of gold, which also serves the goal of economising on gold use, and in the long run abolish this use for monetary purposes."(8)

The other discussant, G.M. Verrijn Stuart, held a plea for value stable money. But he did not condemn all price movements: "Only those price level fluctuations caused by excessive growth or a shrinking of the money supply are a proof of insufficient value stability of the exchange medium. If the price level fluctuates through 'money' causes, these must be counteracted, but if the same happens through 'goods' causes, things must be left to take their course." (9) Following Keynes' 'Tract on monetary reform' (1923), he advocated an essentially a-metallic monetary system. If the powers of central banks would be widened, fears of increased inflation risks would be unjustified. But such a system would only work under strong international coordination: "For a small country it is difficult to introduce an a-metallic system by itself if it does not want to isolate itself and disturb the fixed parity of exchange rates."(10) It is not surprising that Verrijn Stuart would later become one of the prominent members of the pro-devaluationist NVWG *Nederlandsche Vereeniging voor Waardevast Geld*, (Dutch Assocation for Value Stable Money) (see below ch. 6) and that miss van Dorp would refuse to join.

Both these authors examined at some length the problem of measuring the fluctuations of the price level (as an economic and a statistical question) following a number of foreign authors. But the Netherlands had (at least) two own system builders in these matters: J. Goudriaan and W.C. Mees. The engineer J. Goudriaan, a director of Philips (Eindhoven) and part-time professor of economics in Rotterdam (and later in Delft as well) advocated a monetary system founded on a. a 'numeraire' which must be indifferent to 'natural price formation' and b. the requirement that goods should be 'indifferent in time' (i.e. have a constant value). In his inaugural lecture in Delft, he advocated his money, "popularly speaking an index of wholesale prices", as a means of combating unemployment by eliminating its most prominent cause (in his eyes), the synchronous dip of raw materials prices.(11) Goudriaan was also a leading member of the NVWG. But his colleague at the agricultural high school of Wageningen, the economics professor W.C. Mees, was ridiculed in the NVWG organ *Waardevast Geld* for his alternative system, which was only partly based on indexation. His 'reduction system' (*Herleidingsstelsel*) and his lecture to the NVWG were reviewed by W.J.L. van Es in its monthly journal. He called the system "a dragon with a gold head and an indexation tail".(12)

Mees opposed devaluation as it would only (temporarily) cure one of the symptoms and not the underlying cause of the disproportional development of wages, prices and exchange rates. He advocated gold value for money and short-term liabilities against index value for wages and long run debts. Van Es particularly attacked Mees' idea of using the consumer prices index as a pivot of his system; he considered this much too rigid to mirror the true price movements. Mees was one of the few opponents of devaluation who took the trouble (or was given the opportunity) to write a reply in the NVWG's journal. In his opinion, the curve of the consumer prices index would show a parallel development to the one of wholesale prices, and for that reason be acceptable both to the business community and the public.(13)

Another anti-devluationist to write in *Waardevast Geld* on this matter was the economics professor of the Free University (Amsterdam), F.L. van Muiswinkel. He discussed the possible effects of devaluation for the retail trade by looking at the development of gross profits and distribution costs. In his calculation, adaptation of retail prices to wholesale prices (after a devaluation) would lower the profit margin. This could only be compensated by a larger turnover, but he could not see where the increasing purchasing power in the economy was supposed to come from. So the effects of devaluation might benefit producers and exporters but would certainly harm most retailers. Van Muiswinkel expected more results from the government's deflationary policy than from devaluation.(14)

A reply was written by A.W.J. Renaud, a spokesman of the house owners lobby, which provoked an answer by Van Muiswinkel. Renaud pointed to the sorry development of Dutch grocers' net profits between 1928 and 1933. He criticised some of Van Muiswinkel's numerical examples. But his final argument was the improved economic situation in those countries which had devalued and which had experienced larger purchasing power and increased home consumption, while the opposite happened in the remaining gold bloc countries. This switching between micro- and macro-economic reasoning (what will happen to individual firms and households vs. what will happen to the whole economy) is characteristic of a large part of the dispute between the proponents and the opponents of devaluation. Moreover, the theoretical debate – maintaining, lowering or altogether abolishing the gold parity of the guilder – was narrowed down in the political debate to: for or against the gold standard. The 'devaluationists' were unable to bring home the notion that they were only attacking the monetary policy of the government and were otherwise respectable people – as the experience of the NVWG was to show.

Ceteris paribus, "Other things remaining equal" (the famous economists' reserve), one can try to compute the effects of a devaluation or depreciation: higher prices for imported goods and services in terms of the home currency, more competitive export prices in foreign currencies. But the final effect on the balance of payments, and ultimately on employment and national income, is determined by the elasticity with which home and foreign demand will react to the changed terms of trade. And, moreover, it is impossible to predict the psychological effects of devaluation. In practice, other things will not remain equal.

The defenders of the gold standard were apt to condemn the expected rise of the price level as 'inflationary'. Their proposed 'deflationary policy' implied a lowering of wages and prices so as to maintain the standard of living and improve the export position as well. But the downward rigidity of wages and prices in practice was an important handicap in carrying this through. The moral side of their argument pertained to the effect that debts contracted in guilders would be worth less, both in foreign exchange and in purchasing power at home (given a rising price level). In bringing forward the moral argument against devaluation, the prime minister Hendrik Colijn could point to several academic scholars doing the same.

The roman catholic professor, Ch. Raaymakers, spoke on the subject to the 'Association for the Advancement of Science among Dutch catholics' in 1934. He was pessimistic about the possible export stimulus from devaluation – because of foreign protectionism – as well as about debt relief and higher profitability. He founded his moral stand against devaluation upon the government's promise to guarantee the gold value of the guilder and upon the principle of distributive justice. His lecture was reviewed by M.W.Holtrop (who became president of the central bank after the war) who wrote that the only point in the moral argument was about foreign creditors but this was no valid reason to abstain from devaluation.(15)

Another advocate of the gold standard, professor H.W.C. Bordewijk from Groningen, also mixed economic and moral reasoning. Lecturing to solicitors after the devaluation of the pound in 1931, he said: "The abolition of the gold standard entirely fits into a protectionist framework". He called this a "narrow-minded neo-Mercantilism" which would not work. Meanwhile, he saw the Dutch gold standard as stronger than ever: "Should this ever be abolished

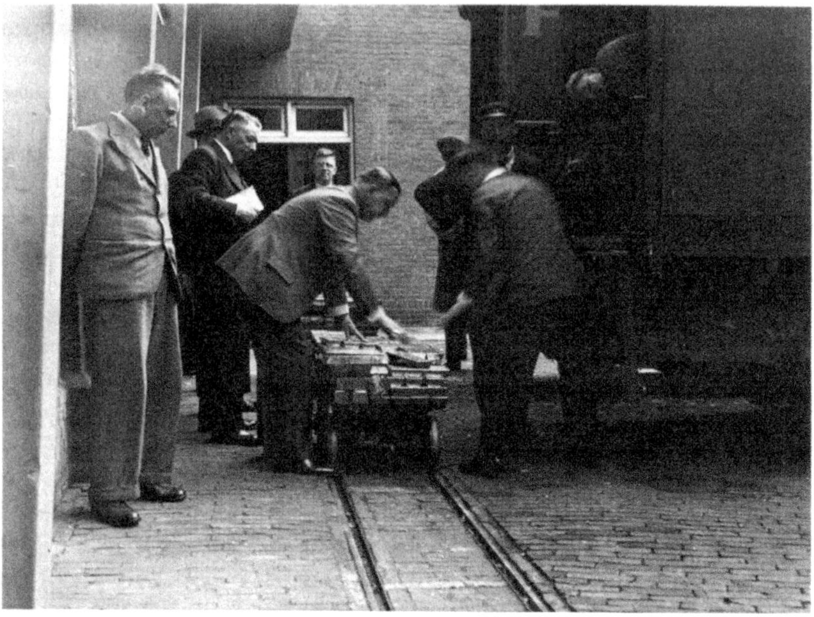

Delivery of gold at the Netherlands Bank (1936). Photo: De Nederlandsche Bank.

then be it never in the way England did, never as an emergency in abnormal times." Only if something better than gold – which by itself is not altogether exempt from value fluctuations – could be found, might gold be abolished by a deliberate act of policy.(16) Looking back in 1936, but still before the Dutch devaluation, he followed the diagnosis of L. Robbins ('The Great Depression', 1934): "In 1925 the British authorities had restored the gold standard at a parity which, in the light of subsequent events, is now generally admitted to have been too high".(17) Thus a stream of *undervalued* monetary gold left the country. At the end, he added his own belief to this analysis: "To me it is a very happy circumstance that the requirements of economics are supported in this respect by those of good faith (....) The gold standard, meaning maintenance of existing gold parities, has, in these times of universal suspicion, the grand task of restoring *trust* in the field of credit and trade – indispensable to combating trade impediments and the autarky fallacy which will become the grave of all welfare."

When we turn to the other side we find the most ardent opponents of the gold standard at the *Economische Hogescholen:* Polak and F. de de Vries in Rotterdam, Gimbrère and Kaag in Tilburg. Father C.A. and son G.M. Verrijn Stuart (who succeeded his father in the economics chair in Utrecht after teaching in Rotterdam), joined the association of these colleagues and a number of worried businessmen in the NVWG in 1934. The most active person in the founding of this society, as well as being its president, was the liberal economist Nico J.

Polak. Most of his writings were concerned with business economics and taxes and only to a lesser extent with economic policy. But in the devaluation debate he was, in the first place, an organiser: of the NVWG, of its petitions and of its journal. He took no active part in the discussion in the leading professional journals *Economisch-Statistische Berichten* and *De Economist* but, of course, as an editor of the former from November 1934, he could exert some influence. Of the five new editors who joined in that month only one, P. Lieftinck, could be called a supporter of the gold standard. The other four were Polak, Tinbergen, H.M.A. van der Valk and De Vries. *Economisch-Statistisch Berichten* was a Rotterdam-based journal – and Rotterdam was a bulwark of the 'devaluationists'. Already a year earlier, in November 1933, the editors had found it necessary to deny rumours that it was their policy to withhold pro-gold standard articles from the journal.(18)

Apart from delivering speeches, Polak contributed two pamphlets to the debate: *Aanpassen, maar hoe?*(To adapt, but how? 1935) and *Devaluatie*(1936) in the series 'Pro and Contra'. 'Adaptation' was the keyword for the government's economic policy. Polak showed how little this meant by identifying how many meanings of the word existed. He distinguished five seperate interpretations: 1. Adaptation of revenue to spending, 2. Adaptation of spending to revenue, 3. Adaptation of costs to revenues, 4. Adaptation of employment to productive capacity, and 5. Adaptation of home to international purchasing power of money, or rather adaptation by devaluation. He rejected the deflationary policy employed to realise the first three goals and he was against promoting the fourth by means of more and more regulation. He reviewed the effects of devaluation for various categories in economic life: investors, employers, farmers, the employed and the unemployed and, finally, government. Most would be better off; and he did not forget to strike the moral note in passing: "Only the foreigner who has fled into the comfortable guilder for fear of his own currency and the Dutchman spending his interest abroad will be heavily hit. Neither of these two hurts our conscience." Polak did not recommend devaluation as a panacea, but as a necessary precondition for economic recovery. He also sketched the favourable psychological effects: "Lack of courage and fear of a further lowering of prices will disappear and employment and purchasing power will increase".(19) In his 1935 pamphlet, he drew the conclusion that the official deflation policy had failed. A year later he concentrated on the choice which remained: between devaluation and "automatic adaptation" (i.e. by the forces of the market).(20) He was now more technical in his examples and calculated that the consumer price index would rise much less as a result of devaluation than the opponents of this measure were predicting. And, as for ethics: "Is not the exaggerated concern for the investor's guilder coinciding with depressed wages and pensions because of money's increased purchasing power, is that not a Janus headed morale?"

A part of the quantitative analysis and of the numerical examples with which the devaluationist illustrated their reasoning, was provided by the statistician and accountant dr. J.G. Stridiron. He also produced the statistical appendix to the pro-devaluation petition to the government in January 1934. His numbers and conclusions were attacked by C. Kool in *Economisch-Statitische Berichten* and by the staff of Trip of the Netherlands Bank (see below pp 175-179).(21) Stridiron's central arguments were that the export performance of non-gold countries was much better than that of the gold countries, that government bonds rated higher in non-gold countries, and, finally, that employment figures developed more favourably in non-gold countries. Against this, Kool argued that Stridiron had forgotten to confront exports with imports figures and to draw conclusions for the balance of payments. On the second point, he suggested that investment in government bonds was rather a sign of lack of profitability in other possible investments. Lastly, he contended that employment figures were not that much better in non-gold countries. Certainly Kool's second point seems convincing.

This exchange between Stridiron and Kool was one of the few examples of a prolonged discussion on certain aspects of devaluation. Much of the rest of the debate consisted largely of a repetition at length of arguments for a once embraced standpoint. Few converts were made on either side. Moreover, the moral twist in the debate did not exactly contribute to the analytical rigour of the discussion. All in all, the debate surrounding the gold standard in the Netherlands was not an example of the advancement of 'high theory'. Some of the best monetary theorists, like de Vries and Koopmans, scarcely came to the foreground at all. If anything, the debate is rather more interesting as an example of how value judgements, sometimes dressed up as analysis, can influence the discussion of economic policy.

Notes

1. J. Foreman-Peck, *A History of the World Economy*, Brighton, 1983, 166. For a short Dutch textbook introduction to the gold standard: J.C.P.A. van Esch, *Internationale economische betrekkingen in hoofdlijnen*, Leiden/Antwerpen, 1982, 100-114.
2. Foreman-Peck, *A History of the World Economy*, 182.
3. *Ibid.*, 240.
4. M.M.G.Fase (ed.) *Neutraal Geld, Keuze uit de geschriften van J.G. Koopmans*, Leiden/Antwerpen, 1982, 29-30.
5. M.H.J. Dullaart, *Regeling of Vrijheid. Nederlands economisch denken tussen de wereldoorlogen*, Alblasserdam, 1984, 229.
6. *Ibid.*, 34.
7. J. Tinbergen, *De Konjunktuur*, Amsterdam, 1933, 180.
8. *Prae-adviezen over het wezen der prijs-stabilisatie*, 's Gravenhage, 1919, 70.
9. *Ibid.*, 96-7.
10. *Ibid.*, 166.
11. J. Goudriaan, *De oorzaken der werkloosheid en de middelen ter bestrijding*, Delft, 1936, 42.
12. *Waardevast Geld*, (1936) 4.
13. *Ibid.*, 20-21.
14. *Ibid.*, 49-65.
15. *Waardevast Geld* (1935) 25-29; *Economische Statistische Berichten* (ESB), 12.12.1934, 1096-1098.

16. H.W.C. Bordewijk, *Om de Gouden Standaard* Groningen/'s-Gravenhage, 1931, 26.
17. W.H.C. Bordewijk, *Het Geld na den Wereldoorlog*, Zwolle, 1936.
18. *ESB*, 15.11.1933, editorial.
19. N.J. Polak, Aanpassen, maar hoe? (1935), *Verspreide Geschriften* II, Purmerend, 1953, 201-217.
20. N.J. Polak, Devaluatie (1936), *Verspreide Geschriften* II, 218-249.
21. J.G. Stridiron and C. Kool in *ESB*, 20.9.1933, 4.10.1933, 10.10.1934, 24.10.1934, 7.11.1934.

CHAPTER THREE

The Employers' Associations

From the devaluation of sterling in September 1931 until the eventual fall of the guilder almost five years later, the various employers' associations wrestled with the question of which position to take in the discussion on monetary policy. The conflict of interests among employers made this far from easy. Exporters complained continuously about the high value of the guilder eroding their competitiveness, whilst businesses which imported their raw materials and sold their products on the domestic market argued against a devaluation of the guilder preferring legislative measures to protect the home market. Efforts in this direction, however, touched a sensitive spot in the export sector since it feared that they would lead to repraisals abroad. Even without the emotions, which alongside the rational arguments also played an important role, the leaders of the employers' associations would have had their hands full just trying to create one line from a membership with such divergent interests. Prompted by an aversion to devaluation, reasoned or not, entrepreneurs could take up positions which with hindsight appeared to be contradictory to their own self-interests. Thus, for example, the ship-owner E. Heldring adopted the slogan of the president of the Netherlands Bank that devaluation was equivalent to coinage debasement. His vision was diametrically opposed to that of his fellow ship-owner A.F. Bronsing, one of the driving forces behind the pro-devaluation NVWG. Incidentally, as we will see, those in favour of devaluation were equally capable of emotional statements. Later in this chapter we will examine the stance adopted by the employers' associations in this difficult situation and their efforts to keep their membership together. Before this, however, we will begin with a short description of the different organisations themselves.

At first sight the Dutch employers were as much affected by the process of 'pillarisation' as the rest of the body politic. In addition to the independant VNW, *Verbond van Nederlandsch Werkgevers* (Union of Dutch Employers), there was the protestant CWV, *Christelijke Werkgeversvereeniging* (Christian Employers' Association) and two catholic organisations, the ARKWV, *Algemeene Roomsch-Katholieke Werkgevers Vereeniging* (General Roman-Catholic Employers' Association) and the RKVWV, *Roomsch-Katholiek Verbond van Werkgeversvakvereenigingen* (Roman catholic Union of Employers' Associations). However, the pillarisation of the business-world was more apparent than real. The VNW was by far the most important organisation. The CWV by contrast was of only marginal significance, whilst the membership of the catholic organisations was limited primarily to the Southern provinces.

Compared with the large political influence of the protestant political parties, the limited significance of the CWV is surprising. Established in 1918, the CWV had reached such a precarious position by 1933 that it was no longer even able to pay the salary of its own secretary.(1) Only in 1936 did it begin to claw its way out of this situation and it was not until after the Second World War that it began to be considered seriously again. The most important factor behind the limited success lay in the attitude of the great protestant leader Abraham Kuyper towards employers' organisations. Kuyper had been of the opinion that employers should limit their organisation strictly to business so as to preserve their neutrality. Most protestant theorists followed Kuypers' line that "a general christian association was sufficient for reflecting the social questions involving theology, whilst the economic interests of the employers could be represented without difficulty by neutral trade associations".(2) Many protestant employers, including committee members of the CWV, were also active in the 'neutral' employers' associations under the umbrella of the VNW. In view of its limited importance as an independent force we will leave the CWV outside the analysis in this chapter.

The catholic employers' associations were much more significant than the CWV. Both the ARKWV (which organised employers by diocese) and the RKVWV (which organised employers by business sector) had a large following among the catholics in the South.(3) They stood for a policy which on a number of points clearly diverged from that of the VNW. Nonetheless, many catholic employers, including big names as Pierre Regout of the cement industry and J. Lips of the safe and lock factory, were also members of the VNW and the secretary of the (catholic) Association of Woollen Manufacturers represented his entire membership in the VNW as well.(4)

The VNW, created in 1926 by a fusion of various neutral employers' associations, was the most representative and the most important of the employers' associations. However, its influence in these years should not be exaggerated either. At the ministry of economic affairs it was the agrarian interests which seemed to carry the most weight.(5) The desire to be consulted more frequently united all the non-agrarian employers associations regardless of political or religious background.

Finally, as a promoter of employers' interests, it is necessary to mention the NMNH, *Nederlandsche Maatschappij voor Nijverheid en Handel* (Dutch Society for Industry and Trade).(6) The NMNH, founded in 1777, had as its aim "the increase of welfare through the promotion of industry and trade". It was composed of about 40 departments which considered matters of general or local importance and a central committee which represented the Society vis-à-vis other bodies. Its membership was drawn from the upper echelons of Dutch society and included entrepreneurs. Although it was not an official employers' association we have included it in the analysis because it often gave voice to views of individual employers which the VNW, for example, preferably kept to itself.

AUTARKY OR FREE TRADE

The fall of sterling on 28 September 1931 gave employers' circles little cause for concern over the strength of the guilder. A commentary in the NMNH journal *Maatschappijbelangen* exuded a sense of superiority which, with hindsight, seems definitely misplaced: "this much is certain, we should not withhold sympathy for England at this difficult moment. There is no reason whatsoever to view England as a competitor with its back to the wall or to pride ourselves on our current superior position."(7) The writer dismissed the thought that England would come to enjoy an advantage over foreign competitors. "As far as a judgement can be made at the moment, it is to be expected that within a short time rising prices and wages will neutralise the artificial advantage."(8) It is interesting to see how "the abdication of the formely so powerful Albion as first and foremost trading power in the world" was explained: "Gambling fever and speculation have replaced entrepreneurial spirit and drive for action. Conservatism and complacency are the reasons why other countries advance more quickly."(9)

The commentary in *De Nederlandsche Werkgever*, the VNW journal, was more sober. Weighing the advantages and disadvantages, it came to the conclusion that the end result of the devaluation would not be favourable for England.(10) It would, moreover, lead to a reduction of incomes among wage-earners and the unemployed. The journal called upon the Dutch trade unions to draw the correct conclusion. What the VNW meant by that last comment became clear in later articles. The trade unions should cooperate with employers in lowering wage costs and reducing government expenditure. "United cooperation of all social groups" was the order of the day.(11) The idea that entrepreneurs were profiting from the crisis should be disposed of once and for all. It was not the employers but the workers employed in local government or in companies such as public utilities, relatively insulated from competition, which had benefitted because their normal wages had not followed deflation. The employers and the less privileged workers were in fact in the same boat.(12) The government was assigned a major responsibility in the realisation of the goal since it would only succeed if it kept a firm hand in pruning its expenditure. According to the VNW these measures were necessary "if we want to protect our country from the disaster which the abandonment of the Gold Standard would entail".(13)

The *R.K. Werkgever*, the organ of both the ARKWV and RKVWV, reacted the most somberly. An article on the English crisis and its consequences made no mention of the compensatory effect of the anticipated inflation. As far as the *R.K. Werkgever* was concerned a 20 per cent devaluation was no different from a 20 per cent wage reduction or the sudden imposition of a 20 per cent import duty. From the catholic side too came a call for government intervention: "since allowing these events to pass over us passively implies the murder and destruction of the largest part of Dutch industry and agriculture".(14) But the measures which the *R.K. Werkgever* envisaged did not include a devaluation of the guilder. At a large 'crisis-congress' held on 10 May 1932 in The Hague and transmitted by the catholic radio, the ARKWV and RKVWV made clear what they wanted: an active trade policy. The general-secretary, L.G. Kortenhorst, expressed it as follows: "Netherlands; buy only there where abroad is bought from us ... and (where they) are willing to pay for it. Thus, back to the pure barter system."(15)

In the eyes of the catholic employers' associations, the repeated calls for purposeful government intervention had little effect. In November 1932, a year after the fall of sterling, the *R.K. Werkgever* noted that there had been precious little by way of an active trade policy. Legislation on quotas, anti-dumping measures and clearing had all remained dead letters. New disasters for businesses loomed on the horizon in the form of tax increases. The municipalities had failed to cut their expenditure and large groups of workers had failed to make the necessary sacrifices. "Is there any other country in Europe which across the board shows such a dilapidated picture such as ours?"(16) There was only one bright spot to be observed. In the same edition of the *R.K. Werkgever* the chairman of the Tilburg Woollen Manufacturers wrote triumphantly about the change in stance of the Twente cotton-mills.(17). Twente, which exported primarily to the Dutch East Indies and other countries without a strong domestic industry, had previously never felt the need for protectionist measures. This had been in contrast to the woollen producers which had had to sell in the markets of industrial countries and were now confronted with a wall of protectionism. Now it appeared the Twente producers were feeling the effects of exchange rate depreciation and were calling for measures to guarantee their colonial markets. He now felt that this "opportunist" change in course made the time ripe for a powerful joint campaign by the most important industrial groups. Industry could now get the help it had missed out on as a result of the conflicting advice often given to the government in the past.

This optimism was somewhat misplaced. Whilst the catholic employers' call for more state intervention, or even autarky,(18) became shriller, the VNW was repeatedly urging the government towards international negotiations with the purpose of reducing trade barriers. It is true that both organisations followed the same line on the need to lower prices and, to effectuate this, wages. The catholics, however, also emphasised the need for concrete government measures to counter unemployment. As far as the VNW was concerned, the recovery of business activity was the greatest problem; solve that and the rest would look after itself. On the question of the gold standard too there were differences in viewpoint between the VNW on the one hand and the ARKWV on the other. To the day of the devaluation itself the VNW was to remain consistently opposed to devaluation, whilst the statements from the catholic employers became ever more nuanced and the desirability of maintaining the gold standard made ever more conditional.

At an extraordinary meeting of the membership of the VNW in February 1932, the members present discussed the gold standard. *De Nederlandsche Werkgever* reported that there had been a lively discussion from which could be concluded "that the meeting was fully aware of the seriousness of the situation".(19) Such a bland conclusion could only mean that the members failed to reach agreement. Whatever the case, the report of a general meeting in September 1934 mentioned explicitly that a number of members had pleaded for devaluation of the guilder. The chairman of the VNW, the textile manufacturer H.P. Gelderman, countered criticism with two arguments. In the first place he contended that it was still too early to evaluate the results of the English devaluation, "besides, the devaluation in England is not yet finished".(20) By way of advice he quoted Asquith: "wait and see". The second argument was political. The VNW had been very unhappy with the weak policy of the cabinet of Ruys de Beerenbrouck which, moreover, had favoured agricultural interests above industrial. After the April 1933 elections Colijn had become minister-president of a broadly based cabinet. The former director of the *Bataafsche Petroleum Maatschappij*, known as a strong personality, had won much more confidence from employers. However, in his cabinet, Colijn had made the maintenance of the gold parity of the guilder one of the pillars of its policy. "Every action in support of devaluation is an action against our ministry, which as a national cabinet should be able to count on the support of every citizen and certainly on the sympathy of organised industry."(21) Not everyone was convinced by this poorly supported appeal for the maintenance of the gold standard. It is even questionable whether Gelderman himself believed in it. Although Gelderman was one of the 63 signatories of the anti-devaluation petition in 1935, as far back as August 1931 Ernst Heldring had noted in his journal that Gelderman and Waller (a predecessor of Gelderman as chairman of the VNW) were sceptical about the future of the guilder. Gelderman is supposed to have said that the guilder should not be defended to the bitter end if industry, trade and shipping were to be threatened as a result.(22) However, to the outside world, the VNW managed to maintain at least the appearance of unity.

A number of businessmen, including some pretty big names, decided to cooperate outside the VNW in an initiative of a number of professors to send a confidential petition to the government (see chapter 7 for more details). In the petition, dated 19th July 1933, a number of the signatories were of the opinion that a devaluation was the only remedy whilst others preferred (unspecified) drastic measures, holding open the option of a devaluation should these not succeed. No mention was made of who supported what. Among the signatories we find names as S. van den Bergh, director of Unilever, Anton Philips of the Philips concern in Eindhoven, G.A. Kessler director of Hoogovens, textile manufacturers as G.J. van Heek and H. ter Kuile and H.F. van Leeuwen of the Twentse Bank. These same names also appear on the petition of 5 January

1934. The tone had changed and the petition was now unambiguously in favour of devaluation. It is noticeable that these pro-devaluation entrepreneurs tried, as far as possible, to hide these activities from publicity. This was perhaps not so surprising in view of the fact that the press, more often than not, portrayed devaluation as being something akin to coinage debasement and the fact that they feared being depicted as opponents of Colijn. Given this need for secrecy, it is probable that rumours inferring that Philips was a substantial contributor to the funds of the pro-devaluation group, the NVWG, contained an element of truth.

Meanwhile, one entrepreneur had deliberately sought the full glare of publicity and that via the NMNH. This was no one less than the practically untouchable Sir Henry Deterding, Director-General of the *Koninklijke Petroleum Maatschappij*, who demanded that a letter from him be read before the members in the general meeting of June 1933.(23) In this letter Deterding unfolded his vision on the problems surrounding the gold standard. To support his arguments he had also sent a foreword which he had written in a book by Dunlop, 'Facts and Figures about the Crisis'. In the foreword he had pleaded for a return to the silver standard and during the meeting itself he was attacked on this point by a number of the members. In his letter he went much further and pleaded for guilder devaluation. "The Netherlands should follow the currency-measure of the majority of trading countries. Fix the dollar at Dfl. 2.50 or sterling at Dfl. 10.00 or take gold at Dfl. 2000 per kilogramme. Yes, I would go even further, make the standard in the Dutch Indies equivalent to that in the Far East, in the same way that you are bringing the Netherlands (down) to (the level of) the Far East..." In highly emotional terms he attacked the legitimacy of the gold standard: "Must the hungry population of China and Russia be denied access to the large quantities of food which are being destroyed by us and others because there exists no means of trade? Should we not abandon the theoretical standard and put a practical one in its place? Is this not our duty as *human beings*? I am not speaking for *Koninklijke*, I make this demand as a human being. You must". Just as many anti-devaluationists urged the Netherlands to remain faithful to the gold standard as a beacon at sea for the rest of the world, Deterding too saw a unique role for his country, but in a completely different sense: "If the people of Holland have the moral courage of President Roosevelt and do what in practical terms *must* be correct but which will probably be condemned in theoretical terms by many economists and monetary theorists, then it will inspire the whole world to do what will save the whole world. However, King Midas will commit suicide even more quickly since he is anyway condemned to death." Whether Deterding was speaking purely as a "human being" and not perhaps a tiny bit as *Koninklijke* is a question we will not enter into. The journal of the non-confessional trade unions, *De Vakbeweging* reported that a devaluation would yield *Koninklijke* a profit of Dfl. 50,000,000, though how it came to this figure was not stated (see also p 109).(24)

Deterding's letter was not well received. The executive of the *Nederlandsche*

Maatschappij refrained from any official comment, but one of its number, J.W. Beyen, in a lecture on the stability of international financial relationships, tackled the question at length.(25) Beyen, an executive of the *Rotterdamsche Bankvereeniging* and Trip's replacement in the Dutch delegation at the World Economic Conference in London, announced that he would be restrained in his criticism: "The gold standard should be an idol for the Dutch people, Sir Henry Deterding is that too. It is to be regretted, therefore, that he set foot on what for him is strange territory and has drawn conclusions the logic behind which the speaker could not accept." We will not go into the technical aspects of his criticism. It was an exposé permeated with the hope that the London Conference would lead to a stabilisation of exchange rates. Even here though, a certain chauvinism was never far from the surface: "The Netherlands and Switzerland are the only ones with a clear conscience (i.e. whose exchange rates were still at their pre-war gold parities – ESAB). Naturally that is for others an unpleasant feeling." Those other members at the meeting who participated in the discussion fell in behind Beyen's standpoint. Deterding, at least in public, never returned to the subject.

TABOE AND CRITICISM

"Through the letter of Mr. Deterding, the question of the value of the guilder was unexpectedly brought into discussion."(26) If we look at the period between October 1931 and September 1936 as a whole, what is noticeable is how few times such a burning issue was raised at annual meetings of the NMNH. The explanation is easily given: the executive had decided that the entire question was to be avoided as far as possible. Directly after the devaluation of the guilder the editor of *Maatschappijbelangen* made this decision public: "For almost five years .....in our country the question of the devaluation of the guilder has been the subject of relatively unfruitful discussions, a subject which contributed to clashes of meanings without bringing the parties closer together, and (a subject) over which it was better not to speak in public. Meanwhile, moreover, because of the stated position of our government .... the question had taken on a political dimension. These circumstances led our executive at the time to decide to touch upon the subject as little as possible within our society."(27)

Not everyone agreed with this policy line and, not surprisingly, this criticism came largely from the ranks of those opposed to maintaining the gold standard. Professor J. Goudriaan, an active member of the pro-devaluation NVWG was able to speak after the devaluation with the authority of someone whose standpoint was borne out by events: "The greatest error which was made in the past was a political, even a moral, error. People had as far as possible supressed freedom of discussion over the monetary question and in the process had forgotten that this freedom, which is embedded deep in Dutch popular conviction, was the most efficient means of arriving at the truth by way of the shortest route."(28) This statement was made during a speech at a branch meeting of the *Maatschappij* in Breda. At the time he did not name those responsible but in a later publication he made clear that he had the executive of the *Maatschappij* in mind.(29) What Goudriaan did not know was that the executive had taken this decision in response to outside pressure. No one other than the president of the Netherlands Bank, L.J.A. Trip, had told the president of the *Maatschappij*, in December 1933, that he was unhappy that the question of the gold standard was still the subject of discussion without the government having been given sufficient time to demonstrate the results of its own policies.(30)

The taboe surrounding the gold standard was also commented upon by professor N.J. Polak, chairman of the NVWG, who was allowed to address a branch meeting of the *Maatschappij* in Den Helder in May 1936. He suggested that it was possible to talk of censorship in this respect: "The major newspapers gloss over the question and from above the advice is given; no longer discuss it."(31) Polak announced that he would not be making propaganda for devaluation in his lecture but only giving information, an intention which would seem to be at odds with his definition of the term 'devaluation'; "devaluation is the realisation of the restoration of balance"! The chairman of the branch had clearly taken a possible one-sidedness in Polak's address into account since even before Polak had spoken he had announced that someone would be invited who would see the question from a completely different standpoint. The speaker invited to redress the balance was A.A. van Sandick, like Beyen a member of the *Rotterdamsche Bankvereeniging*. In his lecture held on 3 June 1936, van Sandick defended the controversial statement once made by Trip that devaluation was synonymous with debasement.(32)

The executive of the *Maatschappij* would have preferred to avoid the question of the gold standard altogether but, if that was impossible, then they attempted to give both sides equal space. In the December 1934 issue of *Maatschappijbelangen*, an account of a pro-devaluation lecture by Goudriaan was matched by one by professor H. Frijda against. In February 1933, the same recipe had been used, that time with dr. R. van Genechten in favour and professor G.M. Verrijn Stuart against (the latter was soon to change sides). In the discussions which ensued on the second occasion the textile manufacturer H. ter Kuile sided with van Genechten, commenting: "It would not surprise me if we were to end up being buried by our money."(33)

Whilst the VNW remained, right to the end, loyal to the monetary policy of the Colijn cabinet and the NMNH tried to steer a neutral course, on the side of the catholic employer' associations ever more critical and cautionary voices were raised against the government. The first shot across the bows was made by the then chairman of the ARKWV, M.P.L. Steenberghe, in a speech on 27 November 1933. He urged his organisations to study the question of the value of the guilder and openly questioned "whether it is correct to present devaluation to the Dutch people as the greatest possible disaster....".(34) Six months later Steenberghe was called to cabinet office and swallowed, at least temporarily, his own criticism of the untarnished guilder policy. It was not until March 1935 that a dissenting voice was heard again in the *R.K. Werkgever*, this time taking the form of a report of a speech made by H. Kersten at a meeting of the membership of the ARKWV. Despite the refinement of argument, Kersten's speech could only be seen as a plea for devaluation: "The last thing I want is the panacea for all our ills. I also know that the simple abandonment of the gold standard is an all too easy, a suspiciously easy, therapy. But if foreigners continue to sabotage our position (i.e. by what was called at the time competitive depreciation – ESAB), we should, without panicking, ask ourselves how we should defend ourselves and whether a controlled currency adjustment is not the least bad thing we could choose to avoid something worse."(35) Kersten ended his talk on a suitably christian note: "After this criticism of our guilder, may I conclude by saying something good about it. Whatever else it may lack, one thing is certainly good, and now more than ever, that is the inscription on the edge: God be with us." That Kersten's speech must indeed be interpreted as a plea for devaluation became apparent from a reaction from the general-secretary Kortenhorst in the following issue of the *R.K. Werkgever*. Kortenhorst disagreed with Kersten and focused on the concluding sentences to clarify his criticism. "If the government allows a devaluation to be unleashed, then the inscription on the edge of the new guilder should be altered to read "God help us."(36) Kortenhorst stated that he was still of the opinion that the advantages of a devaluation could be obtained via a safer route and one without the disadvantages of a devaluation; namely through deflation.

The stance of absolute rejection of devaluation adopted by the ARKWV became increasingly difficult to maintain. The devaluation of the Belgian franc sowed new seeds of doubt. On 3 June 1935, in reaction to proposed legislation aimed at reducing *vaste lasten*, the ARKWV sent a petition to the second chamber of parliament condemning the legislation as totally inadequate.(37) It was simply a measure to reduce the budget deficit and had not even the pretention of reducing prices and costs. The implication of this criticism was spelt out in terms which left no room for misinterpretation: "We do not wish to conceal from you....that we no longer have any confidence that this cabinet will be capable, whilst maintaining the gold standard, of mastering the oppressing problems of these times." Now, this did not mean that the ARKWV saw itself aligned with the pro-devaluationists. On the contrary, it remained of the opinion that together with the catholic parliamentary party it had pointed to the only way of avoiding devaluation, namely by lowering the cost of living by 35 per cent. The problem lay in the fact that the Colijn cabinet did not seem capable of executing such a policy. On 5 July, Kortenhorst formulated this as follows: he suggested that since the ARKWV was overwhelmingly against a devaluation, it was their duty to try to correct government policy. He argued that if the opposite were true and ARKWV were in favour of devaluation it could quite happily allow the Colijn cabinet to go its own way since devaluation was the only possible outcome of the policies being followed.(38) In this way the

ARKWV attempted to subtly shift the blame for what was gradually being seen as the inevitable devaluation squarely onto the shoulders of the government.

This political line of 'devaluation is probable but it is not our fault' continued to be pursued in the months which followed. In September 1935, in the middle of a wave of speculation against the guilder, Kortenhorst ventured the opinion that the money markets and the state of government finances had reached the stage where "the question for or against a controlled and self-chosen devaluation must perhaps soon be formulated differently, namely controlled devaluation or uncontrolled inflation".(39) In December 1935, the ARKWV chairman F.H.E. Guljé made known that he considered devaluation "as a solution, but as a less desirable, a violent solution."(40) Should a devaluation become inevitable, he suggested it was better not to wait until the last moment. Meanwhile, the executive had decided to make its position known by means of a resolution addressed to parliament and government. How this came about will be discussed below, but first a few general remarks about the attitude of the catholic employers' organisations.

It is obvious that the ARKWV and RKVWV were much more critical of the Colijn cabinet than the VNW. Yet the catholic party, with which the employers maintained close links, formed part of that cabinet. Part of the explanation is to be sought in the good relations which the employers wished to maintain with the catholic trade unions. The Colijn cabinet had little to offer the workers in the field of social legislation and for that reason it was important for employers to maintain some distance from it. However, a second factor was to be found in the personality of Colijn himself. Colijn had the tendency to present himself as saviour of the Fatherland and this offended the catholics who had allotted themselves an increasingly important role in national politics. On the other hand they did recognise Colijn's more positive qualities and might well have been reasonably happy with the cabinet if there had been more confidence in their own catholic ministers. The difficult relationship came painfully into the open when, in 1933, the catholic social organisations, including employers and workers, wanted to hand over to the government an emergency economic programme. The ministers Colijn, Oud and J.R. Slotemaker de Bruïne welcomed the delegation warmly. "By contrast, the highly uncooperative attitude of minister Verschuur was disagreeable. (He) originally considered an audience unneccessary and then, after long persuasion, permitted an audience of a quarter of an hour. And indeed, after a quarter of an hour it was ended – with the minister announcing that he had to visit his ear-doctor!"(41) This incident gave rise to an angry article in the *R.K. Werkgever*, written after discussion with Steenberghe who considered publication desirable "in view of the apparently obvious growing disquiet, apparent from the almost daily complaints from members of our organisation, from the catholic employers over the more than offensive way in which minister Verschuur lays aside the well-argued complaints and wishes of the business world".(42) In 1934, Verschuur was succeeded by Steenberghe, in whom the catholics had a great deal of confidence. But his tenure of office was too short to alter much. The arrival of his successor, Gelissen, was awaited argus-eyed because he had allowed himself to be talked by Colijn into joining the cabinet without consulting his catholic colleagues.

Matters such as these contributed to the ambivalent attitude of the ARKWV and RKVWV towards the Colijn cabinet. This hesitancy was also apparent on the point of the gold standard. On the one hand they did not feel bound automatically to support the government line but on the other they had no wish to be portrayed as the cabinet's opponents. The caution involved in dealing with anything to do with the gold standard was reinforced by the fact that no agreement on the question existed within the ranks of its membership. At the general meeting which Kersten had addressed in March 1935 (see above p 38), this had again become apparent. After that meeting a whole series of events (the Belgian devaluation, the resignation of Steenberghe, the July cabinet crisis etc.) forced the executive to take stock anew. Moreover, they thought they could detect "on the part of the government a steadily less forceful formulation in the way in which devaluation was rejected".(43) All of this prompted the executive to conduct a survey of the membership, in the greatest possible secrecy, in an attempt to gauge whether a consensus existed on the devaluation issue and, if so, what it was. The tone of the letter in which the affiliated organisations were asked for their views, suggested that the executive at least expected few benefits from the guilder's adherence to the gold standard.(44) From the replies received, however, there was no indication of the concensus which the executive had presumably hoped for. The report of the meetings in the dioceses portrayed a situation of deep division between committed adherents to both sides and, moreover, large numbers who had refrained from voting either way.(45) Exact figures are missing, but because businessmen from different sectors were represented in each diocese they would probably not reveal much anyway. More interesting in this respect is, therefore, the polling of the employers' associations by the RKVWV. Here too the division appeared great. The association for Ladies Mantles Manufacturers declared itself against devaluation (though it admitted to 'converts' within its ranks). In the men's clothing industry however the opinion seemed to be that a devaluation was unavoidable. Kortenhorst reported that within the metal and engineering industries opinion was divided according to the nature of work. From the survey and the informal questioning(46) it appeared that majorities in favour of devaluation were to be found in the woollen industry, the wax industry, the clog manufacturers, the hatters and the cigar-makers. The construction industry and printers had no clear majorities for one side or the other. The leather manufacturers reported that they had not met; the reason being that opinion was divided! When the latter were surveyed informally it appeared the majority were against devaluation since 70 per cent of the cost price was made up of imported materials.

The results of the survey were discussed at a joint executive meeting of the ARKWV and RKVWV. The ARKWV chairman, Guljé, summed up the situation by stating simply that there was obviously no consensus among the membership and that he doubted whether a lengthy renewed discussion would bring the two sides closer together.(47) In order to avoid an endless debate and to ensure that some result be still forthcoming, he announced that the executive had prepared a resolution which could be sent to the government and members of parliament. The text showed all the signs of being a compromise document and many present found it far too vague. Indeed, one of the delegates went so far as to suggest that, as it stood, the cabinet would be able to read into the proposal's weak conclusion support for its equally weak policies. Suggestions were then made to tighten the text and strengthen the message, though looking at the original and the final versions it is sometimes difficult to appreciate the difference. The original version had concluded by urging government and parliament "to alter the policy followed to date and to urgently take measures, whether in the monetary area or not, to save business from destruction". Under pressure from the meeting, the words "whether in the monetary area or not" were altered to " if necessary also in the monetary area"; apparently to increase the force of the message. On the other hand the term "destruction" was found too strong and replaced by "further decline leading to a disaster." The publication of the resolution produced no discernable change in government policy. Nevertheless, the RKVWV and ARKWV took no further action in this direction.

AT LAST! DEVALUATION

When the devaluation of the guilder eventually occurred it was greeted in employers' circles with scarcely veiled relief. "At last!", proclaimed the headline in *Maatschappijbelangen*.(48) The editor Bierens de Haan sighed: "At last this question .... has not only been freed from the sphere which had made it taboe, but at the same time it has been resolved." Devaluation, he suggested, was something always hanging over the economy and which had been inevitable anyway. It is always easier to prophesy after the event.

The glee of the *R.K. Werkgever* was initially at the expense of the discomfiture of others: "The papers, which had until recently portrayed monetary correction as a crime and a folly, especially when responsibility for it could be shoved onto the catholic population, announced within a few hours that the Netherlands would now pluck the fruits of the deflationary policy".(49) Of course, the *R.K. Werkgever* too had seen it coming all along: "Slowly but surely the returns of government policy had crumbled to such a degree that even without the windfall of the French and Swiss devaluation the abandonment of the gold standard could no longer be avoided." Having had its revenge, the next issue of the *R.K. Werkgever* looked to the future and trumpeted, "Now – Industrialisation", arguing that the time was ripe for large investment projects as a new aluminium factory or the expansion of *Hoogovens*. Two weeks later the journal had returned to earth and the old criticisms of Colijn began to resurface.

After the surgery 'The patient is doing well'. Haagsche Post 3.10.1936.

"Notwithstanding the tractability of the captain on the bridge, we should never forget that right up to the 'Great Day of Reconciliation' of 1936 the general opinion in our circle was that the direction of government economic policy could not lead to the desired goal." This was followed by a list of old demands which the government should implement forthwith, "preferably, and then without recrimination, with Colijn, and only without Colijn if absolutely necessary".

A large part of the membership of the VNW almost certainly also greeted the devaluation with a sigh of relief. We have already seen how a number of prominent industrialists pressured, through informal channels, for a change in monetary policy and that they welcomed the events of 26 September cannot be doubted. But even someone as Ernst Heldring, originally a convinced anti-devaluationist, could not bring himself to mourn the fall of the guilder. The resolution of a situation without perspective was the way he referred to it(52) –

and there must have been many who shared such sentiments. The reaction of the VNW itself, however, was more detatched. In the annual report, mention was made of the fact that discussion after the event of whether the Netherlands had been forced off gold or not had only academic merits.(53) The *Nederlandsche Werkgever* concerned itself largely with technical questions and the consequences of the devaluation for the cost of living. Confidence in the government remained undamaged: "People! trust in the mentality of our Dutch people and assume that they will not allow themselves to be influenced by unnecessary scare-stories and will respond to the call of our minister-president above all to keep calm."(54)

The way in which the three organisations looked at in this chapter reacted to the devaluation was entirely consistent with their stances before that step was taken. One interesting, but difficult to answer, question remains open: how far can the stances adopted by the VNW and the ARKVW/RKVWV be traced back to their respective economic interests (the *Maatschappij* can be ignored because it was not a true employers' organisation)? By asking this question we by no means wish to imply that we desire to reduce everything to vested economic interests. On the contrary, we have been at pains to illustrate the role of emotions in the arguments and the special relationship of the catholics with the Colijn cabinet. Nevertheless, it is worthwhile seeing how close we can come to an economic interpretation.

At first sight the stance ot the VNW was extremely curious. Representatives of highly important concerns such as Philips, Unilever and Hoogovens pleaded for devaluation as too, in his own way, did Deterding. Yet the VNW never wavered from its loyalty to the gold standard. It is natural to assume that this was due to a counter current of those whose interests were perceived in lying with the maintenance of the guilders gold parity and there are indications which point in this direction. At a joint meeting of the executives of the ARKWV and RKVWV in 1933, Steenberghe had pointed out that the VNW was the most obvious partner with which to cooperate in an effort to get the government to take more protectionist measures but, he added, "there is nothing to be expected from such cooperation since in the Union (i.e. VNW) other bodies play a large role, such as the railways, the shipping concerns and the banks, which are still entirely oriented towards free trade....".(55) As far as the shipping companies are concerned, Heldring's diaries nicely illustrate how these increasingly came under pressure from the overvalued guilder and how the once rock-solid confidence in the gold standard rapidly began to crumble. The railways had an interest in free freight transport but the policy of other countries made its realisation difficult. That leaves the banks. For them free trade meant no exchange controls and a stabilisation of exchange-rates, both of which would benefit the Netherlands as an important financial centre. However, even more important was the maintenance of the gold standard. Banking is based on trust. That meant that anyone investing hard guilders had to be sure that they would get hard guilders back. The maintenance of that certainty was in the banks' long-term interests.

In light of the above remarks, it is not surprising that the anti-devaluationist pressure group was dominated by prominent bankers. It is also not surprising to find Beyen and Van Sandick of the *Rotterdamsche Bankvereeniging* among the defenders of the gold standard at meetings of the NMNH. The exception which proves the rule is H.F. van Leeuwen, an early and active pro-devaluationist who was director of the Twentse Bank, but this can be explained by the close involvement of the Twentse Bank with the local textile industry, whose exports to the Dutch East Indies were being eroded by the overvalued guilder. On balance it would seem plausible (the VNW archive has not been opened to researchers) that pressure from the banks provide an important explanation for the rigid adherence of the VNW to the gold standard.

The really important entrepreneurs were members of the VNW and not the catholic associations. The largest industrial concern in the catholic South, Philips, was not catholic. The most important leaders in catholic employers' circles, such as Regout and Lips, were little more than middle-size concerns. Alongside them were many small-scale businessmen. However, the most important difference was that the typical export-industries were more likely to be represented in the VNW than in the ARKWV and RKVWV. The relative over-representation of firms with interests in the domestic market may explain why the policy was so long followed of seeking protection against competing imports and resisting a devaluation which would have raised the costs of imported inputs. Nevertheless, even here, in the course of time, more and more voices were raised in favour of devaluation. The increasing pressure felt by those businesses which were dependent on exports is not sufficient to explain this. The feelings towards the Colijn cabinet in the ranks of the ARKWV and RKVWV, feelings which differed markedly from those of the liberal oriented VNW, undoubtedly also played an important role.

Notes

1. Information on the CWV is based on W.J. Wieringa, Veertig jaren christelijk-sociale ondernemersarbeid, *De Verantwoordelijke Maatschappij. Uitgave t.g.v. 40 jarig bestaan VPCW 1918 – 1958*, Franeker, 1958, 339-367, and on verbal communication from P. Werkman who has studied the CWV archives covering this period.
2. Wieringa, Veertig jaren, 347.
3. See for a general survey G.P. Linssen, *Werkgeversorganisatie in katholiek patroon. Een schets van ontstaan en uitbouw van de diocesane verenigingen van werkgevers in het zuiden van Nederland 1915-1940*, Tilburg, 1978.
4. Na tien jaren 'Verbond van Nederlansche Werkgevers', *10 jaar Verbondswerk, 1936. Uitgave van het Verbond van Nederlandsche Werkgevers*, 's-Gravenhage, 1936, 47-51 (originally published in *Het Volk*, 24.1.1936.
5. P.E. de Hen, *Actieve en reactieve industriepolitiek in Nederland*, Amsterdam, 1980, 86-87; Joh. de Vries (ed.), *Herinneringen en dagboek van Ernst Heldring (1871-1954)*, Groningen, 1970, 976.
6. J. Bierens de Haan, *Van economische Tak tot Nederlandsche Maatschappij voor Nijverheid en Handel 1777-1952,* Haarlem, 1952.
7. *Maatschappijbelangen*, October 1931, 229.

8. *Ibid.*, 228.
9. *Ibid.*, 225.
10. *De Nederlandsche Werkgever*, 1.10.1931, 627-628.
11. *Ibid.*, 31.12.1931, 838.
12. *Ibid.*, 27.10.1931, 616.
13. *Ibid.*, 31.12.1931, 839.
14. *De R.K. Werkgever*, 2.10.1931, 465.
15. *Ibid.*, 13.5.1932, 249.
16. *Ibid.*, 4.11.1932, 535.
17. *Ibid.*, 4.11.1932, 547.
18. *Ibid.*, 7.4.1933, editorial comment: 'If we are asked what, ultimately, an anti-deflationary policy involves, we can give the answer in one word: autarky.'
19. *De Nederlandsche Werkgever*, 25.2.1932, 116.
20. *Ibid.*, 13.9.1934, 440.
21. *Jaarverslag VNW*, 1933, 7.
22. De Vries, *Herinneringen en dagboek*, Vol.2, 948-949.
23. *Maatschappijbelangen*, July 1933, 146-147.
24. Internationaal Instituut voor Sociale Geschiedenis, NVV-archief, minutes of meeting of hoofdbestuur, 29-30.5.1934.
25. *Maatschappijbelangen*, July 1933, 131-134.
26. *Ibid.*, August 1933, 154.
27. *Ibid.*, October 1936, 167.
28. *Ibid.*, November 1936, 195.
29. J. Goudriaan, *Waardevast Geld. De eerste voorwaarde voor het behoud van welvaart, vrijheid en cultuur*, Haarlem, 1937. Reviewed in *Maatschappijbelangen*, August 1937, 147-148.
30. Nederlandsche Maatschappij voor Nijverheid en Handel, (private archive) minutes of meeting of hoofdbestuur, 20.12.1933.
31. *Maatschappijbelangen*, June 1936, 96.
32. *Ibid.*, August 1936, 150.
33. *Ibid.*, April 1933, 60.
34. *De R.K. Werkgever*, 1.12.1933, 565.
35. *Ibid.*, 22.3.1935, 150.
36. *Ibid.*, 29.3.1935, 157.
37. *Ibid.*, 7.6.1935, 281.
38. *Ibid.*, 5.7.1935, 323.
39. *Ibid.*, 20.9.1935, 472.
40. *Ibid.*, 13.12.1935, 620.
41. Katholiek Documentatie Centrum Nijmegen (KDC), KWV-archief (AKWV), 40, minutes of meeting of dagelijks bestuur ARKWV, 17.8.1933.
42. *Ibidem.*
43. KDC, AKWV, 2, Minutes of a combined meeting of the bestuur of the ARKWV and RKVWV, 16.12.1935. Statement made by Guljé.
44. KDC, AKWV, 207, Letter from the general secretary on behalf of the dagelijks bestuur to the executives of the diocesene organisations and the employers' associations affiliated to the RKWV, 14.10.1935. Kortenhorst remained opposed.
45. *Ibid.*, *Nota inzake de meningen der diocesane besturen, ledenvergaderingen en kringvergaderingen over het monetaire vraagstuk*, 29.11.1935.
46. KDC, AKWV, 6, minutes of the meeting of kringsecretarissen of the ARKWV and the associations affiliated to the RKVWV, 18.9.1935.
47. KDC, AKWV, 2, minutes of the combined besturenvergadering of the ARKWV-federatie and RKVWV, 16.12.1935.
48. *Maatschappijbelangen*, October 1936, 167.

49. *De R.K. Werkgever*, 2.10.1936, 479.
50. *Ibid.*, 9.10.1936, 491.
51. *Ibid.*, 16.10.1936, 503.
52. De Vries, *Herinneringen en dagboek*, Vol.2, 1203.
53. *Jaarverslag VNW juli 1936 – juli 1937*, 3.
54. *De Nederlandsche Werkgever*, 1.10.1936, 473.
55. KDC, AKWV, 6, minutes of a combined meeting of the dagelijkse bestuur of the ARKWV and the besturen of the associates affiliated to the RKVWV, 10-7-1933.

CHAPTER FOUR

The Agricultural Lobby

Of the various sectors of the Dutch economy, agriculture was the first and probably hardest hit by the depression of the 1930's. From the early 1920's onwards farmers had to cope with falling agricultural prices on World markets and around 1930 the situation deteriorated further. On the domestic market arable farming had to compete with cheap imports from overseas whilst Dutch exporters of dairy products, bacon, vegetables and other horticultural products were confronted with low prices, increasing protectionism and exchange restrictions abroad. The devaluation of sterling in 1931 made it even worse for those sectors of agriculture dependent upon foreign markets, especially since the decline in trade with Germany had made England the number one export market for Dutch agricultural produce. After the sterling devaluation Dutch exporters received even less for their products when converted into guilders. Whilst income decreased, production costs did not. More and more farmers found themselves unable to pay rents, interest on loans and mortgage debts.(1)

Recognising the severity of the crisis in agriculture the government took steps to guarantee farmers a subsistence income and to save the agricultural sector from bankruptcy. From 1930 onwards a whole series of crisis support measures were passed by parliament. A number of these measures had been proposed by the various farmers' organisations that represented farming interests in the Netherlands. In fact, the large farmers' organisations that operated in this period are often cited in the literature as examples of effectively functioning pressure groups.(2) The severity of the crisis in agriculture, the export orientation of Dutch farming, as well as the fact that the agricultural lobby is considered to be an influential factor in Dutch politics, warrants a closer look at the role played by the farmers' organisations in the national devaluation discussion. Before reconstructing the chronology of events, however, it is necessary to give some facts and figures on the organisations involved, on their activities during the depression and on the government's crisis support legislation.

In the 1930's the farming interest was represented by three general national farmers' associations plus a number of specific organisations that represented only one branch of activity (e.g. the dairy-industry).(3) Of the three general organisations the KNLC *Koninklijk Nederlands Landbouw Comité* (Royal Dutch Agricultural Committee) was the oldest. It dated from 1884 and was a federation of provincial farmers' organisations that had been founded by large farmers and local dignitaries in the second half of the 19th century. Officially there was no adherence to any ideology or political persuasion though in the inter-war years there were strong links with the liberal parties: a number of leading members of the affiliated provincial organisations represented either the LSP or the VDB in the second or first chamber. In 1934 the ten affiliated provincial organisations had a total membership of 50,000. Apart from these regional branches some other, more specific, organisations were members of the Committee, which brought the total membership up to more than 90,000 in 1934.(4)

The KNBTB *Katholieke Nederlandse Boeren- en Tuindersbond* (The Catholic Dutch Farmers' Association) was comparable in size. It was a federation of four regional organisations with a total membership of 75,000 in 1934. Dating from 1896 it had from the start been an organisation of small farmers from the Southern and Eastern parts of the country and the province of Holland.(5) There was a close connection with the catholic church: the national executive had a 'spiritual advisor' among its members as too did the executives of the regional organisations and the local branches. There was also regular contact with the other catholic social organisations. And, lastly, there were some personal links with the catholic party (the RKSP): in the period under study three members of the KNBTB executive also represented the RKSP in the Second Chamber.(6)

Finally, and on a much smaller scale, there was the CBTB *Christelijke Boeren- en Tuindersbond* (Protestant Farmers' Association), founded in 1918 and attaining a membership of 10,000 members in 1934. In spite of being diminutive it probably had more influence than could be expected on the basis of its membership alone, not the least because of close personal connections with national politics: in the 1930's its chairman (P.A. Diepenhorst) and vice-chairman, C. van den Heuvel, represented the ARP in the First and Second Chamber respectively.(7)

Because of their nature – general *zuil*-oriented federations – each of the three farmers' associations represented a wide variety of economic interests. The geographic distribution of the membership of each gives a clue as to which economic interest might have prevailed. The catholic KNBTB had most of its membership in the South and in the East: these were sandy soil regions where small scale family farms specialising in dairy farming and pig breeding (bacon) for export predominated.(8) It also had a large number of market-gardeners in its ranks, members of the Holland branch who were likewise dependent on exports. The liberal KNLC, on the other hand, had hardly any members in the Holland market-gardening districts.(9) Instead, it was the only of the two with a large membership in the arable farming regions of Holland and Groningen. Thus, there seems to have been a difference between the two largest farmers' associations. Which economic interest predominated within the protestant CBTB is not clear: the regional distribution of its membership does not show any distinct pattern.

Neither the *zuil* character of organised agriculture nor the differences in membership stood in the way of the three farmers' organisations acting jointly on agricultural issues. Regular meetings had been held since 1922 and in the 1930's a large number of joint petitions and telegrams were sent to government and parliament. In June 1930 the first Priority Programme *Urgentie-Programma* was published. It had largely been the work of the KNLC; only a few proposals had been added by the other two organisations.(10) Besides a number of indirect measures, the Priority Programme asked for an increase in the level of protectionism and suggested support measures for wheat growers and other arable farmers in particular. In August 1931 the KNLC issued a revised Priority Programme: now urging the government to implement support of cattle farming and asking for tariffs on all agricultural products. Two further priority programmes were formulated by the three farmers' organisations in 1933 and 1935.(11)

Although only part of the proposals in these and other petitions were actually carried out by the government, the agricultural lobby was at any rate succesful in drawing attention to the difficult situation confronting farmers. After 1930 a whole machinery of crisis support legislation for agriculture was set up, even to the point of criticism and discontent on the part of other sectors of society.(12) The sugarbeet farmers, growers of industrial potatoes and wheat farmers were the first to benefit. Support measures for horticulture, dairy farming and pig breeding followed in 1932.

The purpose of all these separate measures was to enable farmers to meet their costs and to save them from bankruptcy. The means by which this was to be accomplished shifted in the course of the period.(13) Primarily, the extension of loans was thought to be sufficient, but soon a system of fixed prices and subsidies was set up, sometimes in combination with measures to guarantee sufficient demand for certain products (wheat, butter). At the same time, steps were taken to achieve a reduction in productive capacity since it was only too natural for farmers to increase output once the system of subsidies had been installed, which would increase the tendency of prices to fall. In the beginning the support measures were partly financed out of the state or municipal budget (as in the case of the extension of credit) and partly out of consumer levies (subsidies on milk and bacon were paid for out of levies on butter and other edible fats and oils and pork respectively). After 1933 the *Landbouwcrisiswet* (Agricultural Support Act) brought all the products hit by crisis under centralised government control and established a uniform system of crisis support management. Import levies on a great number of agricultural products, together with consumer levies on others, provided the income for the *Landbouwcrisisfonds* (Agricultural Crisis Fund) out of which all subsidies etc. were paid. This meant that from 1933 onwards the support measures were no longer (partly) financed out of the budget.(14) There is no hard evidence on the effectiveness of the specific crisis support measures. The system of support for wheat farmers seems to have been very effective, but there was much criticism and discontent in other sectors of agriculture.(15)

The farmers' organisations discussed in this chapter were not really interested in the monetary issue and one plausible explanation for this could be the existence of the crisis support machinery. Moreover, they represented the whole spectrum of different interest groups within the agricultural community – and devaluation would only benefit some agricultural sectors (the export sectors not dependent on imported raw materials). Furthermore, although exports would bring in more guilders (which would serve to decrease the costs of the crisis support measures because fewer subsidies would have to be paid) most probably export volume would not have increased because foreign demand was inelastic (i.e. because of protectionism it would not be sensitive to lower prices).(16) Another reason why one would not necessarily expect proposals on devaluation to come from the farmers' organisations could be that they were not independent pressure groups, but instead part of a hierarchy of political interest groups (the catholic, protestant and 'independent' *zuilen*). This suggests that to some extent they could not afford to act independently but would have to follow party lines. The following account will confirm both sets of expectations.

THE ISSUE IS RAISED

In spite of the negative effects of the fall of sterling on Dutch agricultural exports, the government's monetary policy does not seem to have been questioned by any of the farmers' organisations in the years 1931 and 1932.(17) This situation changed in the course of 1933. The KNLC was the first to consider the issue. It was not the national executive that took the initiative, however, but one of the Committee's affiliated organisations: the *Groninger Maatschappij van Landbouw* (Groningen Agricultural Society).

In March 1933 the Groningen Society was confronted with a request from one of its lower affiliated bodies to set up a commission to study whether the maintenance of the gold standard was beneficial for agriculture or not. The chairman H.D. Louwes tried at first to duck the issue by suggesting that it was such a difficult issue and upon which such divergent opinions existed that he doubted whether it would be possible to find any suitably qualified people for such a commission from the Society's membership. The rest of the executive agreed and it was decided to turn down the suggestion.(18) Three weeks later, however, the issue was on the agenda again. Dr. Oortwijn Botjes, who was an influential agriculturalist and advisory member of the Groningen Agricultural Society executive, pointed out that if the agricultural community did not involve itself in the question but declared itself incompetent in this area, it left the whole issue over to others, perhaps equally incompetent, who might end up steering the decision in a direction ultimately unfavourable for agriculture. As a result of the support he received the executive reversed its previous decision and invited Oortwijn Botjes to draft a discussion paper for the yet to be installed committee to consider. The executive would also invite J.B. Westerdijk, who was previous chairman of the Groningen Agricultural Society and at that time representative of the liberal VDB in the first chamber, to put the case in favour of maintaining the gold standard.(19) Oortwijn Botjes worked quickly (or already had it written) and within two months not only was his advice ready, but he had also managed to arrange for its publication in the influential weekly economic journal *Economisch-Statistische Berichten*. Meanwhile Westerdijk had let it be known that he had neither the time nor the opportunity to entertain the executive's request but, it seemed likely that this lacuna could be filled since the journal's editors had already invited the Rotterdam professor, C.W. Verrijn Stuart, to write a countering piece. The executive agreed to distribute the texts when they appeared and to arrange for them also to be published in the Society's own *Groninger Landbouwblad*.(20) Verrijn Stuart's counter-attack never appeared. As Oortwijn Botjes explained to the executive later, Verrijn Stuart had shifted his opinion on the issue to one not far from his own.(21) In fact both Westerdijk and Verrijn Stuart were among the signatories of the first 'pro-devaluation' petition to be sent to the government in July 1933.

Oortwijn Botjes' article duely appeared in print in June 1933.(22) His plea in favour of devaluation contained a number of arguments. Other countries were also confronted with the problem of falling commodity prices that were increasingly out of balance with production costs, he wrote. But the situation was worse in Switzerland and the Netherlands, the only two important industrial nations that still held on to the gold standard at the pre-1913 rate of exchange. In fact, deflation in the Netherlands was partly a consequence of the devaluation of other currencies. In his opinion, the lowering of costs in a direct way (e.g. by wage cuts) was "not possible" and "unfair". Devaluation, on the other hand, would decrease costs (wages, interest rates etc.) all at once, in a uniform way and would hardly be noticed by the social groups concerned. He did not fear the dangers of devaluation seen by others: there would be an increase in wholesale prices as a result of devaluation, but the cost of living would not go up to the same degree since it was determined by more than only wholesale prices. According to Oortwijn Botjes the cost of living in England, Scandinavia and the United States had in fact gone down to a pre-war level after these countries had left the gold standard, while in the Netherlands and Switzerland the cost of living was still 30 per cent higher than before the war: "When Mr Trip complains about the slow rate by which the cost of living goes down in the Netherlands compared to other countries, he forgets that this is primarily the result of the government's monetary policy and the policy of the Nederlands Bank."

Oortwijn Botjes' plea in favour of devaluation was based on a general argumentation – he did not specifically go into the agricultural situation. This does not seem to have hindered the other members of the Groningen executive over much. When it came to a discussion by the Groningen executive, Oortwijn Botjes had the field virtually to himself. Louwes backed him and since the majority supported his suggestion to send a telegram to the cabinet, so too, presumably, did most of the rest, though as far as can be judged from the minutes of the meeting they did so quietly. The arguments of those opposing him ranged from the out and out deflationary ("the solution should be sought in another way, namely the lowering of costs, wages etc. The speaker is of the opinion that although not much has been achieved in this area so far, much can and must be achieved in the coming years") to the touching faith in the wisdom of higher authority ("someone like Colijn is of a completely different opinion. It goes without saying that he (i.e. the speaker) attaches high value to this opinion. He trusts that when it is no longer possible to maintain the guilder at its current level Mr. Colijn will be sensible enough to take the necessary measures"). Such sentiment, however, failed to carry the day and it was left to the Chairman and Secretary to compose an appropriate text.(23)

The telegram, sent the same day, was innocuous enough. It merely requested the government not to approve any agreement between national banks which would make impossible a change in the value of the guilder at some point in the future. But two days later a covering letter was also sent which went much further: "We consider it thus highly probable that the government will shortly come to the conclusion that the system it proposes (i.e. *aanpassing*) will promote an endless series of government interventions and that the chances are large that they will not accomplish their goal. It will then come to the opinion that there is no possibility left other than to do what countless countries have already done, namely lowering the value of its currency to avoid a catastrophy."(24) The same day the Groningen executive wrote and informed the head-quarters of the KNLC in The Hague of the action they had taken and asked them to publish the text of the telegram and an abridged version of the accompanying letter.(25)

To say that the request was not well received would be to put things mildly. At a meeting of the executive and the members of the 'first section', J.L. Nysingh, chairman of the national organisation, tore into Louwes and A.P. Minderhoud, chairman and secretary respectively of the Groningen branch. He condemned the way in which the executive had operated on its own initiative without referring back to its membership (remember, the meeting had only approved the sending of the telegram, not the accompanying text) and he took exception to the fact that Groningen had taken its action without first consulting The Hague. What, he asked, was the point of having a central organisation if people acted independently on such an important question. "In this way the power of the agricultural organisation will be broken and we will return to the earlier situation when each provincial organisation acted on its own initiative and the influence on the government was nil." The whole question of the gold standard was a difficult one, he argued, upon which opinion was divided and it was, moreover, a question which was larger than agriculture alone. This last point was put more succinctly by P. Dieleman, chairman of the Zeeland branch and ARP politician, who put the matter as follows: "The question of the monetary system is one of the most difficult in the economy. The national interest must prevail. We are here to represent the farming interest but within the context of the national interest." Minderhoud accepted that Groningen might have gone too far, though he felt that the executive had the majority of its membership behind it. His argument, however, that the farmers were affected by the monetary question as much as anyone else and had therefore as much right as anyone else to take up a position appeared, as far as can be judged from the minutes, to have received no support whatsoever.(26)

The Groningen branch continued for a while in its attempt to get the question placed on the agenda of the next annual general meeting but, for reasons not entirely clear, later abandoned the attempt.(27) Louwes – who was also a representative of the Liberal State Party (LSP) in the Second Chamber – defended the pro-devaluationist telegram sent by the Groningen branch against criticism in the LSP's weekly journal. In his opinion, devaluation should be considered as a policy alternative because *aanpassing* could not be brought about fast enough, with the possible result of 'uncontrolled inflation'. Although Louwes also seems to have had some doubts over the inflationary consequences of devaluation itself, he held on to his pro-devaluationist viewpoint in articles in the KNLC's weekly journal in November and December. In the November article he repeated his previous argument: *aanpassing* would be too slow, devaluation was necessary to speed up the process (see pp 111-112).

Apart from Louwes, two other liberal politicians with a career in the Groningen Agricultural Society had professed to be at least not unsympathetic towards the possibility of devaluation: the first 'pro-devaluation' petition sent to the government in July 1933 – coincidentally: on the very same day that the Groningen branch was refuted by national headquarters! – was also signed by Westerdijk, who has already been mentioned, and S.E.B. Bierema. Bierema was parliamentary chairman of Louwes' party, the LSP, in the Second Chamber. Westerdijk also signed the second pro-devaluation letter in January 1934. Bierema however, did not. As has been recalled elsewhere (see pp 110-111) in December 1933 the executive of the LSP decided not to allow any further discussions on devaluation within the party. This probably explains Bierema's absence among the signatories of the January letter.

THE DISCUSSION LINGERS ON

Thus the pro-devaluationists within the KNLC did not succeed in getting their point across. However, while discussions on devaluation within that organisation came to a standstill, devaluation within the two other farmers' associations started to become an issue. In December 1933 the monetary question appeared on the agenda of the catholic KNBTB's national executive. The Holland branch had requested a study of the pro's and contra's of leaving the gold standard. The national executive decided not to accept this proposal. Instead, by way of orientation, some articles would be published in the KNBTB's weekly journal.(28) The minutes of the executive meeting do not give the reasons for the negative decision. The promised articles never appeared, at least not in the coming year 1934.

While the KNBTB's executive apparently did not think it either necessary or opportune to consider the monetary question, the leadership of the protestant CBTB clearly followed another strategy. In January 1934 a series of articles on the gold standard was published in the CBTB's weekly journal, written by one of the editors. The pro-devaluationist views of Oortwijn Botjes, Louwes and Bierema were mentioned, together with the fact that sometimes at meetings of the CBTB voices in favour of devaluation could also be heard. Part of a pro-devaluationist speech by Louwes at the annual general meeting of the Groningen Agricultural Society was cited. His argument that devaluation would lead to an increase of exports was refuted: the problem was not that Dutch export products were too expensive but that export was hindered by increasing protectionism. Devaluation of the guilder would simply be followed by retaliatory measures taken by other countries. There was more to be said against devaluation: it was unethical (because it would distort the credit system it was currency debasement vis-à-vis the creditors); it would lead to inflation (and inflation was silent wage reduction and 'demoralised' society); it would not be possible to have controlled devaluation and, finally, devaluation would hurt the credit position of the government at a time when every penny was needed to finance employment projects.(29)

The fact that such arguments were very similar to those expressed by ARP politicians is not surprising when one considers the close (personal) links between the leadership of the CBTB and ARP circles: after all, the 'anti-devaluationist' Diepenhorst, was the CBTB chairman and editor of its weekly. It is also worth noting that, as in Oortwijn Botjes' article, there was no specific treatment of the effects of devaluation on the different sectors of agriculture.

During 1934 the monetary issue was not discussed at the national level by either the KNLC or the KNBTB. In September of that year, however, some leading members of both organisations were among the signatories of the declaration founding the pro-devaluation NVWG. Besides Louwes – who apparently did not worry too much about the 'ban' on discussion issued by his party in December of the previous year – and Oortwijn Botjes, two catholic members of parliament with strong links with the KNBTB also signed: L.F.J.M. Baron van Voorst tot Voorst, who was chairman of the East-Netherlands branch and vice-chairman of the national organisation, plus M.P. v.d. Weyden, agricultural specialist of the RKSP in the Second Chamber.

In November 1934 the monetary issue was discussed at the annual general meeting of the Holland branch of the KNBTB. A few local branches plus Van der Weyden, who was present as guest, proposed joining the NVWG. Only devaluation could bring a solution in the *vaste lasten* problem. The Holland branch executive did not agree. Its chairman G.W. Kampschoër, who also represented the RKSP in the Second Chamber, expressed the executive's viewpoint: since the government wanted to hold on to the gold standard, *vaste lasten* had to be reduced in a direct way. Apparently it did not occur to the majority of those present that maybe the government could be motivated to change its monetary policy. The executive got its way. The proposals of the dissenters were not accepted.(30)

Apparently, however, the executive of the national organisation felt that it could no longer ignore the pro-devaluation voices within its ranks. In January 1935 an article appeared in the KNBTB's weekly journal, written by the secretary, H. van Haastert. Not surprisingly it started with a discussion of the link between devaluation and the *vaste lasten* issue. Van Haastert explained that devaluation would only lead to a reduction of the burden of *vaste lasten* if there were an increase of (agricultural) prices. But, he pointed out, both pro- and anti-devaluationists were of the opinion that devaluation would not, or not significantly, increase the general price level. Van Haastert furthermore pointed out that those sectors of agriculture which would benefit most from devaluation – and consequently be in a better position to meet their costs – were not those already helped by price guarantees and those producing for export which were not reliant upon imported raw materials such as fodder. This meant that the market-gardening sector especially would benefit greatly.(31)

Having published Van Haastert's article one would have expected that the leadership of the KNBTB no longer considered the devaluation issue taboe. A few weeks after its publication the KNBTB had its annual general meeting. On that occasion, however, the executive once again proved to be very hesitant about any discussion on the question. One of the speakers, H. Ruyter (secretary of the East-Netherlands branch and RKSP representative in the first chamber) was told beforehand not to raise the devaluation issue.(32) The national executive, however, could not gag everyone. One of the delegates raised the question by pleading in favour of membership of the NVWG. In his opinion devaluation was the only solution for the small farmer: "Those opposed to devaluation claim that it is a jump in the dark. I agree as long as they don't say that is a jump *into* the dark because that is no longer at stake; we have already been wandering around in the dark for too long..... When the jump is made, I still have hope that it will be a jump out of the dark – also as far as the small farmer is concerned." In spite of the local delegate's rhetoric his proposal was not taken into consideration.(33)

In the meantime there seems to have been some change in the attitude of at least part of the leadership of the CBTB. In January 1935 a series of articles on the monetary issue was published in its weekly journal. It opened with the remark that there was difference of opinion within the executive about the desirability of devaluation. Although, like the year before, a number of disadvantages of devaluation were mentioned, the conclusion was less negative: the possibility of devaluation should be left open. It was one of a number of policy alternatives, it was not a 'disaster'. The article ended with a declaration of faith in the wisdom of Colijn: Mr. Colijn was wise enough to take the decision and "when it would be obvious that national prosperity would benefit from devaluation (i.e. when it would not be possible to push through cuts in government spending) Colijn would take the decision to devalue."(34)

THE KNBTB TAKES SIDES

In the national discussion about devaluation 1935 was an important year. Within the catholic *zuil* doubts about the government's monetary policy increased. In February, Serrarens had held a pro-devaluation speech in the first chamber. In May, shortly after the devaluation of the Belgian franc, the four catholic social organisations held their *Industrialisatie congres*. On this occasion the Tilburg professor, Kaag, made his famous pro-devaluation speech. The KNBTB had sent two speakers: J. Groen, who was under-chairman of the Holland-branch and also RKSP member of parliament in the Second Chamber, and J.D. de Kok, who also came from the ranks of the Holland-branch but who did not hold an executive position. Groen did not mention the devaluation issue in his speech. De Kok however, did take sides. Instead of *aanpassing* De Kok chose Kaag's 'devaluation': "Mr. Stulemeyer (the speaker who had defended *aanpassing* – RTG/MEdV) praises the Danish poeple because of their enterprising spirit and their energy, but this really makes me angry. Mr. Stulemeyer forgets to add that the Danish people devalued their currency and that this helped enormously in bringing down costs."(35) De Kok, by the way, was the only one of the speakers at the *Industrialisatie congres* besides professor Kaag who clearly spoke in favour of leaving the gold standard.

The political conflict over the direction of the government's social economic policy was increasingly thought of, by the catholic party at least, in terms of a choice between 'consistent deflation' and 'devaluation'. Eventually the majority of the RKSP parliamentary party in the Second Chamber seem to have been in favour of devaluation but did not want to make an issue of it for fear of another cabinet crisis.(36) In the autumn of 1935 the KNBTB's national executive put the devaluation issue on the agenda for the first time since it had briefly discussed it in December 1933. The chronology is not entirely clear, nor is it possible to establish who took the initiative and for what reasons. Fact is that in October one of the regional organisations, the East-Netherlands ABTB, voted in favour of devaluation at its annual general meeting. It is important to note that the chairman of the ABTB, Van Voorst tot Voorst, belonged himself to the NVWG. One week after the ABTB vote, the KNBTB itself had its annual general meeting. In the morning the national executive had its regular monthly meeting and it was decided to discuss the monetary issue at their next meeting in November because the *Raad van Overleg* (joint consultative organ of the catholic social organisations) had put the matter on its own agenda.(37) The details behind the decision of the *Raad van Overleg* unfortunately are not known, so it is not clear which of the four social organisations that together formed the *Raad* had taken the initiative. Neither can it be established whether the ABTB vote in favour of devaluation acted as the catalyst or whether the general political situation had prompted the decision.

At the annual general meeting that same afternoon, devaluation was compared with other solutions to the *vaste lasten* problem by one of the speakers, top civil servant Ir. G.J. Heijmeijer. Among other things, he pointed out that devaluation would only lead to higher import prices (and consequently to higher prices in general) if the import levies that existed under the crisis support legislation were not reduced by the government by the same amount as the devaluation percentage. In the discussion that followed Van der Weyden took the opportunity to propose that the KNBTB should follow the ABTB and declare itself in favour of devaluation. In his opinion 'consistent deflation' or devaluation was a false dilemma since it would not be possible to achieve 'consistant deflation' in the current political economic situation: "Devaluation is possibly .... the only way to get results and not only a lot of words is the way shown by professor Kaag at the *Industrialisatie congres* in The Hague." Van der Weyden's proposal to follow the initiative of the ABTB was not put to a vote. The chairman, J. Th. Verheggen, did not think it opportune to have the matter discussed because of the decision taken by the executive that morning to discuss the question at one of its coming meetings.(38)

The meeting of the KNBTB national executive took place on 18 November. H. Bogaardt, secretary of the NVWG, had been invited as guest speaker. In his speech he compared the merits of deflation and devaluation. He mentioned all the well known arguments in favour of devaluation but did not specify the advantages for agriculture. Only at the end of his speech was agriculture mentioned, in summing up the dismal consequences of deflation: "Deflation is expropriation *without* compensation, and the farmers population will eventually be forced to emigrate – like they were during the Great Depression in the 1880's – from a country that once was counted among the most prosperous nations in the world."(39) After Bogaardt had left the meeting there was "ample discussion" about the pro's and con's of devaluation. What these arguments were is not clear because the minutes are not detailed enough. Then two questions were put to a vote: should the KNBTB executive take sides in the devaluation discussion and, if so, which side should be taken: 'consistent deflation', as propagated by RKSP party leader Aalberse, or devaluation?

In view of the reluctancy of the KNBTB executive to raise the devaluation issue, the results of the vote are rather unexpected: the first question (should the KNBTB take sides) was answered affirmatively (16 in favour, 3 against). The vote on the second question ('consistent deflation' or devaluation) turned out in favour of devaluation (12 in favour, 2 against, 5 abstentions).(40) Most likely because of the pending discussion with the other three catholic social organisations in the *Raad van Overleg* the results of the vote were not made public nor was the KNBTB's membership informed.

One week later, on 25 November, the Holland-branch again discussed devaluation as a solution to the *vaste lasten* problem. The Holland branch executive had slightly changed its view from that of a year before. Instead of their previous position (the government holds on to the gold standard, therefore, *vaste lasten* should be reduced by direct government intervention) there was now a reversal in the argumentation: devaluation would be inevitable if the government would not take steps to reduce *vaste lasten*. The membership, however, did not think this viewpoint radical enough. Speeches of local delegates in favour of devaluation were received with applause and "hear hear". Only devaluation could improve the Netherlands' export position, according to one local branch. It was proposed to send a telegram directly to the Queen, ".... because it is useless to talk to this government". And why not risk another cabinet crisis, like the one in July, in the hope that this time there would be a new government with a new policy? The executive replied that it was best to await the results of the imminent discussion within the KNBTB national executive. Since apparently none of those present besides the executive knew that the KNBTB executive had already discussed the matter, no-one protested. The proposals of the pro-devaluationists were not put to a vote. The telegram to the Queen was never sent.(41)

Ironically, the national executive did not officially declare itself in favour of devaluation either in the period December 1935/September 1936. The reasons for this are not entirely clear. Considering the attitude of both the trade unions and the employers' organisations it is unlikely that the discussions within the *Raad van Overleg* resulted in any consensus over the desirability of leaving the gold standard. This might provide part of the explanation for the KNBTB's 'silence'. On the other hand it is significant that the KNBTB did not take independent action. Maybe this can be explained by the fact that the two other farmers' associations, the KNLC and the CBTB, were not in favour of devaluation and that the KNBTB leadership did not wish to operate on its own in such an important matter.(42)

Whatever the explanation, the leadership of the KNBTB probably did not change its pro-devaluationist viewpoint. In May 1936 the pro-devaluationist petition of "the 250" was signed not only by Van der Weyden and vice-chairman Van Voorst tot Voorst, but also by secretary Van Haastert. And the July letter that followed was signed by both the secretary and deputy secretary of the ABTB.(43) From the independent KNLC circles only Oortwijn Botjes signed this time. Louwes seems to have been no longer convinced of either the desirability or the political feasibility of devaluation.

When, in September 1936, devaluation finally became a fact, it was welcomed by Van Haastert in the KNBTB's weekly journal: ".... we are glad that the Netherlands, where the government has been waking up and going to bed with *aanpassen* for so long, will finally adjust (*aanpassen*) its currency to those of the rest of the world, albeit because it could no longer avoid doing so."(44) The positive, though cynical, reaction of the KNBTB stands in contrast to the reaction in the CBTB's weekly journal: "the protestant association is clearly disappointed that it eventually had to come to this."(45)

None of the the three farmers' associations openly advocated devaluation as a solution to the critical situation in agriculture. Within the 'independent' KNLC the matter was raised early in 1933, but after that it was never discussed again, at least not at the national executive level. Although the details are not known the attitude of the CBTB seems to have shifted from a strongly anti-devaluationist stance to a more flexible one. The national executive of the KNBTB, having ducked the issue for a long time, was, in the end, in favour of devaluation but never said so in public.

The fact that the CBTB was not in favour of devaluation is not surprising, considering the close links with Colijn's party, the ARP. Whether the leadership found it necessary to publish its anti-devaluationist view early in 1934 because of dissent within its ranks is a matter of speculation. Nor is it possible to establish the exact nature of the admitted conflicts within the leadership that may have been responsible for the shift in attitude between 1934 and 1935.

The apparent lack of interest in the monetary issue on the side of the KNLC can partly be explained by the composition of its membership: wheat farmers, who were first to benefit from the crisis support measures and who, as non-exporters, would not be helped much by devaluation anyway; and dairy and cattle farmers dependent on imported fodder which would increase in price.(46) On the other hand, as in the case of the CBTB, the link with national politics is of importance. The fact that the LSP did not want the matter discussed stopped Bierema (and probably hindered Louwes) from getting support for their case within the liberal agricultural circles represented by the KNLC. That the composition of membership alone can only provide a partial explanation for the course and the results of the discussion on devaluation within the farmers' organisations is proved by the fact that within the KNLC it was the Groningen Agricultural Society that came out in favour of devaluation. This seems an anomaly since Groningen was a typical wheat producing area. In this respect it is significant that the argumentation of Oortwijn Botjes (and others) was based on national economic considerations, not on considerations specific to agriculture.

Economic interest can explain why the KNBTB, with its membership among market gardeners and dairy and cattle farms in the East and the South that were only partly dependent on imported fodder(47) was, albeit late, in favour of devaluation. The reluctance of the executive to discuss the matter and the timing of the eventual discussion, however, are left unexplained by the economic interest argument. The chronology of the discussion within the KNBTB executive seems to have been dictated by national political considerations. Those same considerations probably also explain the fact that the pro-devaluationist viewpoint of the KNBTB leadership was never publicly voiced. After all, after 1935, the catholic party followed the same strategy. There is another hypothesis in this respect however: the silence of the KNBTB after November 1935 might also have resulted from the desire on the part of the KNBTB not to jeopardize the good working relations with the two other farmers' associations who were not in favour of devaluation.

A final word should be said about the small group of pro-devaluationists active within the KNLC and the KNBTB. The NVWG did have influence in this way by operating through other organisations. The decision of the ABTB (the East-Netherlands branch of the KNBTB) to declare itself in favour of devaluation thus must be linked with the NVWG-membership of its chairman, Van Voorst tot Voorst. Secondly, it is significant that, except for Oortwijn Botjes, these pro-devaluationists were, besides being leading members of their respective organisations, all politicians. This leads to the question whether their views were a result of their involvement with national politics or whether they were in favour of devaluation because of their agricultural background. In this respect it is noteworthy that Van der Weyden and Van Voorst tot Voorst, when proposing devaluation in meetings of their parliamentary parties, did not use the argument that it would be beneficial to agriculture, but that it would be beneficial to industry and the economy at large.(48) In other words, it is not clear whether this is a case of (members of) an economic interest group influencing politics or whether it was politics influencing a pressure group.

We can conclude that the agricultural lobby was too heterogenous and too much part of a political interest to deal in an efficient way with such a global and politically delicate question as Colijn's monetary policy, and that the element of its strength – a joint policy towards government and parliament – was a handicap in this case: it did not leave any opportunity for independent action by one of the three separately.

Notes

1. G. Minderhoud, Crisis en crisiswetgeving 1930-1940, Z.W. Sneller (ed.), *Geschiedenis van den Nederlandschen landbouw 1795-1940*, Groningen/Batavia, 1943, 498-522. C.H.J. Maliepaard, De Nederlandse landbouw, P.B. Kreukniet (ed.), *De Nederlandse Volkshuishouding tussen twee wereldoorlogen*, Vol. III, Utrecht/Antwerpen, 1952, 13-31.
2. See e.g. Maliepaard, Nederlandse landbouw, 81.
3. P.J. Bouman, Landbouworganisaties, Sneller (ed.), *Geschiedenis van den Nederlandschen landbouw*, 252-268.
4. *De Geschiedenis van het Koninklijk Nederlandsch Landbouw-Comité, 1884 tot 1934*, s.l., 1934.; D.J. Piers, *Wisselend getij. Geschiedenis van het Koninklijk Nederlandsch Landbouw Comité, 1934-1959*, 's-Gravenhage, 1959. The leading members of the KNLC in parliament were: S.E.B. Bierema, H.D. Louwes, A.G.S. Ridder van Rappard (LSP Second Chamber) and J.B. Westerdijk (VDB, first chamber).
5. H.W.G. van der Wielen, Sociale toestanden ten plattelande, Sneller (ed.), *Geschiedenis van den Nederlandschen landbouw*. See for a critical view: M. Bax en A. Nieuwenhuis, Boerenemancipatie in Brabant: Vergruizeling van een beeld, *Tijdschrift voor sociale geschiedenis*, 18, (June 1980) 163-180.
6. These were L.F.J.M. Baron van Voorst tot Voorst, G.W. Kampschoër, J. Groen.
7. *Gedenkboek CBTB, 1918-1948*, s.l., 1948.
8. For membership see: *Verslagen en Mededelingen van de Directie van den Landbouw*, 1934, No.2. For type of agriculture see: *Ibid.*, 1935, No. 3, 233-238, 150-157.
9. *Ibid.*, 1934, No.2, 106-108. *Gedenkboek CBTB*, 189.
10. Piers, *Wisselend Getij*, 80.

11. *Ibid.*, 82-84.
12. H.M.F. Krips-Van der Laan, *Praktijk als antwoord: S.L. Louwes en het landbouwcrisisbeleid*, Groningen, 1985, 86-89. The support for agriculture meant that agricultural prices and consequently cost of living were kept at an artificially 'high' level.
13. For a good overview see: special issue of *Economisch-Statistische Berichten* (ESB), 11.12.1935, 1094-1103 and Minderhoud, *Crisis en crisiswetgeving*. More expansive: *De landbouw-crisiswetgeving. Beknopt overzicht van de totstandkoming en werking van de landbouw-crisiswetgeving in Nederland vanaf 1929*, 3 parts, 's-Gravenhage, 1937, 1938, 1940.
14. The system of consumer levies and import levies meant that the support for agriculture was in fact paid for by the consumer.
15. Van der Wielen, Sociale toestanden, 460. Minderhoud, Crisis en crisiswetgeving, 512-514. Krips-Van der Laan, *Praktijk als antwoord*, 107.
16. The decrease in costs of agricultural support after devaluation could be offset however by a loss of income for the *landbouwcrisisfonds* if the government would decide to lower import levies in order to keep prices of imported goods from rising too much as a result of devaluation.
17. Archief KNLC, Notulen bestuursvergaderingen (eerste afdeling), September 1931 – July 1933; Archief KNBTB, Notulen bestuursvergaderingen, 1931-1933.
18. Rijks Archief Groningen (RAG), Archief Groningen Maatschappij van Landbouw (AGML), Notulen, 8.3.1933.
19. *Ibid.*, Notulen, 24.5.1933.
20. *Ibid.*, Notulen, 12.7.1933.
21. *Ibid.*, Notulen, 12.7.1933.
22. J. Oortwijn Botjes, Is devaluatie van den gulden gewenscht?, *ESB*, 21.6.1933.
23. RAG, AGML, Notulen, 12.7.1933.
24. *Ibid.*, Secretariaat, Correspondentie, Box h/f diversen, M, Letter to Voorzitter van de Raad van Ministers, 14.7.1933.
25. *Ibid.*, Box C/D, D, Letter to KNLC, 14.7.1933.
26. Archief KNLC, Notulen Bestuursvergaderingen (eerste afdeling), 19/20.7.1933.
27. *Ibid.*, 20/21.7.1933.
28. Archief KNBTB, Notulen Dagelijksch Bestuur, 18.12.1933.
29. *Ons platteland. Orgaan van den Christelijken Boeren- en Tuindersbond in Nederland*, 7.2.1934, 14.2.1934, 21.2. 1934, 7.3.1934.
30. Notulen Algemeene Vergadering LTB, 26.11.1934, *De R.K. Boeren- en Tuindersstand*, 29.11.1934, 22.12.1934.
31. *De R.K. Boeren- en Tuindersstand*, 3.1.1935.
32. Notulen Buitengewone Algemeene Vergadering KNBTB, 28.1.1935, *De R.K. Boeren- en Tuindersstand*, 7.2.1935.
33. *Ibidem.*
34. *Ons platteland*, 9.1.1935, 16.1.1935, 23.1.1935, 30.1.1935, 6.2.1935.
35. *Verslag van het Industrialisatie-Congres (Werkherstel-werkverruiming) gehouden te s'Gravenhage op Maandag 13 mei 1935*, s.l., s.a., 59-60.
36. F.J.F.M. Duynster, De Katholieke Tweedekamerfractie na 1918 uit haar notulen, *Opstellen over Recht en Rechtsgeschiedenis*, Deventer, 1965, 126, 130.
37. Archief-KNBTB, Notulen hoofd- en dagelijks Bestuur, 28.10.1935.
38. Notulen Algemeene Vergadering KNBTB, 28.10.1935, *De R.K. Boeren- en Tuindersstand*, 7.11.1935.
39. Bogaardt's speech was printed in *De R.K. Boeren- en Tuindersstand*, 2.1.1936.
40. Archief KNBTB, Notulen hoofd- en dagelijksch bestuur, 18.11.1935.
41. Notulen Algemeene Vergadering LTB, 25.11.1935, *De R.K. Boeren- en Tuinderstand*, 12.12.1935, 2.1.1935, 9.1.1935.
42. Early in 1932 the executives of the three farmers' associations jointly decided not to allow their respective regional branches to undertake independent action in important matters. In a letter sent to the regional branches it was stated that proposals should be addressed to the government by the three farmers' associations jointly. *Jaarverslag van den KNBTB over 1932*, 246-7.

43. J.D. de Kok also signed the petition. The follow-up in July was signed by two other members of the ABTB executive H. Ruyter and W.P. Boshouwers.
44. *De R.K. Boeren- en Tuinderstand*, 1.10.1936.
45. *Ons platteland*, 30.9.1936.
46. In fact much depended on the government policy after devaluation: if import levies on imported goods would be reduced, price increases could be checked.
47. *De Landbouw-crisiswetgeving*, Vol. III, 369-370: in the South and East farmers grew their own fodder.
48. Katholiek Documentatie Centrum, Archief-RKSP, inv. no. 136, 137, 138: notulen RKSP tweede kamer fractie, 21.3.1934, 19.9.1935., 7.10.1935.

CHAPTER FIVE

The Trade Unions (1)

Was there a conflict between the maintenance of the gold standard and the interests of the working class? Was it 'reactionary' to oppose a devaluation of the guilder and 'progressive' to be in favour of it? Such questions were to be heard in the Netherlands, certainly from the end of 1933 onwards.(2) After the devaluation the accusation could often be heard that Colijn had maintained the 'untarnished guilder' over the backs of the working classes.(3) Yet, if that were indeed the case, the curious fact remains to be explained that between 1931 and 1936 there was scarcely any attempt on the part of the unions to exercise organised pressure in favour of a devaluation.

The maintenance of the gold standard by the Netherlands after it had been abandoned elsewhere had as a consequence that many firms were forced to cut production costs were they to be able to compete in international markets with firms from countries which had devalued. The recognition by the trade unions of this fact brought with it an acceptance of the need for an, albeit limited, reduction in wages. This, in turn, could bring the unions' executives and negotiators in a difficult position vis-à-vis their own membership. After the fall of the pound, the news soon appeared in trade union papers that industrial activity in the U.K. was picking up and that the rise in the cost of living was less than had been feared. After the dollar devaluation and the devaluation of the Belgian franc similar stories appeared. Why, then, were there doubts whether the same would not hold true for the Netherlands should it too devalue?

Was it only the uncertainty, the conflicting visions or the doubts about the economic and social consequences of a devaluation for the Netherlands which prevented the trade unions from taking up a clear-cut position, or did conflicting interests within the labour movement itself also play a role? It is natural to expect that the national union organisations could not afford the luxury of choosing between the divergent interests of workers in different sectors. Workers in export industries, for example, could anticipate that a devaluation would end the pressure for wage cuts and stop the job losses. On the other hand, workers in other sectors, and the unemployed for that matter, feared the rise in the cost of living and the reduction in purchasing power which the dearer imports resulting from devaluation would entail. Another possible explanation for the absence of a stand-point could lie in the fact that the solution to the economic crisis was sought by means other than devaluation. Finally, it is possible that the answer may lie in the relationship between the unions and the political parties and the perception of the unions of their own role within the labour movement as a whole. An analysis of the rich diversity of representation within the Dutch trade union movement will permit us to get closer to a resolution of these alternatives.

In the 1930's the Netherlands had no less than seven central trade union organisations which together had approximately 650,000 members. There were an additional 110,000 workers belonging to unions not affiliated nationally. In total nearly 25 per cent of the occupied population were members of some union or other. The three largest organisations were the NVV *Nederlandsch Verbond van Vakvereenigingen,* (Dutch Union of Trade Unions) with approximately 305,000 members, the RKWV *Roomsch Katholiek Werklieden Verbond* (Roman Catholic Workers Union) with approximately 175,000 members and the CNV *Christelijk Nationaal Vakverbond* (Christian National Trade Union) with approximately 105,000 members. Almost 90 per cent of union members affiliated to a national organisation were, thus, affiliated to one of these three.(4)

The NVV was founded in 1905 as a reaction against the increasingly revolutionary socialist leanings of the NAS *Nationaal Arbeidssecretariaat* (National Workers Secretariat), established in 1893. The original objectives of the NVV had not been specifically socialist but very early on links were laid with the largest socialist party in the Netherlands, the SDAP *Sociaal-Democratische Arbeiderspartij* (Social Democratic Workers Party). Towards the end of the 1920's these links were given an organisational form by the creation of the so-called 'General Council', in which the NVV, the SDAP and the SDAP parliamentarians were represented. Some seats in parliament were also occupied by NVV executives.(5)

A national *Bureau voor Roomsch Katholieke Vakorganisatie* (Bureau for Roman Catholic Union Organisation) had been set up at the instigation of the bishops in 1909 as a reaction against the growing influence of the socialist NVV and the growth of inter-confessional unions. Inter-confessional unions gained ground in the partly catholic industrial region of Twente and the predominantly catholic mining area of Limburg and had led to the creation of the CNV earlier in the same year. In 1925 a reorganisation took place, again on the initiative of the bishops, which made the distinction between *standsorganisaties*, caring for general spiritual welfare and general material needs on the one hand, and sectoral organisations, for defending the specific material interests of workers, on the other. At the top, the RKWV linked the two together. Although, when it was first set up, it was intended that the RKWV should refrain from politics, links were forged with the RKSP *Rooms Katholiek Staatspartij* (Roman Catholic State Party) and, in 1926, these too took on an organisational form. From then on the RKWV was represented on the party council of the RKSP and spaces were reserved on the electoral candidate lists, not only for members of the RKWV but for the catholic employers', farmers' etc. organisations as well. Moreover, the chairman of the RKWV, A.C. de Bruyn, was made a member of the party executive.(6)

In the 1930's the CNV was no longer a multi-confessional union with a predominantly orthodox-protestant character. Created in 1909 as a confessional organisation for both protestants and catholics, it was forced (in 1912) by the episcopal support for exclusively catholic trade unions to develop into an exclusively protestant organisation.(7) After about 1920, the CNV (where the officials were primarily drawn from the protestant denomination called *gereformeerd*) began positively to welcome protestant isolationism.(8) Because of the diversity within the protestant section of society the CNV was not officially associated with any political party. In practice, however, it oriented itself almost exclusively towards the ARP *Anti-Revolutionaire Partij* (Anti-Revolutionary Party) for a number of historical, religious and pragmatic motives. Relations with the CHU *Christelijk Historische Unie* (Christian Historical Union), which had from the start harboured doubts over the need for a separate christian trade union movement, remained formal and cool. As far as can be determined all the CNV leaders in the inter-war period were members of the ARP, and from 1931 onwards the CNV secretary, H. Amelink, represented the ARP in the second chamber. The influence of dissident protestant splinter groups, such as the socially progressive CDU *Christelijk Democratische Unie* (Christian Democratic Union), which could have been expected to have exercised some attraction among the lower cadres, was firmly resisted by the CNV leadership. Wherever

TABLE 5.1
SECTORAL DISTRIBUTION OF TRADE UNION MEMBERSHIP

	NVV [1]	RKWV [2]	CNV [3]
Industry and transport workers	163,170 54.7%	101,526 55.6%	45,976 40.5%
Agricultural workers	32,042 10.7%	19,042 10.4%	26,898 23.7%
(Semi-) civil servants	46,315 15.5%	21,070 11.5%	18,528 16.3%
Building workers	29,938 10%	27,351 15%	13,704 12.1%
'White collar' workers	21,270 7.1%	10,843 5.9%	8,460 7.4%
Others	5,827 2%	2,843 1.6%	0 0%
Total	298,562 100%	182,675 100%	113,566 100%

Sources: [1] 16e Jaarverslag NVV, 397.
[2] Leering en Leiding, X (1935), 161.
[3] Amelink, Met ontplooide banieren, 20.
Date: 1.1.1935.

possible the CNV backed the ARP leader and prime-minister H. Colijn – who represented for many the embodiment of protestant emancipation.(9) The result was that of all the national unions the CNV was the least critical of government policy; a policy with which the ARP identified itself.

The three national unions were also characterised by differences in the representation of economic sectors in each, though these were not as great as the differences in religious or political preference. Table 4.1 gives a global picture of the situation prevailing at the beginning of 1935. It reveals that the CNV was under-represented in the industrial and transport sectors, both relatively and absolutely, compared with the NVV and RKWV and was relatively strong among the agricultural workers. On the basis of these figures one would be justified in supposing that the proportion of workers in enterprises exposed to foreign competition was larger in the NVV and RKWV than in the CNV and that, therefore, one could expect a more favourable attitude towards devaluation among the former. Even so, in none of the three were such sectors dominant; the most apparent characteristic common to all was the heterogenity of the membership in terms of economic background. In view of this, a more easily defensible expectation would be that none of the unions would find it easy to establish a standpoint because of the diversity of interests which each represented. Before approaching the question of what factors did then determine the positions taken, it is necessary to examine each group first.

THE SOCIALISTS (NVV)

"The decline in the value of the English pound, of the Swedish Krone and of other currencies, as a result of abandoning the gold standard, has once again let us see how out of control economic life proceeds", stated *De Vakbeweging*, the monthly organ of the NVV after the fall of the pound.(10) The incident gave the writer the opportunity to develop a long exposé on the international chaos caused by the capitalist system. If production, government expenditure and the note circulation could be planned, and if international economic conflict could be brought to an end, then, the author considered, the value produced by an hour of human labour could replace gold as an international measure of value and the international struggle for gold could be stopped. No one could accuse the author of betraying socialist principles, but the analysis was of no great use as a guide-line for a practical policy in the short-term.

The executive of the NVV was forced to make a more pragmatic appraisal of the new situation prevailing after the devaluation of sterling. It immediately protested against the attempts to lower production costs in the export industries exclusively by means of wage cuts. In a letter to Colijn, prompted by a proposal of the *Commissie voor Werkverruiming* (Commission for Work Creation) to call an immediate meeting of employers and employees (see pp 166-167), the NVV advocated measures such as increased protection, increased credit flexibility,

Colijn: 'The workers must learn to adjust'.
From Vrijheid, Arbeid, Brood (NVV and SDAP), 5.9.1936.

cooperation between enterprises etc. as alternatives for wage-cuts. The possibility of devaluing the guilder was not even mentioned.(11) Internally, the need for some wage reduction was quickly accepted(12) but in its external publications the NVV continued to condemn wage-cuts as the policy of the ruling classes.(13)

Around this time, the decision was taken to organise a course for the leaders of affiliated unions on the topic 'The Labour Movement and the Crisis'. At intervals of several months, two-day study conferences were organised which were addressed by both Dutch and foreign speakers. The lectures and summaries of discussions were published by the NVV and sold at cost price to the membership, with the clear intention of spreading the information beyond the immediate circle of the Unions' executives.(14) The first such conference was held on 10 October 1931 and was addressed by the German social democrat Fritz Tarnow and by the Amsterdam economist professor Th. Limperg, later one of the anti-devaluationists. This course had not yet concerned itself with monetary issues but on the occasion of the third conference, held on 25/26 February 1932, professor A.M. de Jong gave a lecture entitled 'Our Money and the Gold Standard', in which he contended that whilst the gold standard might not be functioning optimally, monetary experiment was not the solution. The interests of international trade, he argued, were best served by the maintenance of the gold standard and in any discussion this should be the clinching argument. He too was to become a member of the anti-devaluationist group. The fifth and sixth conferences, held respectively in November 1933 and March 1934, were also devoted to financial questions.

In this period contacts with the SDAP on the question of the gold standard were also intensified. In March 1933 – just before the dollar devaluation – the General Council, the consultative body linking the NVV and the SDAP, set up a commission to examine the devaluation question.(15) The NVV was initially represented by its chairman E. Kupers and secretary, S. de la Bella, both later to become pro-devaluationists. Kupers was soon to be replaced by another of the executive, F.S. Noordhoff, who was to evolve into one of the most militant anti-devaluationists in the NVV. The commissions' report was eventually printed in July 1935. Since no consensus had emerged it was given the title 'Devaluation Pro and Contra'.

After the dollar devaluation in April 1933 *De Vakbeweging* began to interest itself more actively in the devaluation question. One view which was extensively aired was that the working class did not need to form a judgement on the issue. Whatever happened – devaluation, tariff increases, lowered production costs – "the working class always foots the capitalist bill. A result that should not surprise us Marxists". Such was the message of a series of articles towards the end of 1933. The author S. Kleerekoper, later to become professor of economics in Amsterdam, was of the opinion that it was better to confine the movement's energies to resisting wage-cuts and advancing demands for socialist planning. Despite such exhortations the editors did begin to formulate a stance of their own on the question: against devaluation. Every now and then pro-devaluationist articles were placed, but the editorial commentary remained anti-devaluationist to the very end. Quite clearly, they were not in the least intimidated by the suggestion, heard increasingly from the beginning of 1934 onwards, that it was progressive to be pro-devaluationist and reactionary to be against.(16)

The NVV turns out to have been divided on the devaluation question in two ways: the first split was over whether the labour movement should take a position in the debate or not; the second over what that position should be. In the course of time, arguments against taking a position tended to merge with those opposing devaluation. The anti-devaluation section of the devaluation report opened with the statement that currency depreciation should be seen as a symptom of the inevitable crisis of capitalism. Occasionally (and not very convincingly) the observation was made that a pro-devaluationist labour movement would find itself with somewhat curious bed-fellows (see pp 140-152 for more information on the pro-devaluation pressure groups). It is noticable that those approaching the question from a theoretical Marxist position were least inclined towards a pro-devaluationist position.

The executive did not leave the discussion solely to the commission established for the purpose. In November 1933 the heads of affiliated unions were offered a conference on the subject 'Inflation, Deflation, Reflation'. The proceedings were opened by H.F. van Leeuwen, director of the Twentse Bank. In his lecture he stated: "Value stable money can soften the class struggle." He explained this by arguing that "if money creation keeps pace with the development of social production progress can be expressed in wage increases". He went on to say that he thought the Netherlands should have suspended gold payments during the speculation in the Summer of 1933 and that he still considered the step should be taken whilst the Netherlands Bank still had large gold reserves. Ten months later the manifesto establishing the *Nederlandsche Vereeniging voor Waardevast Geld* was published. Among the 49 signatories were to be found not only H.F. van Leeuwen but also the chairman and secretary of the NVV, E. Kupers and S. de la Bella, as well as another member of the executive, J. Brautigam of the Transport Union. But it should be noticed that all signed *à titre personnel* The same names also appeared on the pro-devaluation petition sent to the government in May 1936.

At the study conference in March 1934 professor J. Tinbergen, later famous for founding the Dutch Central Planning Bureau after the War, addressed on the same topic: 'Inflation, Deflation, Reflation'.(17) He was more concerned with explaining the potential of an active counter-cyclical policy than to talk about devaluation but when questioned afterwards he confessed that he considered devaluation to be less painful than wage cuts.

Two speakers favouring devaluation, chairman and secretary both inclined towards the same position, little wonder the SDAP began to fear that the NVV was becoming pro-devaluationist. But in fact the executive remained split on the issue and the replacement of Kupers by Noordhoff in the commission to study devaluation suggests that it was concerned that both strands of opinion be represented. Further proof that such fears were groundless is provided by the fact that nobody considered it necessary to interfere with the stream of anti-devaluationist editorials published in *De Vakbeweging*. Noordhoff remained the editor-in-chief.(18)

Shortly before the study-conference of March 1934 the executive had apparently decided that the leaders of the affiliated unions had been sufficiently informed for the question to be put on the agenda for their next joint meeting. W. Drees, SDAP member of parliament and later minister-president in a number of post-war cabinets, was invited to put the case for devaluation, and the economist J. van den Tempel, a minister for the SDAP in the 1939 cabinet and ex-secretary of the NVV, the case against.(19) The discussions afterwards had been copiously minuted. Among the participants in the discussions six could be identified as pro-devaluation: the NVV secretary, De la Bella, and the leaders of the transport union, the furniture makers, the typographers, the textile workers and the factory workers. In three cases (transport, textile and factory-workers unions) their stand may have been motivated by the fact that devaluation would improve the export chances in their sectors. Four of the discussants were opposed to devaluation including the leaders of the civil-servants union and the lithographers' union, as well as NVV executive member Noordhoff, who had links with the civil servants' union.(20) From the interests which these represented one could summise that fear of domestic inflation weighed heavier as a consideration than the possibility of increasing export opportunities. Looking at the debate within the NVV as a whole, the following arguments can be discerned:(21)

- The pro-devaluationists emphasised that the economic situation in countries which had devalued was better than in Netherlands, whilst their opponents questioned whether this was because of or despite the devaluation. Central to their argumentation was that devaluation was a leap in the dark.
- The parties also differed on the question of policy priorities. For pro-devaluationists as Van der Wal, De la Bella and Rengelink it was the recovery of employment, whilst for anti-devaluationists as P.Verburg, who wrote the rubric 'economic chronicle' in *De Vakbeweging*, it was control of prices.
- The two sides, moreover, differed in their vision of the predominant economic character of the Netherlands. Pro-devaluationist, Muller, emphasised the fact that employment in industry, trade and transport was greater than in agriculture. The Netherlands had to export to survive and two thirds of exports came from industry. Opponents pointed to the Dutch import dependence arguing that in this situation it could not afford the luxury of uncontrolled inflation. Moreover, such inflation, it was argued, would also destroy the attractiveness of the Netherlands for foreign capital.
- The fear of repraisals from abroad in the event of a Dutch devaluation also played a role in the thinking of opponents, whilst pro-devaluationists countered by pointing to the fact that *any* artificial stimulus to exports carried such a risk and anyway they expected the impact of such counter-measures to be small.
- Anti-devaluationists discerned a gradual return of international confidence and suggested that in such circumstances it would be irresponsible to put this at risk with a guilder devaluation. Pro-devaluationists, whilst appreciating the value of a broad international approach, argued that it should not be followed to the extent that it led to sacrificing the interests of the Dutch worker. Further wage reductions, they argued, were impossible now that the cost of living was rising. They conceded that in theory devaluation could also result in reduced real wages but pointed out that in the UK and Sweden this had not been the case. Anti-devaluationist Lindeman, however, considered that the risk was not worth taking unless the country was on the point of collapse, which it was not. Noodhoff also argued that the deflationary process had already accomplished much. In the metal industry, for example, he considered that a further 5 per cent cost reduction sufficient to make the industry competitive once more.

- The pro-devaluationists further argued that not devaluing implied an acceptance of further wage-cuts which would be damaging to the morale of the labour movement and play straight into the hands of the national socialists. This point was made by Brautigam. Anti-devaluationists countered by suggesting that even after a devaluation wage cuts would still be necessary (they pointed to the UK) which would be even more damaging to morale.
- Finally, the pro-devaluationists argued that in the event of devaluation suffering would no longer be confined to working classes. Everyone would have to cut back and Van der Wal, for example, considered that holders of government stock did not need the sympathy of the labour movement. Anti-devaluationists, however, thought that it was those self-same big-capitalists who would manage, as always, to escape the negative consequences. "We would be giving Deterding a Dfl. 50 million present" said Noordhoff "and he is the one who has financed Hitler and the anti-Russian campaign."

Although the pro-devaluationists were probably in the majority; the NVV's stand-point was primarily determined by the internal divisiveness stemming from both the differing assessment of the effects of a devaluation and the differing priorities in economic policy.

The report *Devaluatie Pro en Contra* was reviewed by Tinbergen in the *De Vakbeweging* in September 1935. He agreed with the pro-devaluationists that the devaluations had contributed to the better economic situation in the non-gold countries though he conceded to the opponents the point that the favourable price movements observed were more accurately attributable to the fact that world market prices had been falling at the time. He admitted that it was difficult to quantify the possible impact of repraisals but thought that exports would expand all the same. Finally, he agreed unreservedly with those anti-devaluationists who considered that agitation in favour of devaluation should be avoided by the labour movement. The final decision on devaluation should be left to the central authorities. In this at least, he appeared to have the pro-devaluationists behind him as well. "If we engage in such action and it did not succeed but nonetheless created the impression that a devaluation would possibly come, it would give rise to capital flight and credit difficulties," wrote Drees. "The fear for a devaluation without an actual devaluation brings nothing but disadvantage."(22) He felt that the trade unions should stick to their protest against the working class alone shouldering the burden of internal price deflation. At the same time he suggested that an even fall in prices (including 'fixed costs' like interest and rent) was unattainable so that the people would eventually come to the conclusion that the best way to arrive at the desired result was through devaluation. It is also worth noting that during the meeting of trade union leaders in May 1934 it had also been two pro-devaluationists who had explicitly stated that the trade unions could not publicly agitate in favour of devaluation.(23)

Meanwhile, the socialist labour-movement had formulated an alternative to

Colijn's policy in the form of the *Plan van den Arbeid*(Labour Plan). This allowed some to suggest that all efforts should be thrown behind a constructive welfare policy "without the leap into the dark of devaluation",(24) though others asked themselves whether an abandonment of the gold standard did not form a precondition for the Plans successful implementation.(25) Hein Vos, the first post-war minister for trade and industry, who had played a major role in its drafting, considered that the Plan was not impossible without devaluation and that it would still be necessary even should the guilder devalue.(26) Thus, the Plan failed to bridge the divide within the NVV on the devaluation question.

Nonetheless, from the beginning of 1936 a clear change is apparent in comparison with the previous years in that interest in the devaluation question dropped off sharply. Throughout 1936 the minutes of the executive make no mention at all of the devaluation option, even though such important issues as the actions of the transport and textile workers against wage cuts, the government's attack on social security payments and the role of import quotas, where it might have been a relevant consideration, were all extensively discussed. Nor did *De Vakbeweging* publish any further statements on the question, either for or against.

After the decision to devalue in September 1936, interest in the entire issue immediately returned. On 27 September the executives of the NVV and SDAP held a meeting together with members of parliament Drees, Van de Tempel, Vos and Matthijsen. On 28 September the full executive met and on 5 October a meeting of the leaders of all the affiliated unions was called. From the results of these discussions it appeared that now the "leap into the dark" had been made, the protection of those on fixed incomes by ensuring that the guilders fall in value be limited, was not a consideration. Priority was given to the restoration of the Dutch export position in order to reduce unemployment and to strengthen the wage bargaining position. Thus, first and foremost, they wanted the fall in the guilder's international value to be sufficiently large to ensure this. Although no target figure was ever published, the figure most often suggested in the discussions was around 30 per cent (the devaluation in fact amounted to no more than 20 per cent), purchasing power of the lowest income groups should be protected by government measures rather than by adopting a lower devaluation percentage. The NVV also wanted the guilder to be relinked to gold as soon as possible and the profit accruing from the revalued gold reserves used to finance expansionary budget measures. The government, incidentally, went on to ignore most of this unsollicited advice.

In conclusion, it can be stated that conflicting visions as well as conflicting interests played a part in explaining the lack of a clear cut vision on the part of the NVV. Remarkable is the qualitatively high level at which the NVV attempted to get to grips with the issues, especially through the medium of study-conferences. The discussions were not conducted solely from the standpoint of defending its own sectorial interests but with the aim of obtaining a wide and informed perspective on the nature of the problems. The explanation for this can only partly be found in the cooperation with the SDAP since the discussions were not restricted to the members of parliament and the 'General Council' of NVV and SDAP but were also extended to the leaders of affiliated unions. This demonstrates how far not only the socialist party but also its counterpart among the Dutch trade unions had come from pure opposition to the prevailing 'capitalist' order of Dutch society. Agitation in favour of devaluation was irresponsible! The force of this argument should not be underestimated.

THE CATHOLICS (RKWV)

"Inflation: that is wage cutting with a blindfold" said CHU minister de Geer in a press interview immediately after the fall of sterling. He was cited with approval a week later in an editorial in *Het Verbondsblad*, the weekly organ of the RKWV edited by the unions' executive. The editorial went on to argue that the only way to avoid such a situation was "through taking measures which will maintain the full purchasing power of the guilder". Only in the course of 1935 is there any discernable change in this anti-devaluationist stand-point.

That did not mean, however, that the catholic trade union movement felt very much for active cooperation in an extensive wage-cutting exercise. Together with the NVV and CNV it protested that the discussions begun on the initiative of the *Commissie voor Werkverruiming* (see pp 166-167) were threatening to evolve into a "commission for the regularisation of wage-cuts".(27) Some weeks later *Het Verbondsblad* described how industrial activity in the UK had begun to recover and that the rise in the cost of living was less than predicted. Yet the RKWV executive still considered that the Netherlands' first priority was the maintenance of international creditworthiness.

The journal for the union cadres *Lering en Leiding* (Instruction and Leadership), whose editorial responsibility rested with two RKWV executives, realised the need for further information over the complicated monetary issues. In 1932 it made a start with a series of articles under the umbrella title 'Money and Gold' in which, for example, it analysed the ideas of Verrijn Stuart and Goudriaan for the replacement of the gold standard. The most important message of all these articles was that even academics could not agree among themselves on the best policy to be followed. At the end of 1933 it supported Colijn's rejection of proposals for a 'managed devaluation', even though a number of "scientific people whom we highly respect"(28) were of a different opinion, and in 1934 an article by Dr. Stridiron in *Economische-Statistische Berichten*, which had argued in favour of devaluation, was strongly criticised.(29)

In 1934 the so-called 'education centrals' of the RKWV began to organise study-days for the leaders of affiliated unions.(30) Among the speakers invited were the early pro-devaluationist professors F. de Vries from Rotterdam and H.A. Kaag from Tilburg, professor Cobbenhagen from Tilburg, who signed one of the 1936 pro-devaluation petitions to the government, and B. van Spaendonck, the secretary of the catholic employers' association (the RKWV) and one of the founders of the NVWG. Outspoken anti-devaluationists did not appear to have been invited! Kaag in particular appears to have been influential within the catholic labour movement. The RKWV used his services on a number of occasions as an intermediary in difficult labour disputes and, furthermore, his advice was often sought on economic questions. Kaag was also one of three reporters chosen to prepare the ground for the discussion at the big 'Industrialisation congress' held on 13 May 1935 (the others were Ch. Stulemeijer of the catholic employers and A.C. de Bruijn, RKWV chairman). Their advice was published before the congress in *Het Verbondsblad*, Kaag's conclusion was: "The primary task of the government is to create a healthy basis for the development of enterprise.....(through) a healthy financial situation. Under the present circumstances this requires the abandonment of the gold standard."(31) But De Bruijn did not mention the possibility of devaluation. He concentrated on industrial organisation, industrial protection etc. The final resolutions of the Congress did not mention devaluation either.(32)

Not even the devaluation of the Belgian franc in April 1935 had any effect on the position of the RKWV. The reaction of *Het Verbondsblad* was that a large proportion of the Belgian population had opposed it, that Germany and the UK were preparing repraisal measures which would mute the anticipated export growth, and that the whole operation had been undertaken to rescue the banks (which, it was noted in passing, played a much more important role for industry than did their counterparts in the Netherlands).(33) Thereafter, however, events in Belgium were closely followed; something which was made easier because of the close contacts which existed with the Belgian catholic unions.

Meanwhile, the government had prepared legislation for a further round of deflation through cut-backs in government expenditure. *Het Verbondsblad* mentioned in passing that this had fuelled new speculation on the likelihood of devaluation.(34) However, the RKWV resolution on the issue chose rather to emphasise its demands for a more active industrialisation policy, increased expenditure on public works and industrial subsidies to combat unemployment.(35)

Thus, until the middle of 1935 the position of the RKWV could be characterised as favouring a maintenance of the gold standard. Indirectly, however, (namely through the reports of the economic situation in non-gold countries) a certain hesitancy could be discerned. *Het Verbondsblad* reprinted a series of articles on devaluation from the paper *Libre Belgique*. On 18 June a report on the economic situation in Belgium appeared within this series, which boiled down to the following; higher profits, higher levels of activity, diminished unemployment and an acceptable level of price increases. News of this kind undoubtedly played an important role in the RKWV executive's shift ir thinking on the devaluation question.

On top of this, the resignation in June 1935 of M.P.L. Steenberghe, one of three catholic ministers in the cabinet, also influenced the change in mood. He had resigned on the issue of maintaining the gold standard and *Het Verbondsblad* left no room for doubt that the RKWV backed Steenberghe's stand. It also expressed its frank amazement that Gelissen, who, the paper pointed out, had only some weeks previously spoken in favour of devaluation, should have been willing to take his place.(36) This same point had also disturbed the RKSP itself and on this question the RKWV was inclined to follow the party's lead. Steenberghe's resignation, and the fact that within the party he had received so much support,(37) cleared the way for a more pro-devaluationist stance. Even so, there was no attempt to initiate a wide discussion within the catholic trade union movement. For example, the executive did not consider devaluation a suitable subject for a lecture at a meeting of all affiliated unions that same autumn.(38)

Even after Steenberghe's resignation doubts still lingered within the RKWV over the desirability of devaluation and there was never any question of a forceful plea for abandoning the gold standard. There was plenty of criticism of Colijn's policies but these boiled down to the fact that deflation policies pursued lacked consistency. Like the RKSP, the RKWV kept complaining that too little attention was paid to the need to lower *all* fixed costs and that the load had fallen too heavily and one-sidedly onto the backs of the workers. In December 1935 the RKWV could still point to the fact that it had never openly come out in favour of devaluation.(39)

According to *Het Verbondsblad* the feeling began to gain ground towards the end of the year that the deflationary measures would continue to be too inadequate to forestall an eventual devaluation. It was considered virtually impossible to lower production costs any further by means of wage-cuts. The (unofficial) strike of Tilburg textile workers in the autumn of 1935 was interpreted as an indication that downward pressure on wages was only serving to produce a dangerous radicalisation of the workers – a process which would continue unless a way other than internal price adjustment were found of making the economy more competitive.(40) Some strikes against further wage cuts were even backed by the RKWV.(41)

The annual report of 1935 was written in a clear pro-devaluationist vein. It recalled that Kaag's last sentence at the Industrialisation Congress – "Do it now!" had struck a chord with many, that Steenberghe had been invited in the autumn to expand his views, and that RKWV executive P.J.S.Serrarens had held, in the First Chamber of parliament, a forceful and well-documented speech in favour of devaluation. Nonetheless, the report still noted that although the executive had extensively discussed the monetary question, it had not taken an official position one way or the other.(42)

It is noticeable that, as was the case with the NVV, interest in the devaluation question waned from the early months of 1936 onwards.(43) Only after the fall of the guilder was the RKWV able, relatively painlessly, to distance itself from the policy of adherence to the gold standard. Only then was the policy characterised without any reservation as: "an unhealthy piece of conservatism which has caused the workers especially a great deal more trouble than would have been necessary with any other policy."(44)

Within the RKWV itself there appeared to be little internal tension on the question of the gold standard.(45) The union was far more concerned with other means for combatting the crisis. In May 1931 the papal encyclical *Quadragesimo Anno* was published; a sequel to the encyclical *Rerum Novarum* in which Pope Pius XI had set out the desirable social and economic order. The new encyclical was widely discussed in *Lering en Leiding* and the RKWV itself published translations of both which by the end of 1932 had sold 25,000 copies. Together they were seen as a sort of constitution for the social action of the catholic labour movement.(46) The methods for combatting the crisis advanced by the RKWV were drawn directly from the ideas of *Quadragesimo Anno* – the 'ordering' of production, a constructive welfare policy, reduction in working hours and a prohibition on the employment of married women who were not main bread-winners. *Quadragesimo Anno* was not the place to expect a discussion of financial-technical instruments of economic policy such as currency devaluation. That *Lering en Leiding* blamed the devaluation of sterling on speculative bankers also fitted in with the thinking of *Quadragesimo Anno* which emphasised the pernicious effects of the increasing power of bank capital. The policy of 'consistent deflation', often promoted in catholic circles, (i.e. interest rates, debts, mortgages and rents should be reduced at the same rate as wages and social security payments) was also in the line with the prescriptions of *Quadragesimo Anno*. The parallel existence of other national trade unions federations made it necessary for the RKWV not only to defend the interests of its members but also to carve out its own identity. The stress which these solutions were to receive is understandable in this light since they drew heavily upon catholic principles. The so-called 'double-structure' of catholic labour organisations and the influence of the clergy within them probably also served to strengthen this tendency.(47) But for the RKWV, as for the NVV, agitation against the guilder was out of the question.

THE PROTESTANTS (CNV)

In so far as the CNV devoted any time at all to monetary questions, it did so in a way which characterised the rest of CNV-policy: not to move out of step with the ARP – and in the ARP doubts over maintaining the gold standard were less than in any of the other important political parties.(48) Nonetheless, during these years some differences in nuances could be discerned between the ARP and CNV.

The devaluation of sterling was deeply regretted by H. Amelink, writing almost immediately afterwards in *De Gids* (The Guide), the organ of the CNV. It was feared that Dutch interests in UK markets would suffer and that the

Netherlands would be flooded by cheaper British products; all of which would increase unemployment. The possibility of the guilder following suit was never even considered. In the first place, Amelink feared the kind of hyper-inflation which had occurred in Germany after the war and, secondly, he saw the fall of sterling as a plot by worshippers of Mammon.(49) His anti-capitalist analysis, which was clearly influenced by the crisis in general, and the capitalism debate being held in catholic circles in particular,(50) brought him into conflict with the ARP-member of parliament and chairman of the protestant working class association *Patrimonium*, C. Smeenk, who resented such an attack on the capitalist system.(51) Thereafter, Amelink was noticably more tempered on this subject.(52) Nor did 'controlled inflation', proposed by the leader of the cigar-makers union B. Kruithof(53) at an emergency meeting of the CNV on 16 October 1931, find any positive response.(54) This was resolutely rejected by F. Fuijkschot, the secretary of the office and trade personnel's union who was to become the major economic commentator of the CNV. Although he conceded that such a solution seemed attractive in the short-term he felt that in the longer term, after the inevitable national and international financial/economic adjustments, it would operate against the interests of the workers(55) – a position he maintained throughout his subsequent analyses.(56)

The CNV placed most of its hopes for a normalisation of economic conditions on international efforts to stem the rising tide of protectionism and the unilateral imposition of exchange controls. Even before the crisis this free-trade approach characterised its social-political programme.(57) Unlike the RKWV, the CNV (and NVV) greeted protectionist solutions with a great deal of reservation. Not surprisingly, therefore, the union was sorely disappointed by the fiasco of the World Economic Conference in London in the summer of 1933. *De Gids*, cited with approval the opinion of its sister paper *Patrimonium*, which ascribed the blame for the failure of the conference primarily to President Roosevelt's ill-considered monetary experiment.(58) For a protestant trade union the only remaining path was trust in God. "Politicians may fail, God won't let the faithful down."(59)

Remarkable in this respect was the position adopted by A. Stapelkamp, one of the secretaries of the CNV. During a christian-social course in September 1933 he suggested that maintenance of an undevalued currency was necessary, even though he acknowledged that the Netherlands' competitive position had worsened. "The deliberate creation of inflation or deflation must be considered in conflict with christian morality", he declared.(60) In this opinion he was not alone. A few months earlier the ARP parliamentary leader, J. Schouten, had stated at the CNV general meeting that the monetary policy of the United States and Germany had in "the most terrible way" mocked the fundamental premises of christianity.(61) The fact that neither of these statements roused any serious disagreement (only J. Groote of the civil-servants union protested at Stapelkamp's statement of principle)(62) may be taken as an indication of the mentality of the CNV upper-cadres. Even accepting that the CNV was convinced that christian norms and values should determine social and economic activity (indeed, the union's own separate existence was testimony to this), the lack of discussion is surprising. The rejection of concrete economic or financial measures on the basis of christian principles was far from convincing. Such a position might have gained in strength had the possibie economic and social *results* of devaluation been confronted with christian principles, but this was never done. When the event came, the CNV had to accept the inevitability of devaluation in September 1936. Though the move was regretted, there was no mention of the possibility that it might conflict with christian teaching.(63)

The CNV position on the gold standard did not mean that there was no criticism of the government's deflationary policy but, the margins for opposition were small and any reserves the unions had were generally expressed with great caution. The CNV spokesman in such matters was Fuykschot. He expressed the union's concern at the way in which such government measures seemed to fall mainly on wages and social-security payments whilst leaving leases, mortgages and rents untouched.(64) In this respect the CNV position had more in common with that of the RKSP than with either of the two large protestant parties.(65)

The gulf separating the CNV from the social democrats on the one hand, and from the liberals on the other, remained large. When these two streams seemed to come together in the pro-devaluation pressure group, the NVWG,(66) the development was viewed with deep suspicion. This same unease had led earlier to the cool reception given to an NVV initiative to bring employers and employees together to discuss a common approach to economic problems.(67) The purchasing power policy of the social democrats found little response in protestant union circles either.(68) A balanced budget remained a *conditio sine qua non* for its economic programme – and that was quite flagrantly not the immediate intention of the socialists. In terms quite consistent with the virulent anti-socialism of the time, the *Plan van den Arbeid* was dismissed as "contemptable demagogy".(69)

In the spring of 1935 the question of 'consistent deflation' rose to the surface again. It was not that the CNV objected to the need for further deflation. At an extraordinary meeting of the CNV executive in May 1935, Stapelkamp had again supported the governments position on this and underlined the unavoidable necessity of a lowering of living standards.(70) Nor did the CNV oppose maintaining the gold standard. Two weeks before the Belgian devaluation Fuykschot had characterised Dutch adherence to the gold standard "as a lasting duty, as a satisfaction of our international vocation to hang in to the bitter end. Even if we must make sacrifices".(71) What worried Stapelkamp was that the government seemed to be treating the balancing of the budget and the attack on *vaste lasten* as two seperate issues – a position which came close to that of Aalberse, leader of the catholic parliamentary party, but not to that of Schouten or CHU leader, D.J. de Geer.(72) However, the suggestion made by Aalberse that without 'consistent deflation' devaluation was inevitable, was not accepted by the CNV. If it were forced to choose an alternative for 'consistent deflation' (i.e. with government legislation to lower *vaste lasten*) it was 'natural deflation', though it preferred the former. This position diverged from that of the ARP but the CNV was not prepared to risk a cabinet crisis on the question. "If this government should go, chaos threatens and the call for a strong man will again be heard," declared A. van Driel, chairman of the civil-servants union.(73) Naturally enough, the CNV was extremely unhappy when a cabinet crisis did occur in July 1935 and it was equally unhappy when later the government's proposed deflationary package was finally accepted by parliament.

After the summer of 1935 the CNV rarely returned to a discussion of monetary questions so it is difficult to know whether stand-points shifted. Equally, whether the devaluation was entirely unexpected can only be guessed at. Amelink's statement that "it had to come" creates the impression that the CNV had expected nothing else.(74) However, in view of the fact that there is no trace of any such statement before 27 September 1936, it would seem as though Amelink was merely expressing wisdom after the event. Similarily, although Fuykschot was more or less forced by the position he had adopted throughout the debates to react negatively to the devaluation itself, his analysis of the possible consequences was characterised by a moderate optimism.(75) In this the CNV differed from the protestant working class association *Patrimonium*, which continued to play up the inadequacy of devaluation as a policy instrument (76).

All in all, monetary problems were little discussed within the CNV. The fact that there was little internal difference of opinion certainly helped to make the issue less urgent. Moreover, it is difficult to trace any clear line through those discussions which did take place (in so far as they were captured in the minutes of the executive meetings) other than to note that the office and trade personnel's union played and an unexpectedly large role (considering its size), but then that typified its contribution to virtually all other discussions as well. By contrast, the influence of the large agricultural workers union was extremely small. This might be explained by the fact that the question of the guilder's value usually came up in the context of discussions on government budget-cutting proposals which affected civil servants more than any category – social security recipients excepted. Moreover, the union's leader, Fuykschot, had a strong personal position within the CNV which derived more from his individual qualities than from the strength of the union itself. There is no indication of any systematic pressure or criticism from the membership.(77)

Of all the unions, the CNV identified itself most with the Colijn cabinets, and this undoubtably influenced its approach towards monetary policy. Both before and after the guilder depreciation CNV spokesmen threw themselves into the breach on behalf of the government, though this did not always enhance the quality of argument. One example of this is C. van Baren Jr. of the factory and transport-workers union who, in the middle of 1934, declared himself incompetent to judge the devaluation question but, nonetheless, could still go on to defend Colijn's policies.(78) A second example of the sometimes emotive arguments used and of the influence of Calvinist thought on the CNV's analysis of the crisis is afforded by the speech made by K. Kruithof on retiring as CNV chairman. "The blame for all misery," he contended, "is to be put on disbelief in God Almighty ....People are too apt to think that world misery can be undone by human interference.... Some make mention of a *Plan van Arbeid*, others speak of a 'constructive welfare policy'.... But those who live by the light of the Scriptures will know that it is risky to put high hopes on human ability....I don't know the solution for the crisis. The only one who knows is God."(79)

Colijn's 'untarnished guilder' policy was never a burning issue within the Dutch labour movement. Even pro-devaluationists were convinced that the trade unions could not afford to be identified with propaganda against the gold standard. For this reason the devaluation question was never allowed to threaten the unity on other points of policy.

The different ways in which the unions examined attempted to formulate a position on the gold standard partly supports the traditional Dutch vision that Dutch society can better be interpreted vertically in terms of *zuilen* than horizontally in terms of class. Each union's close association with its 'own' political party undoubtedly influenced the discussions.

But, it is worth stressing that the visions differed not only in the *way* in which standpoints were reached, but also in the *level* of debate. The CNV was the least inclined to call upon outside expertise. The RKWV did far more in this direction. The level of discussion within the NVV, however, was really high; so high in fact that it is difficult to avoid the conclusion that on the basis of all the evidence available it was indeed impossible to formulate a water-tight 'working class' case on the gold standard one way or the other.

Notes

1. For commentary on earlier versions we would like to thank not only the other members of the research group but also Ger Harmsen. We would further like to thank Tineke de Bie for her research assistance in the archives of the NVV and Henk Middelbrink in those of the RKVW.
2. *Handelingen Tweede Kamer*, 1933-34, 283, (10.11.1933) It appeared that Colijn at that moment was under the impression that the left had created the contraposition of maintaining the 'untarnished' guilder and the supression of workers' rights, a formulation with which he strongly disagreed.
3. See in this context P.W. Klein, Depressie en beleid tijdens de jaren dertig, reprinted in P. Geurts en F. Messing, *Economische Ontwikkeling en Sociale Emancipatie*, Vol.II, 's-Gravenhage, 1977, 144-186.
4. G. Harmsen en B. Reinalda, *Voor de bevrijding van de arbeid*, Nijmegen, 1975, 432-423.
5. *Ibid.*, 113 and 166; E. Hueting, F. de Jong Edzn. and R. Neij, *Naar groter eenheid*, Amsterdam, 1983, 79.
6. C.J. Kuiper, *Uit het rijk van den Arbeid*, s.l., 1951.
7. S. Stuurman, *Verzuiling, Kapitalisme en Patriarchaat. Aspecten van de ontwikkeling van de moderne staat in Nederland*, Nijmegen, 1983, 166 et seq.

8. H. Amelink, *Onder eigen banier*, Utrecht, 1940, 194; M. Ruppert, *De Nederlandse vakbeweging*, Vol.I., Haarlem, 1953, 127.
9. The CNV was averse to the cult build up around Colijn. See for example *De Gids*, 13.5.1937. For a posthumus critique see A. Stapelkamp, Dr. H. Colijn en het sociale leven, B. Offringa, (ed.), *Een groot vaderlander. Dr. H. Colijn herdacht door tijdgenooten*, Leiden, 1947.
10. *De Vakbeweging*, No.11, november 1931, in the 'Economische Kroniek' written by P. Verburg.
11. The complete text of this letter, together with the texts of the letters of the RKWV and the CNV, were reprinted in *14e Verslag van de toestand en de werkzaamheden van het NVV over het tijdvak 1.1.1929 tot 31.12.1931*, 186-189. The discussions were not continued.
12. On the agenda stood the wage-cuts in the textile industry. The point was made that the market was being flooded by Japanese, Polish and English textiles. It was observed that it was no longer possible to compete against the English because wage costs were some 50 per cent higher in the Netherlands. The conclusion was that it was difficult to resist the arguments for wage cutting. A discussion of the strikes in the clothing industry in January 1933 in the verbonds bestuur led to the same one-sided conclusion. Internationaal Instituut voor Sociale Geschiedenis (IISG), NVV-archief, minutes of Verbondsbestuur 28.11.1932.
13. See for example *15e Verslag van de toestand en de werkzaamheden van het NVV 1.1.1932 tot 31.12.1934*, 39-40.
14. The complete series can be found in the library of the FNV.
15. IISG, NVV-archief, minutes of the Verbondsbestuur 20.1.1933.
16. In *De Vakbeweging*, February 1934, Dr K. Mendelsohn stated that the "opponents of devaluation were not exclusively to be found among the social reactionaries nor were proponents exclusively among the socially progressive" which would suggest that such an idea had already caught on.
17. Both introductions were published as brochures.
18. The minutes of the meeting of the Verbondsbestuur for the period 2.6.1933 to 17.2.1936 are missing from the NVV archives deposited at the IISG.
19. The meeting took place on 29/30 May 1934; the lectures were published in July 1934 by the NVV in a brochure under the title *Devaluatie*. The brochure can be found in the library of the FNV.
20. The fourth was a certain L. Soesan, about whom we have been unable to find any further information.
21. IISG, NVV-archief, Notulen Hoofdbesturenvergadering, Vol.IV, 29/30.5.1934, 427-43.
22. *Devaluatie*, 1934, 19.
23. De la Bella said that he supported the stance taken by Drees and Van de Tempel, "that we cannot make devaluation an issue for agitation". Van der Wal said: "We cannot make propoganda for devaluation and not do we have to decide whether it will happen or not, but we would certainly stand much stronger (if we did – WF) against the employers who are still pushing for wage cuts". The fact that nobody in the meeting opposed these views would suggest that the matter was already *communis opinio*.
24. J. Koedijk in *De Vakbeweging*, December 1935.
25. Roelofs during a meeting of the Hoofdbesturen on 17.10.1935; see minutes.
26. H. Vos at the same meeting.
27. The letter is reprinted in *14e Verslag van de toestand en de werkzaamheden van het NVV over het tijdvak 1.1.1929 tot 31.12.1931*,188-189, together with the reaction of the CNV and of the NVV itself.
28. *Lering en Leiding*, December 1933, in the 'Sociaal-Economische Kroniek' by K. (= editor C.J. Kuiper).
29. *Lering en Leiding*, January 1934, 28 by C.J. van Eyndthoven.
30. Kuiper, *Uit het rijk van den Arbeid*, Vol. III, 750.
31. *Het Verbondsblad*, 3.5.1935.
32. *Ibid.*, 17.5.1935.
33. *Ibid.*, 5.4.1935.
34. *Ibid.*, 24.5.1935.
35. *Ibid.*, 7.6.1935.

36. *Ibidem.*
37. P.J. Oud, *Het jongste verleden*, Vol V, Assen, 1950, 205.
38. Katholiek Documentatie Centrum (KDC) Archief-RKWV, minutes of meeting of dagelijks bestuur, 11.6.1935.
39. *Het Verbondsblad*, 20.12.1935.
40. *Het Verbondsblad*, 15.11.1935.
41. In the mining industry and in the zink factory at Budel; see *Het Verbondsblad*, 19.7.1935.
42. *Elfde Jaarboek van het RKWV in Nederland, betrekking hebbende op omvang en werkzaamheden gedurende het jaar 1935*, 139.
43. In the *Twaalfde Jaarboek van het RKWV etc.*, 1936, 125 one can read on the question of devaluation "people do not any longer want to talk about it.....".
44. *Het Verbondsblad*, 2.10.1935.
45. It is impossible to be certain on this point because no extensive minutes have survived after 10.10.1931. The RKWV-archive at the KDC does have summary minutes for 15.10.1932 and for the period after 30.10.1933.
46. According to *Zevende Jaarboek van het RKWV*, 1931, 208
47. The spiritual advisor in the Verbondsbestuur, Father D. Beaufort O.F.M., was the organisor of the economic study days; see KDC, Archief-RKWV, minutes of the meeting of dagelijks bestuur 16.4.1934.
48. J.A. de Wilde and C. Smeenk, *Het Volk ten baat. De geschiedenis van de AR.-partij*, Groningen, 1949, 632.
49. *De Gids*, 8.10.1931. Within the CNV Amelink was the only one who strongly advocated christian reform ideals for restrictions to the freedom of enterprise.
50. P.E. Werkman, Herman Amelink (1881-1957). De denker van het CNV, *Bulletin Nederlandse Arbeidersbeweging*, 1985, No.5, 3-30.
51 See *Patrimonium*, 25 .6.1931, 27.3.1931, 30.7.1931 and *Christelijk Geloof en Economische Crisis. Verslag van den Vijfden Christelijke Socialen Cursus*, Hoorn, 1932.
52. Something similar occurred in the discussion in catholic circles. See T. Salemink, *Krisis en konfessie, ideologie in katholiek Nederland 1917-1933*, Zeist, 1980, 273.
53. Not to be confused with his brother K. Kruithof, who was chairman of the CNV from 1916 to 1935.
54. Archief CNV, Utrecht, minutes of the Algemeen bestuur, 16.10.1931.
55. *Ons Beginsel*, 15.11.1931.
56. See for example *De Gids*, 18.4.1935, 2.5.1935, 16.5.1935.
57. Compare *Dertiende verslag van het Christelijk Nationaal Vakverbond in Nederland. 1 januari 1927 tot 31 december 1928*, 248 with *Harmonie van het individueele en het collectieve. Verslag van den zesden Christelijk-Socialen Cursus*, Hoorn, 1933, 86.
58. *De Gids*, 13.7.1933.
59. *Vijftiende Verslag van het Christelijk Nationaal Vakverbond in Nederland. 1 januari 1931 tot 31 december 1932*. See also *De Gids*, 13.7.1933.
60. *Harmonie*, 87.
61. *Verslag van de algemene vergadering van het Christelijk Nationaal Vakverbond op Maandag 26 en Dinsdag 27 juni 1933*, s.l., s.a., 28.
62. *Harmonie*, 132.
63. See for example, the implicit recognition of this fact by Stapelkamp in May 1935 when he commented that, "it has not been established, that in every circumstance the christian trade union movement opposes devaluation." Archief CNV, minutes of extraordinary meeting of the Algemeen Bestuur, 31.5.1935.
64. *De Gids*, 23.8.1934.
65. Oud, *Het jongste verleden*, Vol.V, 142 et seq.
66. *De Gids*, 1.11.1934.
67. Archief CNV, minutes of meeting of Algemeen Bestuur, 5.2.1934.
68. *De Gids*, 27.6.1935. For a discordant note see *De Gids*, 25.7.1935.

69. Archief CNV, minutes of meeting of Algemeen Bestuur 31.5.1935 and *De Gids*, 31.10.1935.
70. Archief CNV, minutes of an extraordinary meeting of the algemene bestuur, 31.5.1935.
71. *De Gids*, 17.5.1935. Compare Oud, *Het jongste verleden*, Vol.V, 218.
72. Oud, *Het jongste verleden*, Vol.V, 213 et seq.
73. Archief CNV, minutes of extraordinary meeting of Algemeen Bestuur, 31.5.1935.
74. *De Gids*, 15.10.1936.
75. *De Gids*, 1.10.1936, 15.10.1936.
76. C.J. van Laren en G.M.T. Trienekens, De jaren dertig: van liberale naar gemengde ekonomie?, P.W. Klein en G.J. Borger (eds.) *De Jaren Dertig. Aspecten van crisis en werkloosheid*, Amsterdam, 1979, 52 et seq.
77. A note of caution is required here. Firstly virtually all the CNV archive was lost during the Second World War. And secondly the research has been restricted to the national level and has not included separate work on the affiliated unions.
78. *De Gids*, 9.8.1934. See also *De Gids*, 29.10.1936.
79. *Verslag van de zeventiende algemeene vergadering van het Christelijk Nationaal Vakverbond, gehouden Donderdag 27 en Vrijdag 28 juni 1935.*

CHAPTER SIX

The Political Parties

The introduction in 1918 of proportional representation and universal male suffrage, soon to be followed by the introduction of female suffrage, marked the beginning of a new period in Dutch political history characterised by a large degree of stability in the relative positions of the major political tendencies. This stability can be explained by the phenomenon of pillarisation, discussed more extensively in Chapter One (see pp 13-16), and by the system of proportional representation itself, which contributed to fewer large shifts in parliamentary representation between the different parties than the district system.

Despite difficulties in working together, the 1920's and early 1930's formed a period of uninterrupted governmental responsibility for the confessional parties. Numerically the confessional parties were dominated by the catholics. Their party, which in 1926 attained its definitive form as the RKSP, *Roomsch Katholieke Staats Partij* (Roman Catholic Party), averaged 30 seats in the Second Chamber (out of a total of 100) and was larger than both the protestant coalition partners put together. Of these the ARP, *Anti-Revolutionaire Partij* (Anti-revolutionary Party) with an average of 13 seats, was larger than the CHU, *Christelijk-Historische Unie* (Christian Historical Union) which had an average of 10. The birth of the CHU alongside the older ARP can be explained in social-political as well as in religious terms; in contrast to the somewhat more progressive ARP, the CHU had a more conservative character and whilst the CHU drew its support largely from the *Nederlandse Hervormde Kerk* the ARP was supported primarily by the members of the *Gereformeerde Kerken*. Although the religious split remained as definite as ever, if measured by their progressivity, the two parties had grown together in the 1930's: the ARP under its new leader Hendrik Colijn (since 1922) had altered course – taking a more conservative path, whilst the CHU had begun to attract a number of more progressive younger members – though they had yet to succeed in shifting the party from its overwhelmingly conservative direction.

Universal sufferage and proportional representation had transformed the SDAP, *Sociaal-Democratische Arbeiders Partij* (Social Democratic Labour Party) into the second largest political group in the country, but in the 1930's it had failed to increase its support, the party had to remain satisfied with between one fifth and one quarter of the votes; the 22 seats it achieved in 1918 was equalled in 1933. This was, however, sufficient for social democracy to replace liberalism as the biggest non-confessional political stream in the country.

In the beginning of the 1920's Dutch liberalism was concentrated in a conservative and in a more progressive party. Of the two, the conservative LSP *Liberale Staats Partij* (Liberal Party) was originally the largest but was affected the most by the general fall in liberal support and saw its number of seats sink from 7 in 1933 to 4 in 1937. The more progressive VDB *Vrijzinnig-Democratische Bond* (Free-Democratic Union) succeeded better in maintaining its not very large number of seats; during the inter-war period as a whole it averaged 6 seats in the Second Chamber, a number it also achieved in 1933.

In the Dutch political system the key for the composition of any coalition lay with the RKSP. Only if it were prepared to work together with the SDAP was an alternative to the confessional or confessionally dominated cabinets possible. However, in the course of the 1920's the RKSP had formulated a number of stringent conditions which had to be satisfied before it was prepared to join a cabinet with the social democrats; together known as the law of the 'ultimate necessity'. Firstly, there had to be no other alternative; a coalition with the SDAP had to form the last possible option. Secondly, this 'ultimate necessity' could not be forced or provoked; the RKSP did not want to be put into a position by other groups in which it had no alternative other than to work together with the SDAP; furthermore, at least one other party had to participate in the cabinet; the RKSP was not prepared to be the only party which carried the responsibility for bringing the social democrats into government. And finally, the parliamentary party had to decide on this step unanimously.

After the 1929 elections the conditions of 'ultimate necessity' could scarcely be said to have existed as far as the RKSP was concerned. The economic development was favourable and there were no other immediate large social or political problems. The cabinet formation therefore ended with the traditional result in the form of a confessional cabinet, this time under the leadership of the RKSP politician Ch.J.M. Ruys de Beerenbrouck. The two key economic ministries were lead by D.J. de Geer (finance) and T.J. Verschuur (economic affairs), whereby it is worth mentioning that the relatively unknown Verschuur was not the first choice.(1) For a long time it had appeared that the cabinet would last its full parliamentary life but shortly before the end of its journey it ran into a parliamentary defeat on its deflationary budget plans. The government decided to call for early elections. In the event these elections of April 1933 were not dominated by the proposed budgetary cuts nor by the cabinet's social-economic policy as a whole but by the issue of law and order. This was a consequence of the mutiny on the Dutch battleship 'The Seven Provinces' several months before and of the ensuing general outrage, which was great. Only the SDAP showed a measure of ambivalence: officially the mutiny was condemned, but the indignancy of the social democrats was directed less against the mutineers than against the violent way in which the government had brought the mutiny to an end.

This ambivalent position had certainly not strengthened the chances of the SDAP being included in a new government after the elections. This time the decision on the form of the cabinet lay not with a RKSP politician but with Colijn. His ARP was the only coalition party which had improved its position, largely attributed to the forceful way in which Colijn had presented himself as the man of law and order. He was entrusted with the formation of a parliamentary cabinet. 'Parliamentary' meaning in this context that the government programme would be based on agreements between the various parliamentary parties upon whose support the government could then count. Colijn's attempt involved not only the three confessional parties (who with 52 seats had managed to achieve a small majority) but also representatives of both liberal parties. In view of the extremely small confessional majority there is little doubt that the deteriorating economic situation formed a motive for attempting to construct a broadly based cabinet, although account must also be taken of the difficulties which had arisen between the confessional coalition partners themselves.

The RKSP refused to cooperate. It was not prepared to participate in a parliamentary cabinet which included the too conservative LSP. Because of this refusal Colijn was forced to surrender his mandate. However, he was immediately reappointed; this time with the goal of forming a 'crisis cabinet'. Without a new round of consultation with the parliamentary parties Colijn approached a number of the most prominent politicians from the three confessional parties and the two liberal parties, inviting them to join the cabinet on the basis of his own programme. Most declared themselves willing to do so and within days the crisis cabinet of Colijn became a reality. Verschuur retained his position in economic affairs. For the portfolio of minister of finance Colijn had brought in the VDB politician P.J. Oud, probably from the consideration that the necessary budgetry cuts would be more easily accepted by parliament if they originated from a liberal, progressive politician.(2) Because Oud was not prepared to accept this post unless the political leader of the VDB, H.P. Marchant, was also brought into the government Colijn invited him as well. This explains why the VDB was represented in the cabinet by two ministers whilst both the larger CHU and LSP had each to be satisfied with one.

In the course of the next cabinet period a clear division of opinion emerged between the RKSP and the four others. Because the RKSP had objected to a cabinet on the basis of five parties (this had come nonetheless, albeit without the outspoken approval of the parliamentary parties) the catholics did not consider themselves bound to the government. In practice this meant that the RKSP parliamentary party exercised increasing criticism on the governments social-economic policy. By contrast, the parliamentary parties of the ARP, CHU, VDB and LSP were most of the time loyal. The tension between the RKSP and the government reached a high point in July 1935 when a speech by its parliamentary leader P.J. Aalberse was so critical on the government's expenditure cutting legislation that Colijn, irritated, demanded a vote of confidence from the chamber. When it became apparent that the RKSP would probably vote against the government, he asked that the parliamentary discussions on the proposed legislation be suspended and two days later tendered his cabinet's resignation.

Following the unwritten rule 'he who breaks pays', the task of forming a parliamentary cabinet fell to Aalberse. The most obvious course for him to follow was to attempt to include the SDAP. However, the CHU and the VDB were not prepared to participate in any cabinet formed by Aalberse. On the other hand, the RKSP parliamentary party, in line with the condition that a third party had always to be found, was not prepared to accept an exclusive 'Rome/red' coalition – which would only have half the parliamentary seats anyway. As a result Aalberse failed and he had to surrender his mandate.

Apparently the CHU leader, De Geer, was then approached as to whether he would consider forming a government but he refused,(3) among other reasons because he had considered the crisis totally unnecessary in the first place. It was then the turn of Colijn, who was asked to form a new extra-parliamentary cabinet (i.e. again, one whose programme did not need to be approved by the parliamentary parties beforehand) which he succeeded in doing in the shortest possible time. The new cabinet differed little in its composition from the previous one. It was clear to all that Colijn had achieved a victory over the rebellious RKSP parliamentary party, in the course of which Aalberse's powerlessness had been painfully exposed. For the rest of the parliamentary period, the RKSP was to cause the government no real problems in the execution of its social-economic policy.

It is perhaps helpful at this juncture to recapitulate on the meanings of a number of terms used in the political debate on economic policy. The Dutch term used to describe the government's policy is *aanpassing*. This was something more than merely trying to balance the budget: by lowering the civil servants' wages and unemployment benefits it was hoped to alter the entire context of wage bargaining and so contribute towards the restoration of the economy's competitiveness. The government was often inclined to describe this as 'natural deflation' since it left the rest of the process of domestic price adjustment to market forces. For a few remaining 'laissez-faire' liberals the term 'natural deflation' went even further; it meant not only that the government should continue with its positive contribution (expenditure and wage cuts) but that it should also refrain from taking measures which thwarted the realisation of its policy (i.e. the subsidies to businesses and public services, price-increasing agricultural support schemes etc.). There were others who considered that the government's efforts were too lop-sided; pushing down prices in certain areas where it had control but leaving the rest untouched. Their demand was for 'consistent deflation' which meant taking legislative measures to reduce prices and charges which were proving downwardly inflexible, more often than not because they had been fixed by private contract when the prevailing price level had been much higher. These fixed charges were grouped under the collective term *vaste lasten* and included interest, mortgage, rent and tenancy payments (and, in some cases, thinking even went so far as to include the principle as well).

In previous chapters we have attempted to explain the terms as they arose in the text but in this chapter they come so thick and fast that such an option is neither possible nor desirable.

THE ANTI-REVOLUTIONARY PARTY (ARP)

Looking at the standpoints of the political parties with regard to the gold standard and trying to answer the question which support or opposition they gave to the government, it is logical to start with the ARP. The obvious reason for this lies in the person of Hendrik Colijn who, as prime-minister, was the main architect of the financial-economic policy of the governments from 1933 onwards, but who was also the uncrowned king of the ARP. However, as will be shown, it was not only Colijn's ideas and position that made the ARP stick to the gold standard.

There was little theorising in political circles about the gold standard. That the Netherlands should adhere to this monetary standard was not a matter for political struggle in the 1930's. In general people assumed that the value of the guilder was fixed to that of precious metal and, since 1875, that precious metal had been gold. The ARP was no exception to this. On monetary questions there was little conflict within the orthodox-protestant group represented by the ARP though, occasionally, differences in nuances could be discerned. However, since within orthodox political circles people were fully aware of each others opinions on religious, social and political questions, it is possible to talk about a separate anti-revolutionary consensus. In the following paragraphs we will examine the tradition of anti-revolutionary thought on financial and economic policy, the view of a small group of orthodox-protestant economists, the opinions in the anti-revolutionary press, the stand of the party in parliament and finally the monetary theory of the ARP leader Dr H. Colijn.

The tradition of ARP thought on the question of the gold-standard was not a long one. A researcher will look in vain for any mention of the concept of the gold standard in the parties first political programme. *Ons program* (Our Programme) did indeed devote a chapter to the question of finance but this was chiefly concerned with government fiscal/financial policy.(4) In other words, one can speak of an anti-revolutionary vision on the execution of monetary policy but not on the basic principles underlying the monetary system as such. When, in 1874, Kuyper explained *Ons Program* in the daily paper *De Standaard* the question of a choice between a gold or a silver standard was one of the burning issues of the day, but not one word was devoted to the issue.(5)

Indeed, the question of the value of money was avoided in all subsequent commentaries on the programme until, in 1934, Colijn published his commentary on a revised ARP political programme.(6) In his exposition on finance he unambiguously chose a metallic stand-point. He made a clear distinction in the economic process between the phenomenon of depreciation and inflation. He attributed depreciation to an "unbridled issue of paper money", a phenomenon

Colijn used the radio as a medium to reassure the public the government would defend the parity of the guilder to the utmost. (Behind him minister of finance Oud.) (Photo: Historisch Documentatiecentrum voor het Nederlands Protestantisme)

he termed "money decay".(7) Inflation, on the other hand, stemmed from a scarcity of goods which, for example, could occur in times of war when a sudden and unanticipated surge of demand for certain goods could arise, pushing up their price.

It is evident that neither Kuyper nor Colijn considered the gold standard a matter of principle for the anti-revolutionary party. No space is devoted to the subject either in the original version of the programme of 1878 or in the revisions of 1916 and 1934. In 1934 the gold standard was just as hot a topic for discussion as it had been in 1874, but, as before in the eyes of most anti-revolutionaries, the question lay in the sphere of the practical application of the party's principles and not in the principles themselves. It was a purely technical matter; suitable for discussion in commentaries on the programme or in election manifestos.

Alongside the programme of principles economic science had a role in shaping anti-revolutionary opinion. Party contacts with the law faculty of the Free University played an important role, as too did the party's own scientific bureau, established in 1921, in the form of the *Dr Abraham Kuyper Stichting*. In this connection we will concentrate on an analysis of the ideas of two anti-revolutionary economists: Dr J.A. Nederbragt, recipient of the first Ph.D. in economics from the Rotterdam Trade High School and the chief civil servant in the ministry of foreign affairs, and Dr P.A. Diepenhorst, who from 1904 until 1948 was professor of economics in the faculty of law at the Free University. In their publications both repeatedly returned to the question of the gold standard and both directly involved their calvinist philosophy in doing so.

This was done most explicitly by Nederbragt who distanced himself from the general opinion that the role of gold depended ultimately upon a political choice. Nederbragt thought that the curious historical development of the monetary system stood under God's guidance since He had endowed gold with special qualities. We could classify Nederbragt as a 'biblical monetarist'. "The fact that money gave people power over goods and services, rests, not on any invention of mankind, but on a gift of God."(8) P.A. Diepenhorst, by contrast, never allowed himself to form such a one-sided interpretation of the link between the bible and economic science. Because of having written a thesis on 'Calvin and the Economy' he was reluctant to be explicit about the link between Calvinist values and economic theory. His active role in Dutch society enabled him to base his economic and political opinions upon practical matters.(9) His membership of the first chamber, his chairmanship of the *Christelijke Boeren- en Tuindersbond* (Christian Farmers Union) and the *Vereniging voor Actieve Handelspolitiek* (Society for active Trade Policy) enabled him to assume a relatively independant position vis-à-vis Colijn and his opinions on economic matters can be considered to have been influential within the party.

When, in 1934, Diepenhorst added a paragraph on the devaluation question to his economic text book, he considered extensively the pro's and con's before coming down in favour of the governments stand-point.(10) The most important consideration was the social one, namely that devaluation implied a blindly executed wage-cut for the workers. He admitted that deflation had aggravated the position of small independent businessmen and that of numerous mortgage payers, but he considered that devaluation would endanger the flow of capital upon which they depended. Besides, he went on to note, mortgage bank capital was largely contributed by small savers who had invested in mortgage bonds. Such a comment placed Diephorst in the social tradition of his party, whose 'programme of principles' called on the government to protect the weaker in society(11).

It is worth noting that Diepenhorst devoted much more space and thought to monetary questions in his later publications than he had done earlier. The first edition of his text book, published in 1914, had no chapter on money at all, in the 1930's, on the other hand, he devoted not only space in his text book to the gold standard question, but also wrote frequently in learned articles on the subject. He regretted that so many countries had abandoned gold, which he saw as the cause of the stunted growth of international trade, but warned against defending the gold standard with such mystical arguments as the existence of an independent national tradition or on the grounds of one of God's Commandments. His own arguments, were based primarily on pure economic grounds, yet moral and juridic considerations also played a role: "commitment once assumed must be honoured, because coinage debasement is an unlawful act."(12)

Besides the party programme and the judgement of party economists, the anti-revolutionary politician also had to take into account the opinions expressed in the friendly press when formulating his stand-point on the gold standard. The first thing which stands out is the emphasis upon the uncontrollability of events. For example, in July 1933 the *Nieuwe Provinciale Groninger Courant* wrote: "Once we are on the road to inflation, (then) we must go on. There is no end in sight."(13) It then went on to mention the German hyper-inflation of the 1920's. It was in those very years that the anti-revolutionary Colijn was prime-minister, and it was he that saved the Netherlands from such a fate, commented the *Friesch Dagblad,* mentioning for good measure the catastrophic fall in the value of the French franc in 1925. "Under God's rule and through the measures of Colijn we were spared that."(14) In the second place a heavy emphasis was laid upon the disadvantageous effects of devaluation for all income groups. Not only workers, but all minority groups and social institutions dependant upon a fixed income would be affected: "With inflation real wages decline violently, widows and pensioners increasingly feel the pinch. Savings melt away like snow. The reserves of the trade unions lose a great deal of their real value. Social security suffers serious damage. Churches and philanthropic institutions are confronted with the greatest difficulties."(15)

To us, the dividing line between the social/political arguments and the ethical/juridical side of the question may seem small but for the anti-revolutionaries in the 1930's there was a clear difference. The former concerned the way in which the interest of the parties' own favoured social groups were promoted, the latter was more a religous/cultural question and, as such, it was scarcely a topic for discussion. The essence of the ethical/juridical argument lay in keeping faith with one's word. A questioner once asked C.A. Verrijn Stuart, who had just given a pro-devaluation speech, whether a devaluation did not imply that the government and the Netherlands Bank would be breaking their word. By way of answer Verrijn Stuart quoted a remark of Bismark. Bismark had solved a similar problem by declaring that "if one is not able to poison in the evening someone with whom one had had a friendly lunch in the afternoon, one is unsuitable for diplomacy". On the basis of this machiavellian answer *De Standaard* drew the conclusion that the devaluation alternative should be rejected on principle since "devaluation leads to a weakening of moral responsibility".(16)

Within anti-revolutionary circles devaluation was primarily viewed from the stand-point of the middle classes who were used to defending their own interests and who depended upon the good faith of their trade partners. The *Nieuwe Provinciale Groninger Courant* expressed this as follows: "We should not seek to better our position through not paying our debts, but by living more frugally. Hard work and frugality, soberiety and solidarity will restore our position. That is an old saying, but it only expresses the moral law." (17) Devaluation was seen as a dishonourable weapon. A government which resorted to devaluation did not fight with an open visor. As the christian social journal *Patrimonium* expressed it: "What people do not dare openly to do, or consider impossible, they attempt to achieve through experimentation with the currency."(18) Strictly speaking an anti-revolutionary did not consider that devaluation constituted a rational policy because the results were too unpredictable. If a government lowered salaries by 4 per cent "then one knows exactly what it means for those affected. But if the guilder is devalued by 25 per cent then one cannot directly see what this implies".(19)

Turning to the parliamentary party, it would be unrealistic to expect it to adopt a standpoint other than that of the cabinet since it was represented in the government. In both chambers of parliament the ARP supported the government on the question of the gold standard, often violently debating with speakers from the socialist opposition or from the increasingly critical RKSP. For the ARP, these debates were almost exclusively conducted by J. Schouten in the Second Chamber and by P.A. Diepenhorst in the First.(20) Since we have already analysed Diepenhorst's ideas, we will concentrate in this section on those of J. Schouten, leader of the parliamentary party, a self-made man who as councillor for the city of Rotterdam had aquired much experience in financial matters.

In the course of the parliamentary debate following the devaluation of sterling, Schouten had revealed himself as a loyal disciple of Colijn.(21) His analysis of the causes of the economic depression were exactly the same as those of his party leader, in his eyes, the most fundamental being the large scale destruction of capital during the First World War and the rising level of protectionism. He stressed his confidence in the parity of the Dutch currency.

Pointing to the German banking crisis in the summer of 1931 and the fall of sterling in September, he urged the government in unambiguous terms to maintain equilibrium in public finance. "Solid finances" were essential preconditions for the the government's ability to continue work creation schemes and support for the unemployed.(22) When, in 1933, the process of international monetary and economic discussion in which Colijn had over the years invested so much energy, finally collapsed, Schouten's conclusion remained unaltered: "No change is required in our monetary policy; we must keep our currency unweakened."(23)

Above all else the ARP parliamentary party looked for certainty. This attitude is continuously apparent in Schouten's phraseology. A devaluation of the guilder would only increase international uncertainty. "There are more than enough dancing currencies." Devaluation was seen as an artificial measure that increased the price of imports and which rendered exports vulnerable to reprisals abroad. The ARP preferred to expand exports by taking real measures, i.e. by reducing costs to the level of its competitors.(24) This objective fitted in with their structural analysis of the causes of the depression and in this monetary experiments had no role: "They dislocate international cooperation even further and serve to increase uncertainty."

The primary political reason for their rejection of devaluation was that no one could predict what the results of such an operation would be for domestic social economic relationships. Devaluation, it was argued, causes "the most capricious and arbitrary and therefore unjustifiable shifts in assets and debts and takes no account of what has or has not been done to put the economy on a sound basis....".(25) However, although the ARP wished to achieve an adjustment of costs and prices to a level prevailing abroad, it was not willing to go as far as the RSKP leader Aalberse who counterposed the alternatives of 'consistent deflation' or devaluation. Schouten repeatedly resisted the formulation of the dilemma in these terms. The giving of such global powers to the government and the judicial consequences for the value of private contract, which the 'consistent' deflation policy implied, went too far for the ARP, a position which they shared with the CHU. It involved an unacceptable degree of interference in, to quote Abraham Kuyper, the "organic life of society".

As leader of the parliamentary party in the Second Chamber Schouten succeeded in giving the government the broadest possible support, but in the course of time hairline splits began to appear in the ARP front. In the Autumn of 1934, during the debate on the next year's budget, the unanimity of the party came under heavy pressure. In the extremely summary minutes one can read that the parliamentary party supported the economic and social policy of the government, "in essentials" but that "one of its members expressed a dissenting opinion". A year later, after the Belgian devaluation, the parliamentary party once again discussed the deflationary measures proposed by the government. The minutes recorded that most members "agreed with Schouten that devaluation must be rejected and equally that foreign trade policy should not be adjusted in an autarkic direction." The minutes recorded that there were now two deviant members but also that "some others" could no longer support the moral objection to devaluation, or at least felt that it should no longer be introduced into the argument. Two months later, in July 1935, the subject resurfaced and again the difference of opinion was noted in the minutes.(26) It is not clear who the dissenting members were but, in any event, it is apparent that within the ARP parliamentary party the question of the ethical argument for or against an eventual devaluation was the subject of deep seated debate. However, to the outside world the official line of support for the policy of *aanpassing* was maintained. The economic and social objections against devaluation remained intact.

The disunity within the ARP spilled into the open during the parliamentary debate on the so called *vaste lasten* legislation in June 1936. Schouten argued that such an intervention in private contractual agreements would weaken the preparedness of mortgage banks to advance credit in the future. A majority of the ARP party, eight of the thirteen including all those who had had a legal education, voted against the government proposals. Only a minority, under the leadership of the vice-chairman of the *Christelijk Boeren- en Tuindersbond* Chr. van den Heuvel supported the government, together with the VDB and the SDAP. The ARP was the only parliamentary party which was so sharply divided.(27) The others were either unanimously against the government proposals (CHU, RKSP, SGP) or for (VDB and SDAP). This division shows clearly the seriousness with which ARP had thought through the consequences of the *aanpassings*-policy and the difficulty which they found in coming up with any real alternative.

Let us finally consider the monetary views of Dr. H. Colijn. There is no room to analyse the social/economic policy followed by the cabinets which he led, nor would it be useful in answering the question of 'how and why' the Netherlands devalued in 1936 and not earlier. It is, however, relevent to consider his views on financial policy and on monetary affairs. We will restrict ourselves to his fundamental ideas and the most important motives for his policy as minister-president. In particular, we will consider him as leader and the major financial economic expert of the anti-revolutionary party who, in 1933 at the age of 64, once again accepted the office of prime minister. The country had long before become acquainted with his views on government finances and his proclamations on monetary questions. He had become minister of finance in the beginning of the 1920's when various European currencies came into difficulties and left no room for misunderstanding on the question.

Colijn saw little difference between abandonment of the gold standard and inflation. Looking at the experience of Germany at that time, he had described inflation as a "fall in the value of money" which, he went on to explain, involved "a gradual expropriation of all property and a wretched poverty for all those dispossessed and for all people living from a fixed income".(28) As long ago as 1924, in a speech to the christian employers, he had unfolded his views on the economic difficulties after the first World War. The problem in the long term lay not in satisfying the supply of goods, but in estimating the level of demand. A great deal of capital had been destroyed, only the external trappings remained in the form of a large mass of unused and valueless paper. Inflation had become a fact.(29) It is quite clear that Colijn considered inflation an evil to be avoided at all costs. The most important policy instrument in this respect he saw as the maintainance of an absolute balance between government income and expenditure.(30)

In Colijn's eyes devaluation always represented the start of inflation. In order to illustrate this position he pointed to England, which had begun by allowing the pound to depreciate by ten per cent and where the percentage had, in the meantime, climbed to forty.(31) When the SDAP leader, Albarda, had asked the government not to exclude the possibility of a managed depreciation (i.e. a devaluation), Colijn had replied by asking him where such a situation had ever occurred. When in the first chamber the catholic jurist W.M. van Lanschot had made a similar suggestion, Colijn's reaction had been that his arguments against a legal devaluation were to some extent precisely the same as those against inflation and managed currency. He made a distinction between a country such as the U.K., which was faced by speculative pressures to abandon gold, and a country which would consider doing so as an act of deliberate government policy. The latter would "deliberately and premeditatively cause a change in all the monetary relationships without in any way taking account of the time in which or the circumstances under which those relationships came into existence."(32)

Colijns chief objection against devaluation is concisely expressed in this quote. He saw devaluation as being too crude a measure because it worked unfairly, taking insufficient account of individual persons or groups. As minister-president this point weighed very heavily in his considerations as he worked from the premise that a government was directly responsible for the changes in property and income of its subjects which would result from a devaluation. In the event of a forced abandonment of gold, he implied, the question of who was responsible was different. This can be called an ethical objection, but it also has a juridic side. This issue was hotly debated among politicians and among economists. H.W.C. Bordewijk chose as the subject for his inaugural lecture in 1934 the topic of the relationship between ethics and economics. His conclusion was that the shifts in income and wealth which would occur as a result of devaluation could not possibly be justified, a conclusion which Colijn could endorse unreservedly.(33)

The second fundamental objection which Colijn had against devaluation lay in the fact that it was an artificial measure in contrast to a natural policy of price adjustment. This policy had both quantative and qualitative aspects. Not only did the level of wages and prices have to conform with those abroad but the structure of the Dutch production apparatus had also to be adjusted to take into account the changed relationships within the world economy. Colijn did not wish to break opposition within the Netherlands to this policy by means of government decree. The government "lacks the power and the authority to intervene in a free society".(34) This second argument against devaluation did not mean that Colijn rejected any intervention in the economy. He only wished to do so in a more nuanced way. When in July 1935 Aalberse cited the success of Chancellor Brüning's policy in support of his plea for 'consistent' deflation Colijn rejected such intervention out of hand as being too sweeping. What he wanted to do was "to slow down ...where it goes too fast, stimulate where it does not go fast enough".(35) His objections to 'consistent' deflation were the same as those against devaluation, namely that the results were unpredictable and could not be anticipated in advance. As far as possible the government had to take account of the divergent circumstances affecting different firms as well as the differences between individual persons.(36)

Alongside the ethical/juridical and the purely political objections that Colijn had against devaluation, he also repeatedly introduced a treasury argument, namely that of the credit worthiness of the state in the eyes of its creditors. In this respect Colijn remained a typical ex-manager of an international company. Although the Netherlands Bank was obliged by law to advance the state the sum of up to Dfl. 15,000,000 beyond that Colijn considered the state should be treated just like any other debtor and should be judged on the basis of its solvency.(37) What was true for the national bank was also true for individual banks, and for citizens who subscribed to a government bond issue. Should The Netherlands leave the gold standard or, more figuratively, should "the guilder be released from its anchor" this would have immediate consequences for the financing of government expenditure. In this event Colijn foresaw an extremely sombre future: "It would mean an end to the possibility of consolidating the floating debt and to the financing of the floating debt itself."(38) The fact that the actual developments after 1936 did not support such pessimism does nothing to diminish the weight attributed to this argument.

The businessman and the anti-revolutionary politician were interwoven in the person of Colijn. As the politician responsible he wished, both in the 20's and in the crisis of the 30's, to maintain and protect the creditworthiness and therefore the continuity of the state. At the same time, he attempted as far as possible to limit the expansion of the role of the state in the economic field. Socially, he considered the task of the state to be that of helping the weak within society, especially in those cases where private initiative was incapable of doing so. In this Colijn based himself upon the anti-revolutionary principle of sovereignty within ones own circle.(39) In both society and the economy the organic units which had evolved had the right to develop according to their own laws. Within Colijn's interpretation of this ARP principle the government had no role in guaranteeing the individual welfare of the citizen or guaranteeing a safe return for business.(40) On the other hand, it was responsible for preserving as far as possible the sources of national income and national welfare. In 1924 he had already formulated this as a central objective for the social economic policy of the government in years of depression. As minister-president in the 1930's he remained true to this task.

THE CHRISTIAN HISTORICAL UNION (CHU)

As an orthodox-protestant party the CHU had the same political-religious background as the ARP. However, being represented in the Colijn-governments with only one minister and with its political leader, D.J. de Geer, outside the cabinet, the CHU was much less narrowly tied to the government's policy. What did that mean for the position of the CHU in the monetary debate? And on which grounds and in what way did it arrive at that position?

From 1918 onward, after the introduction of proportional representation, the CHU had been continually represented in the government. Of its leaders who had filled cabinet posts in the 1920's and 30's, De Geer was one of the most important. The high point of his long career had come in the years 1926-29 when he combined his position as minister-president with the portfolio of minister of finance. Though in 1929 he had had to make way for C.J.M. Ruys de Beerenbrouck as minister-president, he continued as minister of finance until 1933. In this capacity he had been responsible for coping with the sterling losses of the Netherlands Bank after the British devaluation. Although his policy of accepting part of the losses for the state had come in for sharp criticism from parliament,(41) he succeeded in pushing it through and his reputation as a financial expert emerged from the debacle virtually unscathed. Perhaps more surprisingly, that reputation had also survived the failure in the last years of his ministry to achieve a balanced budget. After the 1933 elections De Geer, who had headed the CHU-list, did not return as minister, although he was elected as chairman of the parliamentary party. The fact that from 1933 on De Geer was both party chairman and editor-in-chief of the party's daily newspaper *De Nederlander*, illustrates his matchless position within the CHU in the 1930's. Moreover, in all the debates in the Second Chamber involving the devaluation he was the party's only spokesman.

The first occasion on which De Geer addressed the devaluation question at any length was during the budget debates in November 1934, when he clearly supported the Government in its rejection of devaluation as a policy-option. That did not mean, however, that he could not envisage a situation in which he could support such a policy. He went on to explain that should all the "civilised countries" agree to return to the gold standard, those countries which had not devalued since 1914 (i.e. including the Netherlands) should then do so to come into line with the others. The chances of such a situation arising, he felt, were remote.(43) His nuancering went even further and much closer to the realms of political reality when he counter-posed devaluation with the question of *vaste lasten*. He explicitly rejected any attempt to reduce the weight of such payments other than by 'natural' means since any such attempt would irrevocably damage the credit structure. "Credit is the foundation of our society. That it has remained free from shocks, I consider to be one of the most important factors in the welfare which still remains. Should credit collapse, it will be the beginning of the end." Weighing both evils against each other, De Geer stated that he would, if forced to choose, unconditionally plumb for devaluation. "The latter is a leap in the dark, the result is highly doubtful. The former (compulsory reduction of mortgage interest – HJL) is a leap into the abyss; there is no doubt about the result."(44) De Geer devoted a great deal of attention to the *vaste lasten* problem during these debates in order to head off pressure from the RKSP-leader Aalberse in favour of comprehensive intervention in this field. He could also assume that the minister-president was on his side since Colijn had openly supported his position in rejecting legislation on mortgage rates.(45)

The next occasion on which devaluation was extensively debated in the Second Chamber was in connection with the deflationary package presented in July 1935. The fact that Belgium had devalued only a couple of months earlier must be held responsible for the first, and only, evidence of any hesitancy in the CHU-parliamentary party's position. At a meeting held in mid-May 1935 J.W.H. Rutgers van Rozenburg, who had been the CHU financial specialist before 1933, announced that he was no longer so strongly opposed to devaluation.(46) There is no evidence, however, that this had any influence on the party's standpoint which remained loyal to that of De Geer. What De Geer explained in the May meeting and what he unfolded during the parliamentary debate in July was a complex set of circumstances in which devaluation would be acceptable, while rejecting it for the present. To his previous position, which he reaffirmed, he added one further condition: in a situation in which it would become apparent to the government that adherence to the gold standard had become untenable, he postulated, he would prefer an early and deliberate choice to be made in favour of devaluation to waiting for panic selling of guilders to force the issue. "The semi-voluntary should be chosen above the forced." He had the grace to add that he did not consider such a moment to be close at hand!(47)

The budget-package led directly to the cabinet crisis of July 1935, but this had been resolved without any change in the political composition of the government. As a result the budgetry measures were presented afresh in September 1935. Once again De Geer made the connection between legislation on *vaste lasten* and devaluation. "Devaluation is a painful operation which I abhor. But I would chose a painful, technically well executed operation above a series of haphazardly applied crude knife cuts which, indeed, make wounds but which are incapable of effecting a cure. Should it ever, unfortunately, have to come to a devaluation, it should not be as a result of a parliamentary debate or conflict but as a result of a decision taken by the government, the only authority with access to all the necessary information." De Geer returned to his medical analogy: "Whoever undertakes such an operation should ensure beforehand that it is done by the best surgeon, with the most modern equipment, in a sterile environment and well away from restless spectators." As usual he added that the results of such an operation were far from certain.(48)

De Geer's formulation attracted a rebuttal from J. Schouten, who argued that the way De Geer approached the devaluation issue only served to increase uncertainty. If one were really opposed to devaluation, one should withhold from publicly discussing how the "operation could be executed in the most attractive and appetizing way".(49) In this respect Schouten was on the same wave-length as Colijn who, the following day, appealed to parliament to avoid further discussion of the devaluation issue.(50) More fundamental was the criticism of RKSP-chairman Aalberse who suggested that in counterposing 'consistent deflation' and 'devaluation' he would make precisely the opposite choice to that made by De Geer.(51) In September 1935 we can establish that, of the leaders of the three large confessional parties, De Geer was the most willing to consider devaluation as a policy option, albeit that he still rejected it.

Given De Geer's position it was not surprising that when devaluation became reality a year later it did not exactly come as a shock. It is true that in the subsequent parliamentary debate he lamented "the tragedy that the exceptionally honourable position, which our country had been able to occupy until now, no longer appeared tenable", but in the rest of his speech the positive considerations far outweighed the negative.(52) Addressing the next meeting of the parliamentary party De Geer's appreciation of the situation was mostly positive. Devaluation would give the country economic and political breathing space. He did add, however, that further deflation would remain necessary.(53) One month later he had the satisfaction of pointing out to the die-hard proponents of the gold standard who had argued that devaluation would ruin the market for state-borrowing and force up interest rates, as well as to those who in July 1936 had lost the parliamentary struggle for legislation to lower *vaste lasten*(54) that devaluation itself had brought an interest-rate reduction in sight; "in a better, more natural, healthier and therefore more permanent way than through the legislative interference with contracts. Here (i.e. in the event of devaluation – HJL) a fall in interest rates does not involve undermining credit, but on the contrary is related to, indeed, is a consequence of a raising of credit-worthiness. That is the true way."(55) In this way De Geer was able to present himself not only as the moral victor over the cabinet but as someone whose opposition to *vaste lasten* legislation was thoroughly vindicated.

The description so far has focused on the CHU parliamentary party in the Second Chamber because that was where the real parliamentary power lay. It was always highly unlikely that the First Chamber would force the government to alter course on monetary policy. There are two other reasons why a treatment of the CHU in the First Chamber can be brief – firstly, there was no important difference in stance from the party in the Second Chamber and secondly, there was no financial specialist in the First Chamber of the caliber of De Geer. The main spokesman in the debates in which devaluation was discussed was professor B.C. de Savornin Lohman, even though he readily conceded that he was no financial expert. In February 1935 he stated, "Nowadays ....every messenger boy and every charwoman talks about deflation, inflation, gold standard etc. Therefore I am a little embarassed to admit honestly that I am confronted with a scientific economic question which is extremely difficult to grasp." Nonetheless, Lohman argued, the chamber had to formulate a standpoint and since he had great confidence in the minister of finance, the minister-president and the president of the Netherlands Bank, he had every reason to support the government's position. He did, however, offer the suggestion that if the danger of having to abandon the gold standard should threaten, the government should consider the lesser evil of doing so voluntarily rather than waiting to be forced off. It is worthwhile noting that this comment was made before the Belgian devaluation and before a similar statement by De Geer. He added that he recognised that "if devaluation *per se* was immoral" it would be wrong to talk in terms of (semi-) voluntary devaluation, "but it isn't".(56) This, too, would seem to be broadly in line with De Geer's position. Indeed, the only discernable difference between the two men appeared on the appreciation of the pro-devaluation lobby. Whilst De Geer spoke positively about the best among them, (57) Lohman described the lot as "an army of devaluationists who disagree among themselves over practically everything, except for the point that the monetary policy of the government does not work",(58) a judgement which was not far from the mark.

Looking at the CHU so far one could be forgiven for believing that the party *en bloc* was opposed to devaluation but this was not completely true. At least one prominent member, professor F. de Vries, was an early and active protagonist in favour of devaluation. Although he was both a member of the party executive and a member of the supervisory board of the party daily *De Nederlander*, there is no evidence that he attempted to shift the party towards a pro-devaluation standpoint. It is possible that there were others. When the party secretary H.W. Tilanus compiled his report for the year 1936, he observed that the guilder devaluation had removed a source of difference which had cut right across party lines and also went on to mention that it had long been a matter of discussion within the CHU.(59) The lack of any record of minutes of executive meetings makes this line of inquiry impossible to pursue.

One source of dissent, not on the devaluation question *per se* but on de Geer's formulation of the choice between devaluation and 'consistent deflation' was the party's own newspaper *De Nederlander*. Its editorial board was made up of group of relatively young intellectuals who attempted to establish a seperate political identity. Its central figure was G.E. van Walsum, secretary of the Rotterdam Chamber of Commerce, who had succeeded De Geer as chairman of the editorial board in September 1934. From this position, the group was able to push its own political ideas to the fore.(60) The monetary expert of this group was P. Lieftinck who, shortly after his nomination to the board, was made professor of economics at the Trade Highschool in Rotterdam(61) and whose greatest claim to a place in history was as the first post-war minister of finance.

Lieftinck was also a member of the anti-devaluationist group led by Professor H.W.C. Bordewijk.

Lieftinck's position made it unlikely that *De Nederlander* would deviate from the party line by agitating for an abandoment of the gold standard but in October 1934, only a month after De Geer had surrendered control, the editorial board veered away from De Geer's position on the *vaste lasten* question. It pronounced itself in favour of bringing down the nominal burden involved in these private agreements and demanded legislation for the reduction of mortgage rates in the common interest.(62) This conflict spilled fully into the open in July 1935 when Lieftinck addressed the party's summer conference on the question of "the future of our monetary policy". Lieftinck still adhered to the view that the gold standard should be maintained, not from any theoretical conviction but, because it formed the best basis for the implementation of a programme for general economic recovery. Such a programme, he felt, should combine both deflationary and reflationary elements – deflationary in the sense of reducing the weight of *vaste lasten* and reflationary in the sense of a relaxation of credit conditions and the introduction of a large-scale programme of public works.(63)

Lieftinck was aware that in formulating the issue in this way he was challenging the leadership of de Geer, but he confided to Van Walsum afterwards that he felt that his address had struck a chord among the majority of those present, including a number of CHU parliamentarians.(64) The latter did not include H.W. Tilanus, who, in the discussion following Lieftinck's speech, defended De Geer's position by emphasising the juridical problems involved in legislation to reduce *vaste lasten*. He further suggested that 'natural deflation' was a third alternative for restoring the economy's competitiveness. Lieftinck, in turn, replied that he shared Tilanus' reserves on the actual *vaste lasten* legislation proposed by the government but not to the extent of rejecting such intervention. "By too great an emphasis on the juridical difficulties ... one probably does the law a disservice." He ended by arguing that a selective deflationary policy permitted a case by case examination of where price/cost reductions were necessary whereas devaluation was akin to putting a red pencil through the lot.(65) The last point was broadly similar to the postion adopted by the RKSP leader Aalberse from September 1935 onwards. Indeed, with its emphasis on the need to tackle the *vaste lasten* problem, the editorial position of *De Nederlander* came very close to that of the RKSP parliamentary party.

Until the Summer of 1935 there was no difference between the CHU parliamentary party and *De Nederlander* on the desirability of maintaining the gold standard. Although neither went so far as to make it an issue of principle, the editorial position of *De Nederlander* could be considered more anti-devaluationist since it was prepared to consider legislative interference in *vaste-lasten* whereas De Geer would have preferred devaluation rather that countenance such a move. Nevertheless, the editors recognised that a situation could arise forcing the government to devalue; in such an event there would be nothing to condemn.(66) However, *De Nederlander's* position underwent a subtle but significant change in the Spring of 1936. On 3 April Lieftinck wrote to the editorial board announcing his conversion to the pro-devaluationist camp. By way of motive he pointed to the increasing political tension in Europe which, on the one hand, had seriously reduced the chances of economic and monetary stabilisation and which, on the other, would require increased Dutch military expenditure making the goal of a balanced budget unattainable. In principle, he admitted, he would have preferred a more active government policy in reducing costs above a devaluation but he considered that the cabinet was incapable of immediate and positive action "given the dominating influences on the economic departments". "Because of the deteriorating political situation I consider us *periculum in mora*. Under these circumstances the better-in-the-long-run must make way for the good-in-the-short-term." Lieftinck concluded by suggesting an exchange of ideas in the meeting of the editorial board the next week.(67)

It is unrealistic to expect that Lieftinck's conversion would have led to a fundamental change of course by *De Nederlander*, if only because an openly pro-devaluation standpoint would have brought it into conflict with its own parliamentary party and with the government. However, from that moment on, a change was apparent. The editorials could be described as neutral or ambivalent. An important element in this policy was a reexamination of the arguments for and against devaluation, in the course of which it is noticable that the anti-devaluationist standpoint was the more forcefully attacked, implying a not openly articulated preference for devaluation. For example, when Trip pleaded for the government to desist from placing obstacles in the way of natural deflation (i.e. reducing agricultural support measures, social security payments etc) *De Nederlander* rounded on him, suggesting that any such alternative to such a policy would be preferable "whether active intervention or monetary correction".(68) This was apparently the limit which the editors had set themselves; devaluation was recognised as an option worth considering but no one would be able to accuse *De Nederlander* of coming out openly in its favour.

When the gold standard was eventually abandoned, its passing was not mourned by *De Nederlander*. In its first commentary after the event it stated: "Since from the beginning we have never suggested that devaluation would be a disaster, we don't now have to compromise our position if we call for calm and confidence." (69) A few days later the paper published a deeper analysis written by Lieftinck, who praised the government's decision to allow the guilder to float since it would increase the margins of freedom for economic policy. "The main precondition for business expansion has hereby been realised."(70)

THE FREE DEMOCRATS (VDB)

Aside from the two protestant parties, the government relied for its support also on the two Liberal parties and the Roman-Catholic party. Of the two liberal parties, the VDB became most closely associated with the financial policy of the Colijn governments. This was a consequence of the fact that the VDB's financial specialist P.J. Oud was chosen by Colijn for the position of minister of finance in his 1933- and 1935-governments. After the eclipse of party-leader, H.P. Marchant, in May 1935, Oud was the most prominent politician of the VDB. Did this double position of Oud – as a finance-minister responsible for maintaining the gold standard and, from 1935 on, as de facto political leader of the VDB – diminish the political possibilities of the VDB with respect to the monetary question?

The VDB, established in 1901, was a relatively small party with a progressive liberal character whose aims were social reform and the reduction of the inequalities within society. In the 1920's it had adopted a relatively dogmatic position on the points of free trade and government finances. It was in favour of selective government intervention aimed at preventing abuses of economic power. This policy had nothing to do with protectionism and the VDB saw no conflict between this selective intervention and its basic laissez-faire ideology. The second point which the VDB emphasised was the need for equilibrium in government finances. Neoclassical economics played an important role in shaping Free Democratic thinking on this point and on the corollary of the need for a strong currency linked to gold.

The onset of the economic crisis rapidly shook the VDB's faith in the efficacy of free trade. At the VDB congress in Alkmaar in November 1931 the agricultural expert, S.L. Louwes, openly condemned making free trade an article of dogma and pleaded for the implementation of protectionist measures, especially for agriculture. Even the financial expert in the second chamber, P.J. Oud, felt that it was possible to take ad hoc emergency measures in the interest of the national economy without having to abandon the liberal laissez-faire principles. This careful formulation of the issue received the congress' support. The same meeting discussed a motion from the constituency party in Friesland directed against any attempts to inflate the Dutch currency "in order to save large groups of the population from ruin". This motion was accepted by acclamation.(71) Thus, in the aftermath of the sterling devaluation, the VDB had opted for a policy in which the adjustment of the economy to the changed international circumstances, mitigated by government intervention where necessary, and the maintenance of the gold standard formed a logical whole.

Since the introduction of proportional representation the VDB had never been in government. It had seen its role as trying to form a progressive alternative to the succesive confessional and conservative cabinets. In practice what was hoped for was a coalition government drawn from "Democrats from different houses" (i.e. the SDAP, the RKSP and, of course, the VDB itself). However, the party's reaction to the crisis had driven a wedge between itself and the SDAP since, in all main respects, the VDB found itself in complete agreement with the financial/economic policies followed by the confessional cabinet led by Ruys de Beerenbrouck.(72) The economy was depressed and this called for a policy of retrenchment by the state. Its only difference with cabinet policy was over the question of how the burden should be shared. The VDB's anti-militaristic character, expressed in a call for national disarmament, made military expenditure the primary target for the budgetary knife, a priority not shared by the goverment.

Given the alienation from the SDAP and the rapprochement towards the confessional parties, it was only a small step for the VDB to make from perpetual opposition to participation in the second Colijn cabinet, formed after the general elections of April 1933. In this 'crisis cabinet' the VDB was represented by its political leader H.P. Marchant as minister of education and by Oud as minister of finance. The cabinet was committed to a rigorous deflationary policy aimed at restoring international competitiveness in which the rationalisation of government expenditure and the maintenance of the gold standard were central points. As minister of finance Oud, despite being more a fiscal than a monetary specialist,(73) was the cabinet minister most directly responsible for the implementation of this policy. In a radio speech in 1933 he declared: "healthy government finances are a condition for any administration. National bankruptcy, manifested in a falling value of our money, hits the poorest the most. In those countries where people have personally experienced the horror of inflation this one thought prevails: 'Never again!'."(74) In his analysis currency depreciation, and the disastrous inflation which was bound to follow, could only occur as a result of financial mismanagement. This one-way logic in considering the currency question broached no pro-devaluationist alternative policy.

Generally speaking, in 1933 the VDB had a great deal of faith in Oud's financial economic policy. This confidence was expressed in the party weekly, *De Vrijzinnig-Democraat*, by L.G. van Dam, who had succeeded Oud as party secretary. Van Dam argued that everything possible should be done to avoid the disaster of devaluation and that the cabinet deserved wholehearted support in its struggle to trim back government expenditure.(75) At its first general meeting since the installation of the new cabinet, in Groningen in November 1933, the VDB supported the policy of its ministers because it was felt that the budgetry measures announced were demanded by circumstances.(76) Nonetheless, there was an undertone of discontent because the cuts affected a number of concerns dear to the party's heart; it was particularly aggrieved at the lowering of civil service salaries and Marchant's proposals to close a number of public (i.e. non-religious) schools. Although there was much grumbling, the alternative of devaluation was not openly discussed. But, even at the time, not everyone within the VDB was so happy with the cabinet's rejection of devaluation. Among the signatories of the 'pro-devaluation' address to the government in July 1933 were two important Free Democrats. These were S.J. van den Bergh, director of Unilever and, at the time, a member of the VDB executive, and J.B. Westerdijk, member of the first chamber and party expert of agriculture and the economy. Westerdijk was seriously ill at the time and was to die within the year. Van den

Bergh, however, continued to be an active pro-devaluationist throughout the thirties.

In March 1934 the *Vrijzinnig-Democraat* published its first pro-devaluation article: 'Sacred Objects' by D. Kloppenburg.(77) The author complained that an earlier article written in the same vein had been turned down by the editors. The editorial board was led by A.M. Joekes, who had succeeded Marchant as chairman of the parliamentary party and Oud as editor-in-chief of the paper. It replied at length to Kloppenburg's article which had considered the restoration of the pre-1931 relationship between the guilder and the pound a precondition for economic recovery. The editorial board rejected this position, arguing that the consequences of devaluation could not be overseen and that it would create uncertainty at a time when economic recovery depended primarily on the stability of international relationships. Moreover, devaluation would increase the cost of imported materials, would lead to disadvantage for savers and holders of debt and would create the conditions making capital flight likely, which, in turn, would make the capital market inaccessible for the state.(78) In the parliamentary year 1934/35 Joekers repeatedly used such terms in opposing devaluation, thereby throwing the journal's editorial support behind Oud.

Meanwhile Oud repeatedly warned against devaluation, arguing that it would create more moral and material damage than the slow working process of *aanpassing*.(79) Feeling that moral arguments alone were unlikely to be convincing, A. Plate wrote a number of 'practical' reflections on the monetary question which were published in November 1934 in the *Vrijzinnig-Democraat*. Plate was chairman of the *Scheepvaart Vereeniging Zuid* in Rotterdam, an association of harbour employers. Because the over-valued guilder was relatively unpopular in shipping circles his stand-point against devaluation is somewhat surprising to say the least but he considered that the British government would respond immediately to any devaluation with help for its own fleet. He also emphasised the desirability of currency stabilisation (i.e. sterling and the dollar should be relinked with gold). He ended by suggesting that the Dutch economy was not in the doldrums and that the recovery in the United States was disappointing: "Things are not so bad, the Dutch people only come good when they are in a fix."(80) Plate, together with his fellow party member, professor I.B. Cohen, belonged to the Group of anti-devaluationists. Both signed the anti-devaluationist letter addressed to the government in 1935, as too did D. van Embden, professor of economics at the University of Amsterdam and chairman of the parliamentary party in the first chamber, A.C. Josephus Jitta, and the chairman of the VDB, R. Kranenburg. All of these may be numbered among the party's big guns.

At the VDB congress of November 1934 in Rotterdam, there were complaints about the way in which government deflation was going.(81) The increasing discontent was directed primarily at the policy of its own minister, Marchant. In the context of the budgetry cuts Marchant had closed numerous public schools, whilst exempting protestant or catholic schools because of constitutional objections. This was totally unacceptable to VDB supporters who, from the very first, had stood up for the interests of public education. When in May 1935 it was learned that Marchant had secretly joined the roman catholic church his position as Free Democratic minister became untenable. Many lay a direct connection between his conversion and the school policy he had followed. Marchant felt himself compelled to resign both from the cabinet and from the party, leaving Oud the undisputed leader of the Party.

Marchant remained in the cabinet long enough to participate in a discussion in April 1935 on monetary policy stemming from the devaluation of the Belgian franc and the pro-devaluation note compiled by the minister of economic affairs M.P.L. Steenberghe (see pp 179-181). From the comments which he made on Oud's reply it is clear that Marchant was no longer convinced of the success of the government's *aanpassings* policy which, he felt, had reached its limits.(82) Later, after his resignation, and probably after the devaluation of the guilder, Marchant wrote a memo for himself: "During my period as minister nothing happened to convice me that my cabinet colleagues knew more about the real importance of gold as a unit of value than I did, namely nothing. As far as I was concerned I admitted this openly. ..... (illegible name) mentioned once: You say that, but others think it without saying it. I left the matter to the experts. It was in fact Trip, president of the Netherlands Bank, who decided these issues. Oud is a technician in the area of taxation; nothing more. He lacks any originality. He has one overwhelming goal: He wants to stay as minister. His dealings with me were ruled by that consideration."(83) In interpreting this quotation one must remember that Marchant had still not forgiven Oud for his role in his political demise.

April 1935 was also marked by provincial elections. The VDB obtained only 4.2 per cent of the vote against the 5.6 per cent it had achieved in 1931. Because shifts in voting preferences were usually relatively small, this was seen as a painful defeat. In *De Vrijzinnig Democrat* Van den Bergh wrote an analysis of the election results ascribing the defeat exclusively to the VDB support for the governments *aanpassing* policy. He linked his unambiguously pro-devaluation stand-point to the need to formulate an active welfare policy, "like Roosevelt with his New Deal, we must have a clear programme for social construction, for work creation, for improvements which even in these times are possible".(84) It was the first time that *De Vrijzinnig Democraat* had published such open criticism by an important party member. The article acted as a catalyst for others who had been suppressing their criticism to come into the open. It soon became apparent that the number of VDB members who favoured devaluation was growing.

In the spring of 1935 the government proposed a further set of deflationary measures. This had provided the occasion for a conflict with the catholics which in July 1935 had resulted in a cabinet crisis. After the crisis Colijn had formed a new cabinet in which Oud remained minister of finance and VDB party member M. Slingenberg, who had built up a reputation as a financier, became minister of social affairs. The VDB parliamentary party had also been critical on the proposed measures because they included nothing for the reduction of *vaste lasten* and nothing for the creation of employment but this criticism had been kept behind closed doors; in public the VDB supported the cabinet on this matter.(85) However, the concern with unemployment had prompted the party executive, in May 1935, to install a commission to study the problem.

Before it could report its findings, the annual conference of the *Radicale Entente*, an association of progressive European liberal parties, took place in London in July 1935.(86) The VDB was represented by the pro-devaluationist Van den Bergh and the anti-devaluationists Van Dam and Josephus Jitta. At the conference the American Democrats made a number of speeches describing the New Deal and the British Liberals too advocated an active welfare policy. Both groups emphasised that international stabilisation was unlikely without a prior devaluation by the gold bloc countries.(87) The congress probably contributed to the change of heart experienced by Van Dam and Josephus Jitta on monetary policy. Van Dam, who in the summer had become acting editor of *De Vrijzinnig-Democraat*, now wrote uninterruptedly in favour of devaluation. So too did Josephus Jitta who, in May 1936, went so far as to sign a pro-devaluation address to the government. Another possible contributory factor to Van Dam's about-turn was his membership of the VDB employment creation committee in which the devaluation question played an important role.

A. van Raalte, who was a member of another VDB commission entrusted with examining crisis measures, still cherished the illusion in August 1935 that the Free Democrats were unanimously opposed to devaluation. Van Dam helped him out of his anti-devaluationist dream; "In our party too there are proponents for devaluation"(88); a statement which was immediately confirmed by a number of articles submitted to the *Vrijzinnig Democraat*. The direct cause of this stream of devaluationist letters had been the cabinet crisis which had pushed the devaluation question to the foreground. Most had expressed the disillusionment with the failure of *aanpassing*. The alternative of devaluation, which would enable economic recovery to take place, became increasingly more attractive.

The increasing split in VDB ranks also became evident during a meeting of the parliamentary party in September 1935. Two of the six members of parliament, namely parliamentary leader Joekes and B. Bakker-Nort, considered that the Netherlands should abandon the gold standard immediately. They argued that devaluation was unavoidable in light of the fact that confidence in the success of the government's deflationary policy was evaporating but the others were not convinced.(89) The following month the employment creation commission published its report but without a unanimous conclusion since the members were divided on the question of the effects of the *aanpassing* policy. This resulted in the publication of two separate notes in which the proponents and opponents of devaluation attempted to dismiss the arguments of the other.(90) The proponents of devaluation, primarily Van den Bergh and Van Dam, considered a reduction in the value of the guilder a precondition for economic recovery; an economic recovery which was already visible outside the gold bloc. Their opponents, represented primarily by Plate and the second chamber member J. Schilthuis, countered by suggesting that monetary intervention could do no more than create a temporary upturn. Notwithstanding the battery of statistics employed by the pro-devaluationists to support their case, the two sides remained at the end as far apart as ever. No decision was ever taken on the report, partly because of the divisivness on major issues but also because there was insufficient time to prepare the discussion before the party's annual conference in November and partly because the deteriorating international situation had pushed the issue of national disarmament back into to the forefront of party discussion. At the annual conference in Arnhem, the majority still supported the financial economic policy of the cabinet, primarily because they had confidence in the person of Oud.(91)

Throughout 1936 the *Vrijzinnig Democraat* was the forum for a lively polemic on the devaluation question with Van Dam and Schilthuis as the major contenders. Van Dam had the advantage in that he had a regular weekly column in the paper in which he published news of the economic recovery in those countries which had previously devalued. His opponents became increasingly annoyed with this "uninterrupted propaganda" of which the following is one of the more colourful examples: "We are already over the edge of the abyss and are falling full speed downwards. The only thing that can save us is to grasp for the rope before we are smashed to pieces at the bottom."(92)

The rope to which Van Dam had referred was grasped by the government on 26 September 1936 when the Netherlands became the last gold bloc country to abandon the gold standard. Van Dam was satisfied. He called the decision a "turning point" which would enable economic recovery to begin.(93) The *Vrijzinnig-Democraat* too greeted the decision with approval. It anticipated an expansion of business activity and a recovery in profitability.(94) Less happy was the pro-devaluationist A.W. Schippers, who considered that the devaluation of the guilder had not gone far enough to restore the former parity with sterling.(95) The parliamentary party acknowledged that the cabinet had had no alternative other than the temporary abandonment of the gold standard.(96) In the light of its division it was logical that within the Second Chamber the VDB decided to say as little as possible on the issue.

THE LIBERALS (LSP)

That it would be wrong to suppose that a pro-devaluationist position was progressive, and an anti-devaluationist option conservative, can best be demonstrated on the LSP. Of the five parties supporting the Colijn-governments, the LSP was the most conservative, i.e. it counted the most influential group adherents to orthodox liberal economic principles among its members. However, as will be shown, from the summer of 1933 on there was a strong current in the party pro-devaluation. Did this lead to a pro-devaluation position for the LSP as such, or was the party-leadership able to cope with this current?

Within the LSP the discussion on the gold standard began in the course of 1933 after the devaluation of the dollar. In May 1933 the economist Max de Vries wrote an article in *Het Liberale Weekblad*(97) on the currency question in which he condemned any reduction in the guilder's gold value as "debasement on a large scale". He contended that the gold stocks of the Netherlands Bank were sufficiently large to enable the Netherlands to resist speculative pressures. Only a marked loss of domestic confidence could bring the guilder into the danger zone. In this way the question of the maintenance of the gold standard was made an issue of sound and decisive government policy. He considered any deviation from this course fatal and supported this by citing a metaphor of De Geer, in which a little bit of devaluation was compared with a little bit of derailment of a train.(98) The occasion for a further development on this theme was provided by the written plea for devaluation by Sir Henry Deterding at the general meeting of the *Nederlandsche Maatschappij voor Nijverheid en Handel* in June 1933 (see p. 36). An editorial article in *Het Liberale Weekblad* mentioned the opposition to Deterding's proposals at the meeting and added its own rejection, arguing that the results of a devaluation could not be predicted and that the English and American situations were not comparable to that of the Netherlands.(99) In his rejection De Vries went even further. In an emotional argumentation he deplored what he described as an attempt "at a moment when the currency was threatened, to try to kick the guilder to pulp". This he condemned as "scandalous". As a possible motive for Deterding's action he mentioned the currency position of *Koninklijke Petroleum*. In 1932 he argued the Dfl.343,000,000 in liquid capital had almost been entirely invested in dollars and pounds. He made no mention of the composition of the Dfl. 422,000,000 in liquid capital in 1933 but suggested that these too included a dollar or two. As a result, he argued, *Koninklijk* would gain considerably from a relative rise in the value of the dollar and sterling should the guilder depreciate.(100)

Meanwhile, the editor of the LSP weekly *De Vrijheid*,(101) J.J. Belinfante, had also shown himself as an opponent of devaluation by reacting negatively to a telegram from the *De Groninger Maatschappij van Landbouw* (the Groningen Society of Agriculture) to the government which pleaded that it hold open the option of devaluation. (see pp 50-53) This attracted a rebuttal from the president of the *Groninger Maatschappij* and LSP Second Chamber member, H.D. Louwes, in which he argued that the rigidity of social structures served to retard the *aanpassing* process. In these circumstances, he argued, devaluation should be considered as a policy alternative.(102) Later he was to express this even more forcefully: "Not from a preference for the easiest way but from the realisation that the above named way (deflation – JPV) is far from fast enough, there are many, and I belong to them, who consider that a lowering of the gold value of the guilder will greatly speed up the *aanpassing* process."(103)

Thus, in the summer and autumn of 1933 there was a clear conflict of opinion beginning to emerge on the devaluation question within the LSP. In this context, the position of the party leader S.E.B. Bierema was of the utmost importance. As well as being chairman of the parliamentary party, Bierema was also an executive member of various agricultural organisations and on these grounds can be considered one of the party's agricultural specialists. In July 1933 Bierema had signed the first 'pro-devaluation' address to the government. This is an indication that at least he doubted the eventual success of the governments *aanpassing* policy but, because the address did not unambiguously come out in favour of devaluation, it is impossible to go further than that. Indeed, in November 1933 during the budgetry debate in parliament, Bierma had pleaded for a 'consistent' deflationary policy. In the process, however, he asked himself if, in view of the problems which this course entailed and in light of the prevailing international monetary situation, the maintenance of the gold standard was not as much an experiment as its abandonment.(104) Although in this speech Bierema took great care not to come out openly in favour of devaluation, the impression was created that such a step would not have been unwelcome.

Much less ambiguous in his criticism of the government's monetary policy was Polak himself. At a meeting of LSP members he spoke out in favour of devaluation.(105) This attracted a negative reaction from the editor of *Het Liberale Weekblad*, A.W. Abspoel, in which he declared that the overwhelming majority of liberals, given the choice, would prefer 'natural' deflation above the uncertain effects of devaluation.(106)

This mounting public display of doubt about the government's monetary policy caused great concern within the party executive and it considered it necessary to take matters in hand. On the agenda of the executive meeting of December 1933 appeared the question: "If it can be permitted that the party, in public or in local party meetings, argue in favour of devaluation." The need for a decision was made necessary by the fact that the LSP was represented in the government – a government one of whose main planks of policy was adherence to the gold standard. The chairman, W.C. Wendelaar, expressed the opinion that the impression had been created to the outside world that the LSP was in favour of devaluation. Presumably with Bierema's parliamentary speech in mind, he suggested that in its official pronouncements the party should no longer come out in favour of devaluation. In any event, Bierema interpreted the remarks as addressed to him. He replied that he was *not* a proponent of devaluation and that his speech in parliament had not been intended as a plea for devaluation: what he wanted to emphasise was the necessity for a dramatic reduction in production costs. There was not much discussion though in the course of the discussion that did take place Bierema had expressed the opinion that the supression of any debate on the devaluation issue would be too extreme a measure. Before putting his proposal to muzzle all discussion to the vote Wendelaar urged the meeting to accept the standpoint that the party supported the government and would therefore reject devaluation as long as the government rejected it. The proposal was accepted without needing to register individual votes making it impossible to determine who was for or against.(107)

That same meeting also discussed the rumours that attempts had been undertaken to ban the devaluation discussion in the press. J.J. van Bolhuis, editor-in-chief of the *De Vrijheid* and the liberal daily *Het Vaderland*, stated that as far as he was concerned he knew of no such pressure, whether from the government or from the newspaper directorships. Nonetheless Bierema stood by his impression that the press was presenting a too one sided standpoint by systematically glossing over reports of the favourable results of devaluation abroad.(108)

Within days the first results of the party's decision became apparent. K. Jansma, member of the executive and chairman of the Amsterdam constituency party, declared at an LSP meeting that the gold standard was not in question as far as the LSP was concerned. He described all earlier liberal statements in favour of devaluation as "an accidental coincidence of circumstances" which had unfortunately created the impression that the LSP was no longer determined to maintain the gold standard. He disputed this impression in the following terms: "there is no question that the liberal party will abandon the gold standard ...people can rest assured that also with respect to monetary policy, our parliamentary parties will stand behind the government."(109) This statement was followed by a lecture from the director of the Amsterdamse Bank, H.A. van Nierop, entitled: "Keep your gold".

That the executive intended stringently to enforce its prohibition on pro-devaluation statements became obvious at its next meeting when it discussed a written request from professor Polak to place the devaluation question on the agenda for the next general meeting of party members. The executive decided to reply that such a discussion was considered undesirable. At the same meeting Bierema announced that he had left the group centered around Professor Polak because its petitions to the government had taken on an unambiguously pro-devaluation character. Wendelaar expressed himself delighted.(110) A dissatisfied Polak repeated his request the following month; without success.(111)

The decision taken by the executive was not without result. From the beginning of 1934 the discussion within the party appears to have come to a full stop, though it is difficult to be absolutely dogmatic on this point because the source material for the period 1934 to 1936 is more limited than for the previous period. In any event the LSP periodicals *De Vrijheid* and *Het Liberale Weekblad* were very sparing in the articles they placed concerning the devaluation question.(112) It is true that Polak and a number of other pro-devaluation professors within the party continued to express their opinons. But they did this outside the party context and they were not important within the party either.

An obvious exception was Louwes and it is worth dwelling on his position a little longer. He was an important member in the party, he was in favour of devaluation and he did not wish to conform with the executive's decision. In September 1934 he was one of the signatories to the manifesto establishing the

Nederlandsche Vereeniging voor waardevast geld. Louwes too confined his campaign outside the party and this could be the reason why the executive never reacted (though we have to take account of the lacunes in the sources). It is possible that Louwes was put under some informal pressure because after September 1934 he never again expressed himself openly in favour of devaluation. During the general meeting of the *Koninklijk Nederlandsch Landbouw Comite* in October 1934 he described the gold standard only as a vexed question in which farmers should become involved.(113) On another occasion he emphasised that adequate *aanpassing* was more important than the way in which it was reached.(114) In this way he held open the possibility of devaluation without, however, speaking out directly in its favour.

An interesting question is what influence Louwes, with his preference for devaluation (openly expressed or not), exercised on the standpoint of the parliamentary party. It was, after all, the parliamentary party and not the executive which had primarily to decide on the question whether the LSP would support the government's monetary policy. The answer would seem to be: very little. Bierema was the only spokesman for the LSP on monetary questions and he had never spoken in favour of an abandonment of the gold standard. On the other hand, it is difficult to describe Bierema's position as unqualified support for government policy. In his speech in the budgetary debate on November 1934 he expressed his doubts over the chances of success for the governments policy of 'natural deflation'(115) and during the debate on the government's budget cutting proposals of July 1935 his position was so critical that Oud (afterwards) thought that he could discern "that Bierema had already crossed the rubicon of devaluation".(116) In October 1935 during the budgetary debate Ernst Heldring, an influential member of the LSP, thought that that the party was steering towards devaluation.(117) This is certainly not apparent from Bierema's speech which limited itself to a plea for further deflation and wage cuts.(118) It seems probable that, despite clearly articulated doubts about the appropriateness of the governments economic policy and an unarticulated preference for devaluation among at least part of their number, the parliamentary party nevertheless wanted to avoid an open confrontation with the government on monetary policy.

The dissatisfaction with government economic policy extended beyond the parliamentary party. This became apparent in September 1934 from an address sent by 26 prominent party members to the executive and to members of both chambers of parliament which advocated a change in the course of economic policy. The address expressed its regret at the way in which the various so-called 'crisis laws' had increased the governments influence over the economy. This implied criticism of the LSP parliamentary party as well since it had wholeheartedly supported the government in the extention of agricultural crisis measures: a policy which can be explained by the strong postion of agricultrual interests in the parliamentary party (Bierema, Louwes). It is worth noting that the signatories of the address included both proponents of devaluation (Polak, C.A. Verrijn Stuart, G.M. Verrijn Stuart) and opponents (T. Ligthart, dr.E.C.

van Dorp). These two currents managed to find each other in an agreement that a gradual restoration of free trade in all sectors of the economy was an absolute must, whatever they thought about the gold standard. So it was that pro- and anti-devaluationists within the LSP, who can be classified as orthodox liberals, were able to find each other in criticism of the far too interventionistically inclined government policy and the support which that policy had been given by the parliamentary party.

The executive's reaction to this address had everything in common with its earlier reaction to criticism on monetary policy, namely to attempt to keep the criticism as far as possible from becoming public. At least, that much can be read into a letter from the constituency party in Utrecht to the executive, which complained about the fact that the address of the 26th had not been distributed to the constituency parties which made any resulting discussion superficial at best.(120) Of course, the policy of the executive was directed at avoiding, as far as possible, open criticism of the government's social/economic policy. One important consideration was that openly expressed doubts about the deflationary policy would weaken the position of the guilder and that if this unleashed a wave of speculation the government could be forced to abandon the gold standard at an unfavourable moment. Another was that pleas in favour of devaluation meant that the party was no longer behind the government and its own minister on monetary questions. It was not a position that the party, now that after a long period of opposition it could participate in government, wished to take. Finally, there was no reason to believe that any other course of action would have reduced the tensions within the party and it may even have increased them. In so far as *Het Liberal Weekblad* and *De Vrijheid* still expressed any opinion at all on the devaluation question, it lined up one hundred per cent behind the government.

The difference in approach between the liberal weeklies, which could be seen as the mouth piece of the executive, and the parliamentary party also became apparent in the reactions to the devaluation in September 1936. Whilst the Liberal weeklies were of the opinion that given the gold stocks of the Netherlands Bank it had been technically possible to maintain the gold standard, they felt that it had been an act of wise policy which had allowed the guilder to perish on the field of honour.(121) Louwes drew his analogy closer to home, comparing the devaluation with a visit by a child to the dentist. What was important, he considered, was how that child had been prepared for the visit. The government, he felt, had portrayed the waiting room as "the place of terror", which had not helped create an atmosphere of calm when the event had come.(122)

THE CATHOLICS (RKSP)

The position of the RKSP with regard to the government differed from that of the four parties treated thus far; it never gave more than lukewarm support. For its social policy, the RKSP had a clear point of departure in the papal encyclical *Quadragesimo Anno* (1931). On this basis the RKSP often criticised the government but for its financial-economic policy the RKSP lacked such a stronghold. Did the RKSP nevertheless reach a unanimous standpoint on the monetary question? And if this was not the case, which standpoint prevailed, and on what grounds?In view of the fact that catholics were to be found in all layers of society, the RKSP was a typical *zuil* party with different and often conflicting social economic interests. Such a party, which saw itself as a people's party in the widest sense of the word, was mostly forced to compromise in order to arrive at a general party standpoint.(123) Within the Dutch political spectrum the RKSP had a pivotal position in that it was virtually indespensable in the formation of any viable governmental coalition. This brought with it great responsibility but, at the same time, gave it the power to force cardinal questions. The party found it difficult to cope with such a position. Fear of the electorate and a continuous need to keep in step with its own religious support group had a paralysing effect at those moments when drastic political decisions had to be taken.(124) Roman catholic politicians were very governmentally minded. Fear of not being taken as good Dutchmen played a role in this: the perceived threat of anti-papalism was a theme which continually reemerged in the deliberations of RKSP leaders. Most party politicians in the Netherlands, including those within the RKSP, had little economic training. In discussions on the causes, consequences and solutions of the world crisis interest focussed primarily on the social and ethical aspects.(125) Even catholic economists saw economics as a normative science.(126)

It was a cabinet under RKSP leadership which was confronted in September 1931 with the devaluation of sterling. The government, in the person of RKSP minister Verschuur of economic affairs, gave no thought to following the English example. Nor within the parliamentary party, was there any discussion on the question of whether or not the guilder should maintain its gold value. L.G. Kortenhorst, parliamentary represtentative of the catholic employers' interests, advocated cost reductions in production as the most obvious way to the restoration of profitability. "The only and absolutely necessary policy which can save the guilder" was for him the encouragement of exports and the limitation of government expenditure. C.J. Kuiper, representative of the catholic trade unions, considered that "without planned leadership" no positive results could be achieved.(128) For the time being the cabinet chose in favour of a solution in the spirit of Kortenhorst.

An extremely confidential RKSP report on government economic policy in May 1932 came to the conclusion that the government had created the impression among the population that it lacked both direction and conviction.(129) Criticism within party ranks began to swell. The demand for a more active trade policy had been articulated at the second crisis conference of the roman catholic employers' association. The parliamentarians A.J. Loerakker and M.J.M. van Poll were the first to articulate demands for 'consistent' deflation, a policy which from 1934 onwards would be seen by the RKSP as the only possible alternative for devaluation. Van Poll pointed out how the government attempts at income reduction had been one-sided, attacking those who depended for their income on labour whilst not demanding any extra sacrifice from those who derived their income from government stocks, mortgages, rents, etc.(130) When the budget for 1933 proposed reducing expenditure by Dfl. 71,500,000, of which Dfl. 14,500,000 had to come from the reduction of salaries of civil servants, the patience of the RKSP was exhausted.(131) The proposals were defeated in the Second Chamber, parliament was dissolved and elections were called for 26 April.

The Colijn cabinet formed after these elections received a number of urgent requests from catholic circles to adopt a more active economic policy. None of these, however, suggested devaluation.(132) In November 1933 the RKSP leader Aalberse spoke out strongly against devaluation. In his arguments the fear of inflation and the memory of the hyper-inflation in Germany after the First World War played an important role. But the criticism of Colijn's *aanpassing* policy grew. In the spring of 1934 Aalberse began to tie his anti-devaluation standpoint with the demand for a 'consistent deflation' in which not only wages but also *vaste lasten* would be tackled. At almost the same time, however, the first voices in favour of devaluation were to be heard. In the First Chamber Blomjous pointed out that since the devaluation of sterling the British economy had improved. On these grounds, he explained, he had doubts about the monetary policy being followed. In February 1935 the First Chamber was able to hear the first undisguised pro-devaluation speech and that from the mouth of a catholic representative, P.J.S. Serrarens of the Catholic Employees' Association. In his speech he sketched the advantages of a timely and quick devaluation: "We must devalue whilst we can technically still control events." He was not of the opinion that the crisis would disappear with devaluation but felt that it was the only way to adjusting the Dutch price level to that of world prices. He added that he thought it was somewhat strange still to talk of devaluation in terms of a "leap in the dark", in the light of the fact that 35 countries had already abandoned the gold standard. Yet, despite the increasing demands for devaluation, the parliamentary party and the party executive were basically split on the issue. Within the party executive for example, A.C. de Bruyn, chairman of the RKWV, was still against devaluation in September 1934, whilst the chairman, Goseling, and secretary, F.G.C.J.M. Teulings, were both early converts to the devaluationist cause.

It would be wrong to create the impression that the devaluation question was intensively discussed within the RKSP in these years. Only from the autumn of 1934 did requests for information of this problem begin to come in from the rank and file. In the forty five meetings of the parliamentary party, held between May 1933 and May 1935, the possibility of devaluation was only advanced eight times, and then often in passing: economic science had not yet adequately explained the consequences, the discussion was not politically oppertune and it was considered a subject too dangerous for party unity.

This last consideration was all the more conclusive because at this very moment the party was beginning to split up into two camps. One group formed itself around the party chairman and the vice chairman of the parliamentary party, C.M.J.F. Goseling, and a second group identified with the parliamentary party chairman, P.J.M. Aalberse. The split focussed on the attitude towards the cabinet in general and towards monetary policy in particular. The cautious, velvet gloves approach of Aalberse was increasingly challenged by Goseling and Teulings who wanted the RKSP to be more strident in putting its demands to the Colijn cabinet. It was in the Goseling/Teulings circle that the number of proponents of devaluation steadily increased; the Aalberse group would remain shaky on this point right to the end.(133)

On 17 April 1934 it was announced that the RKSP minister for economic affairs, Verschuur, had resigned for reasons of ill health. In the RKSP press there is no word to be found about other possible motives but, according to P.J. Oud, minister of finance at the time, other causes did play a role, namely the growing opposition from within his own party by proponents of increased protectionism and proponents of devaluation.(134) After a short interim period Colijn had found M.P.L. Steenberghe, chairman of the *Algemeene R K Werkgevers Vereeniging*, willing to succeed Verschuur. It is true that Colijn had some objections against Steenberghe, on the other hand, bringing him into the cabinet could serve to silence catholic opposition. He found Steenberghe's economic thinking too protectionist and he was even more unhappy about Steenberghe's doubts on the desirability of maintaining the gold standard. Colijn got Steenberghe to agree that for the time being there would be no change in the monetary policy. If, however, financial circumstances should change to such a degree that they raised an acute problem Steenberghe was permitted to place the question on the cabinet agenda. In catholic circles this new ministerial appointment was greeted with general applause and high expectations.(135)

The presence of Steenberghe in the cabinet could not prevent the enthusiasm of the RKSP for continuing support of the cabinet from sinking even further. 'Consistent deflation' became the slogan on the RKSP banner; a banner behind which they hoped to get the government to march. As soon as it became apparent that the cabinet had no such intention the call for devaluation became ever louder, especially in RKSP circles.(136) The catholic economic high school in Tilburg joined the economic high school in Rotterdam as a devaluationist bulwork.(137) But, it took the Belgian devaluation and the resignation of Steenberghe to harden the RKSP standpoint against the Colijn cabinet and to stimulate at last real discussions within the RKSP on the desirability of devaluation, support for which had meanwhile increased even further.

In the parliamentary party's preliminary reports on the government's budgetry proposals (completed at the end of April 1935) Goseling and Teulings had already expressed their dissatisfaction that the question of *vaste lasten* had not been included in the proposed legislation. By this omission, they argued, the government was merely increasing the pressure for devaluation.(138) At the meeting of the parliamentary party on 18 June 1935 a verbal report was given of a conversation between the executive and the three RKSP ministers a month earlier at which the ministers had been warned that the RKSP parliamentary party could no longer support Colijn's economic policy.(139) On 17 July 1935 the parliamentary debate on the budgetary proposals began in the second chamber. Aalberse took up a key position: "Was the government still rock fast in the conviction that devaluation could still be avoided? Was the cabinet still convinced that its policy of 'natural deflation', whilst maintaining the untarnished guilder, would still lead to the desired goal? Why had minister Steenberghe resigned? Did his resignation have anything to do with the Belgian devaluation, and if so, why did he consider that the results of the Belgian measures were so serious?"(140) Aalberse then suggested that the government had only two possible alternatives for economic recovery, 'consistent deflation' or devaluation. If Colijn was not prepared to choose between these two alternatives, he warned, the RKSP could not continue to support the cabinet in parliament.(141)

The government refused to abandon its policy. Colijn rejected both consistent deflation and devaluation and demanded a vote of confidence from the catholics.(142) Perhaps Colijn was trying to exploit the internal tension within the RKSP on this very issue. But that was not the only dilemma facing the RKSP. Was it justifiable to let the cabinet fall or was it in the general national interest to continue to support it, even though one no longer had confidence in it? Whatever choice it made, the catholics would be branded as the scapegoat.(143) When the RKSP parliamentary party refused to make the submission Colijn demanded, he tendered his cabinets resignation. *Het dagblad van Noord Brabant* commented mischieviously: "Steenberghe triumphs."(144)

Aalberse was immediately charged with the formation of a parliamentary cabinet on the broadest possible basis. It has been suggested that Aalberse's mandate was framed in this way because the Queen wanted Colijn back and for this reason she had given Aalberse an impossible task. "Mama (= Queen Willhelmina) wanted to keep her Hendrik (= Colijn)", wrote Marchant (who after his conversion to catholicism had joined the RKSP) to Steenberghe, and "good old Aalberse fell for it beautifully." The RKSP press service, however, rejected any such suggestion. Whatever lay behind it, the fact remained that Aalberse accepted the task. The pro's and con's of joining a cabinet including the SDAP were thoroughly considered by the RKSP. On the one hand it was recognised that a new cabinet would have to accommodate the "experimental inflationist economic" policies of the socialists.(145) On the other it was realised that the legitimacy of the cabinet would be strengthened among a large part of the population if it included the SDAP.(146) However, for the time being, the RKSP wanted to keep faith with the old preconditions of not being the only party in a cabinet together with the SDAP (see p 85). Moreover, Aalberse's mandate to form a broadly based cabinet pointed in the same direction. That came unstuck when neither the CHU nor the VDB were prepared to participate.

Since the RKSP did not dare go it alone, Aalberse returned his mandate: a not very honourable retreat.(147)

To the utter incomprehension of the RKSP, Colijn was then recalled to form a government.(148) Not only that, but it was to be an extra parliamentary cabinet with a broad composition. Colijn attempted to bring the RKSP parliamentary party into harness by offering it a fourth minister's post, that of defence, for Goseling. Colijn would then be able to assimilate and neutralise this "evil genius" behind Aalberse within the new cabinet. Goseling refused because he considered that the standpoints of the catholic parliamentary party and the cabinet had too little in common.(149) Nonetheless, Colijn quickly completed his task. The result appeared as a hastily corrected edition of the previous cabinet. The three RKSP members of the old cabinet were also in the new but, it was to appear later on their own responsibility and without permission of the RKSP parliamentary party.(150)

The favourable press reports on the situation in Belgium served to reawaken the discussion among the catholics on the desirability of maintaining the gold standard. It increased almost daily in intensity. In October 1935 the first edition of the monthly *Economie* appeared under the editorship of a number of Tilburg professors. The new journal immediately revealed itself as an advocate for the devaluation of the guilder. In the first issue, professor H.A. Kaag noted that the Netherlands would have been better off if it had followed the English monetary policy in 1931.(151) In the third number, Dr. H.M.A. van der Valk drew a parallel between the period directly preceding the devaluation in Belgium and the situation in the Netherlands at the end of 1935. In Belgium too one saw a practically deadlocked deflationary policy. In Belgium too the government had failed to balance the budget. In Belgium too the government refused to accept proposals for legislative interference in *vaste lasten*. In Belgium too there was steadily increasing social resistance to government policy.(152) But in RKSP circles there was no consensus. Although the increasing disenchantment with government policy and the sharply contrasting optimistic news from Belgium helped swell recruitment to devaluationist ranks, the division on the devaluation issue, following on the fiasco of the cabinet crisis, contributed to a feeling that the party had begun to lose its way. The need was felt for a dramatic policy manifestation which would reaffirm the RKSP as national party and demonstrate catholic unity.(153) The party executive announced that it was planning, in January or February 1936, to organise a political *Landdag* (national day) in Amsterdam.(154)

The party chairman, Goseling, was mandated by the executive to select the speakers and to steer the discussion as far as possible towards the issues of unemployment and the need for work creation.(155) Goseling invited ex-minister Steenberghe to come and speak on the subject "Labour for our people" and the party executive approved the choice. Goseling did not consult Aalberse in the selection of the speakers, which was to create an unpleasant after-taste directly after.(156) The *Landdag* eventually took place on the 2 February. 7,000 people attended to hear speeches from Goseling, Mgr. Poels and Steenberghe.(157) It was Steenberghe's speech which provided the largest political fireworks as he made use of the opportunity to plead forcefully for devaluation and to condemn the deflationary policy of the government as inappropriate. "We won't get there with devaluation alone. Devaluation provides the necessary foundation for an active economic policy."(158) Goseling had been informed before hand by Steenberghe that, in his opinion, devaluation ran as a red thread through the question of economic policy and that he could not avoid mentioning it on the *Landdag*.(159) After Steenberghe's speech it fell to Goseling to close the day. He used the opportunity to endorse Steenberghe's economic programme, suggesting that "certainly among ourselves but also outside our own circle (it) will find little opposition". He ended his closing remarks with the sentence: "I cannot avoid saying it. We are not on the right path, (the path) which leads to more labour for our people."(160) So it was that the *Landdag* was seen, more than anything else, as propoganda for devaluation. Goseling had deliberately steered it in that direction and in his concluding speech he had created the impression that Steenberghe's position was supported by the party executive.(161) The *Landdag* released a whole spectrum of political emotions.

The government was extremely worried about the results of the *Landdag* and instructed the radio control commission to prohibit an integral broadcast of the speeches by the catholic radio station. Censored were the entire speech by Steenberghe and a number of passages from Goseling's concluding speech in which he had summed up Steenberghe's position.(162) The three catholic ministers were equally none too pleased about the *Landdag* either. In the first place, they had not received a special invitation and secondly, they had been confronted with a complete condemnation of government policy.(163) The RKSP parliamentary chairman Aalberse felt himself completely by-passed and even attacked. According to the party's statute, the political leadership lay with the parliamentary chairman and not with the party chairman. Goseling's endorsement of Steenberghe's position had not only created the impression that the party executive was behind him but, it also implied an attack on the parliamentary party. A *Landdag* held under the slogan 'Our Unity: The Country's Strength' should not be the occasion for driving a wedge through the middle of the party.(164)

Aalberse even played with the idea of resigning as parliamentary chairman.(165) *De Maasbode* of 9 March 1936 commented that various catholic daily papers seemed to have made it their task to begin a political witch-hunt against Aalberse.(166) In the event he did not have to resign. He was unanimously proposed by the catholic parliamentary party as candidate for the chairmanship of the second chamber and on 6 May 1936 the candidature was succesful.(167) Goseling immediately added the position of chairman of the parliamentary party to his function of party chairman, thereby becoming at one stroke the most dominant politician within the RKSP.(168)

The RKSP kept hammering on the inevitable choice between devaluation and consistent deflation. In view of the fact that the new Colijn cabinet took as little notice of the party's demands as the previous one, Goseling proposed a parliamentary vote against the government's plans but he failed to convince the parliamentary party which wanted at all costs to avoid a new cabinet crisis. Aalberse's failure to form a cabinet in 1935 had shown that, for the time being at least, there was no real alternative for the present government.(169)

In prominent RKSP circles the number of proponents for devaluation kept increasing. Ex-minister of economic affairs, Verschuur, expressed the opinion of many when, in an openly pro-devaluation speech in June 1936 entitled 'Our People in Need', he said: "Now that we have attempted the impossible, a currency correction must help us over the dead point. With much effort we will probably thereafter, if we do not slacken, find ourselves in calmer waters. Without monetary correction, we will not."(170) Nonetheless, Goseling still feared the potentially divisive nature of the devaluation issue. On 23 May 1936 he suggested to the party executive that the leadership should ensure that the people understood that the devaluation question was not a political problem in the sense that the RKSP, as a party, had to take an official position one way or the other.

After the fall of the guilder on 26 September 1936 Goseling expressed the party's satisfaction with the monetary measures taken by the government and declared that he was prepared to support the cabinet right up to the elections of 1937.(171) On more than one occasion catholic parliamentarians commented with satisfaction that the Dutch people had obviously maintained their calm in the face of the sudden news of devaluation. The RKSP took for itself the credit for the calm reactions because the RKSP was the party which had continuously and in an objective way enlightened the Dutch people on the problems surrounding the issue.(172)

THE SOCIAL DEMOCRATS (SDAP)

Trying to bridge the gap with the other parties with a view to future government participation, the SDAP in the 1930's no longer pursued a policy of opposition for the sake of opposition. On the other hand, as criticism within Dutch society on the monetary policy of the government rose from 1933 onwards the opportunities for the SDAP for an appealing alternative policy on this point increased. This entailed a certain dilemma for the party and in the following pages will be shown how the party, under the not very strong leadership of J.W. Albarda, resolved this dilemma.

"I do not condemn the government for its monetary policy." These words were spoken by the chairman of the parliamentary party of the SDAP, J.W. Albarda, during the budgetary debate of November 1934.(173) The fact that the only large opposition party, and its leader in particular, should so unambiguously support the monetary course chosen by Colijn raises a number of questions, not the least of which is why the party was so passive in opposing the government on this very point whilst being against so many other aspects of Colijn's policies. Notwithstanding the fact that a number of important historical sources have not survived, there is sufficient material to reconstruct the way policy on this question was arrived at within the top echelons of the party. Admittedly, the SDAP consisted of more than the top but there is no evidence that the party congress or even the party council played a role of any importance. This means that the various discussions in the press or during stúdy conferences only served as a safety-valve for the opinions held by the lower ranks. Although the controversies are interesting in their own right, they were of no real significance for the policy formation within the party. Whenever there were aspirations in this direction Albarda immediately took steps to kill the attempt.(174) An indication of the character of the debate in socialist circles is afforded by the section of this book devoted to an analysis of the socialist trade union movement, the NVV (see above pp 69-71).

The British devaluation in 1931 apparently left the SDAP-executive unmoved. Only in March 1933 did the turn of events prompt more concern for monetary questions. Although at that time German developments dominated the list of events requiring a party standpoint, executive member J.W. Matthijsen pointed to the dangers for the economy entailed in the devaluation of the American dollar. His own solution was drastically simple namely "that we.... will have to adjust to the international money market. If we don't, then our entire export will disappear and unemployment will become even greater". He considered that a special commission together with the NVV (later called the 'financial commission') should be set up immediately; an idea supported unreservedly by Albarda in the following terms: "We have thought through the political difficulties with which we are presently confronted, but not the economic. If at this moment something should befall us, we cannot assess the situation."(175)

It has been deduced from Albarda's first public statement on the devaluation question, made in the context of the budget in November 1933, that he was advocating a devaluation of the guilder.(176) The first to make this interpretation, presumably from political motives, was Colijn himself, but this prompted a reply from Albarda that he most definitely had not intended any such thing.(177) Since the spring of 1933 he had taken the opportunity of informing himself on the issue and he only wanted to suggest that the government should do likewise. That way it would be better able to present its case by means other than resorting to crude dogmatism. What he wanted was "clear and concrete motives" for maintaining the gold standard and not merely an "appeal to a tenet of faith".(178)

The developments within the 'financial commission', set up in March 1933 (see p 68), are crucially important in understanding the position of the SDAP. The process of opinion forming in the commission had two clearly seperate phases. The first was from the spring of 1933 until the autumn of the same year, the second from the summer of 1934 to the spring of 1935. The first phase was immediately decisive for the establishment of the SDAP standpoint. On 2 December 1933 the commission came to a definite, albeit divided, conclusion. Of the sixteen members of the commission, nine spoke out against devaluation and four in favour. The names of the four pro-devaluationists were: J.W. Matthijsen, J.F. Ankersmit, editor-in-chief of the socialist daily *Het Volk*, professor J. van Gelderen, one of the party's economic experts, and the NVV secretary S. de la Bella. Among those voting against we find J.W. Albarda.(179)

After the vote of 2 December the financial commission was immediately adjourned. The anti-devaluationists had won the day. From later internal party communications, however, we can deduce that the majority of the commission in 1933 did not unambiguously come out against reduction in the value of the guilder. According to a later statement of Ankersmit, the commission had only rejected "devaluation at that moment". Moreover, it had produced no report at the time because it had not wanted to exclude the possibility of making a different statement should circumstances change.(180) We can conclude from this that the large anti-devaluation majority in the financial commission in 1933 did not imply a statement in principle against an eventual reduction of the gold value of the guilder. No one wanted openly to adopt such a political platform. There is nothing in the internal documentation, either, to suggest that the commission decided not to publish a report in order to cover up its own division. On the contrary, its standpoint was obviously that the party should take no definte position. That a number of anti-devaluationists would be prepared to countenance devaluation should circumstances alter also appeared from a letter from the secretary of the financial commission, S. Mok, in September 1934. In a reaction to the question from the party executive whether people in the commission still stood by the decision taken in the autumn of 1933, he emphasised that there was still a majority backing but, he added, "that there are members among the majority of the commission that stand by the position that, if there is no change in the economic situation, devaluation for the Netherlands will become inevitable, or the Netherlands will be forced to devalue if Great Britain and the United States of America go over to stabilisation of their currencies."(181) It was the timing and the circumstances, and not the act itself, which seemed to have motivated the majority and it was they who determined the party's course.

The second phase of the activity of the financial commission differed from the first in that it was decided to publicise its findings by the SDAP and NVV leadership. In view of the fact that there was no unanimous opinion space was given to both proponents and opponents of devaluation. Presumably in connection with problems in the formulation of the text it was not until the summer of 1935 that the reports reached the public.

The lengthy report 'Devaluation Pro and Contra'(182) demonstrated the great amount of thought the social democratic movement had devoted to the devaluation question, but neither the actual relationships between the proponents and opponents nor the difference between those who opposed as a point of principle and those who did so as a point of policy were really explained. If one wants to characterise this report, it could be said that its thoroughness and expansiveness acted as a fig leaf with which the party leadership wanted to cover its unwillingness to come to a public standpoint. Put more positively; it expressed the deliberate choice not to make "any statement on behalf of the party", as the young party chairman, Koos Vorrink, had expressed it to the party executive in April 1935, (i.e. after the Belgian devaluation). Somewhat cynically he had added that such a party standpoint left both sides free to express their opinions outside.

The SDAP was consistent in maintaining its official neutrality as a party. This is especially noticeable in the contributions of Albarda in the parliamentary debates on the budget proposals. In the first of the two 'extraordinary budget' debates in 1935 and the ordinary budgetry debate of November 1935 he made no mention whatsoever of the devaluation question. He even managed to avoid making any statement on the so-called 'Aalberse alternative' of 'consistent' deflation or devaluation.(184) The qualified pro-devaluation speech of F.M. Wibaut in the First Chamber was purely a personal expression of opinion.(185)

It must be emphasised again that this silence was not an attempt to conceal the internal division of the SDAP but a deliberate tactical choice. Alberda emphasised this at the meeting of the SDAP party executive of 2 June 1934. For him one thing was certain, "that the party should take no responsibility unto itself for devaluation". At the same time he made clear his own scepticism over the future of the 'untarnished' guilder: "Speaker has the feeling that Holland will not avoid devaluation." However, this statement did not mean that he considered such a development desirable, as he repeatedly made clear. He ended his speech with a repetition of his position: "If it can be avoided, the speaker does not want our party to carry the responsibility. If we were in the government then we would probably have to make a decision."(186) In subsequent internal party discussions he remained true to this position.(187) In April 1935, after the devaluation of the Belgian franc he quoted Hendrik de Man, whom he had just visited with Koos Vorrink, in his support with the statement "the problem of devaluation is purely a matter for a government, not even for a parliament."(188)

The effects of Colijn's monetary policy were frequently considered in the party's internal discussions. The Amsterdam councillor, S.R. de Miranda, expressed this in the following way at a meeting of the executive in April 1935: "At this very moment as a result of the devaluation in surrounding countries the whole of Dutch industry is bleeding dry."(189) The importance of the devaluation question for the economic welfare of the Netherlands had already been emphasised by W. Drees some months before. More than anyone else in parliament and in the party executive he had consistently opposed Albarda's position in the internal party debates and had defended devaluation. As early as the summer of 1934 he stated that the devaluation question formed "at this moment the most important problem for our movement" touching upon "the kernel of our economic policy".(190) Even the opponents of devaluation were prepared to concede this point but his standpoint could make no headway against the closed front of the party leadership. It was not only Albarda who held the door shut. Both the party chairman, Koos Vorrink, and party chairman of the financial commission, W.H. Vliegen,(191) supported Albarda's position, to name but two of the more important.

Although the internal division within the party worried the leadership, of far greater importance was the threat of a split in the social democratic movement along organisatorial lines, with the party on the one side and the trade union movement on the other. The latent conflict between the SDAP and the NVV leaderships forms a fascinating aspect in the decision making process on the devaluation question. Sources are scarce but sufficient to get some insight into the nature and extent of the conflict. The trade unions too were divided on the issue but, unlike the party, their top figures (including both the chairman and the secretary, E. Kuypers and S. de la Bella) were proponants of devaluation. Although today we can deduce from the NVV archives that this worry was exaggerated, the SDAP leadership considered NVV activity as requiring some action on its own part.

In a letter to the secretary of the SDAP in April 1934 Albarda mentioned for the first time the concern in the SDAP leadership. The letter was directed against the creation of a pro-devaluation atmosphere in the socialist press.(192) He ended his letter with the warning: "I do not consider it an impossibility that the NVV will cause us difficulties in this affair in the same way as it did at the time in the Belgian-Netherlands treaty. Our press must not cooperate in this." When the letter was discussed by the executive its anti NVV tenour prompted a number of comments. Koos Vorrink stated emphatically, "the situation where the NVV confronts the party with decisions must be avoided."(193) This did not end the matter. Only two and a half weeks later at a meeting of the executive of the General Council, the joint executive organ of the SDAP and the NVV, the decision was taken that before any other statements the financial commission should speak out first.(194) This was exactly what the SDAP leadership had hoped for. The NVV leadership would be bound by the commission's statement. But of course, anti-devaluationists had already in 1933 formed a clear majority (and there was no reason to believe this would change after the summer of 1934). By this manoeuvre what had threatened to become a major split was reduced to a small difference in opinion. For the SDAP leadership this was a great relief because otherwise it would have been doubtful whether it could have continued to stick to its own course.

Would the SDAP leadership have taken another position if the party had been in government? This is not a purely academic question. After the fall of the Colijn cabinet in July 1935, the SDAP was confronted with this very question. On 24 and 29 July the various options were discussed in private meetings of the parliamentary party.(195) The devaluation question was only raised in passing. Central to the discussion on 24 July were the socialist demands in return for participation in a coalition government and the reaction to those of the

AMSTERDAMSCHE EDITIE

Het Liberale Weekblad

OFF. PROPAGANDA-ORGAAN VAN DE LIBERALE STAATSPARTIJ DE VRIJHEIDSBOND

ADRES VAN DIRECTIE EN ADMINISTRATIE HEERENGRACHT 390, AMSTERDAM-CENTRUM
ABONNEMENTSPRIJS f 2 50 PER JAAR (VOOR LEDEN DER PARTIJ f 1 75). AFZ NUMMERS 5 CT.
UITGAVE A J G STRENGHOLT'S UITGEVERSMAATSCHAPPIJ N V HEERENGRACHT 390, AMSTERDAM-CENTRUM
TELEFOON 36886 33421 • POSTGIRO 172884 • BANKIERS AMSTERDAMSCHE BANK
ADVERTENTIES PER REGEL 75 CT TUSSCHEN TEKST 50 VERHOOGING BIJ CONTRACT BELANGRIJKE REDUCTIE
COMMISSIE VAN AANBEVELING Z EXC Mr D FOCK EN Z EXC JHR IR O C A VAN LIDTH DE JEUDE TE 's-GRAVENHAGE A ASSCHER TE AMSTERDAM Mr J DROST EN ED G SCHURMANN TE ROTTERDAM

GECONTR OPLAGE 10.000 EX.
VRIJDAG 2 OCT 1936 • 1e JAAR No 22

De blàren vallen en de munten

Minister Colijn uitgegleden op den Zwitserschen franc

'The laves are falling ... and the money'. The liberal weekly blames the Swiss Franc for the fall of the guilder.

catholics. There is no room here to discuss either of these. Suffice is to say only Drees emphasised the need for devaluation. The NVV chairman Kupers also warned that the SDAP could not remain passive: "If the guilder does not fall by itself, we will be confronted with the question whether we will cooperate towards a devaluation or not."

But what if the guilder did not fall of itself? Albarda certainly reacted as though this would be unlikely. In his introductory remarks to the parliamentary party he mentioned the possiblility that should the Colijn cabinet fall devaluation would be a fact, adding: "Then the question which many of us think that we cannot avoid will resolve itself." This sentence stands out because throughout his lengthy exposition on the SDAP demands for a forceful "recovery cabinet" he said nothing else on the issue. Apparently devaluation would already have happened or else the question would in some miraculous way resolve itself during the negotiations. Similarly, in reacting to the catholic demands Albarda never mentioned the devaluation once. He did, however, react to the catholic demand for 'consistent deflation' which he thought concealed an acceptance of further wage-cuts. Only if this were not the case was he prepared to accept a lowering of *vaste lasten*.(196)

In the subsequent discussion Vliegen left little room for the belief that a miracle would absolve the SDAP from the need to come to a decision itself. He commented perceptively: "Colijn will want to hold on to the guilder at any price and leave the odium of a devaluation to his successor." Albarda did not react to this. He did agree however with Wibaut's statement that the gold countries would have to go over to devaluation "if the urgently necessary international stabilisation comes about"; a position shared by many. However, at a decisive moment when leadership on the question was necessary he provided his party with nothing more than hesitancy. When Albarda informed the parliamentary party about the failure of the catholic attempt to form a cabinet, he again took up no firm position. He only mentioned that the negotiators had failed to come to any agreement either on the question of *vaste lasten* or on the question of devaluation, adding the comment: "though also the opponents of devaluation feared that a continuation of the gold losses would lead to it."(197)

This impression of a lack of decisiveness on Albarda's part was strengthened by a number of statements before and during the second round of the 'extraordinary budget' debate in September 1935. At an internal parliamentary party meeting Vliegen commented that should the newly reconstructed Colijn cabinet fall it would indeed mean a devaluation. Drees immediately supported him by adding that the Colijn cabinet itself seemed to be less convinced than before that the guilder could be held at its current parity. Albarda reacted with the characteristic comment: "The chairman also considers it unlikely that the guilder will survive. That is, however, not the same thing as advocating devaluation." When Drees replied that he considered it important that such a step should be considered because uncontrolled depreciation was also undesirable, he was left without an answer.(198) The following day in the parliamentary debate Albarda discussed extensively the "danger for the guilder" and proposed various measures for its defense, including the introduction of exchange controls. He went on to mention that should a devaluation become inevitable measures should be taken to ensure that the devaluation profit flowed into the exchequer. Not surprisingly in the light of the above, Albarda coupled his reflections on the measures necessary in the event of a devaluation with the statement: "Which I hope will not be the case."(199)

Albarda's comments in defense of the guilder during the September debate of 1935 was the last time that the SDAP spoke on this subject. The full twelve months leading up to the guilder devaluation passed in complete silence on the part of the party. The increasing unrest experienced within catholic circles found no reflection in the SDAP. Instead, its full attention was absorbed by the preparation of the *Plan van de Arbeid* (Labour Plan) The party slogan on the devaluation subject remained: take no official stand.

When the gold standard was eventually abandoned Albarda announced his party as being in full agreement with the decision to devalue. According to him it had long been clear to the entire parliamentary party that "If the French franc succumbed, the guilder could not be maintained at its old level". He did let some relief show through: "Most recently, especially, a cloud of uncertainty about the guilder has hung over our economic life. It is a relief now that the cloud has broken; the atmosphere has been purified; one can again see new possibilities. Optimism will return."(200)

Looking at the disunity within the SDAP a distinction needs to be made not only between proponents and opponents of a guilder devaluation but also between opponents in principle and opponents in practice. Ideological considerations could make some principled opponents say: within a capitalist society there is no room for improvement. Such voices however remained isolated. The SDAP in the 1930's found itself at the frontier of two worlds, the Marxist ideology of the past and a realistic reformism of the future.(201) Among the realists in the party were to be found the practical opponents as well as the proponents of a devaluation. Nonetheless, the point needs to be emphasised again that the monetary neutralism of the SDAP was a deliberate choice and not the result of internal division.

What alternative could there have been? Certainly not an open agitation for devaluation. In this both proponents and opponents of devaluation were unanimous. This was however not the real problem. Nor could one expect the SDAP to try to exercise indirect pressure for a change in government policy. But, when the occasion arose that the SDAP might become a coalition partner should it not then have made its position clear? It is noticable that the question along these lines, formulated by the trade unions, was never answered by the party leadership. So why then was the party leadership, and especially Albarda, unwilling to take up a position? There were three main factors which determined the position of the SDAP leadership: the specific position of the SDAP in the 1930's, the doubts within the leadership on the positive results of a devaluation and Albarda's own personality.

The position of the SDAP in the early 1930's was determined by the double threat of the economic crisis and the rise of fascism. The party leadership had been primarily on the defensive until the *Plan van de Arbeid* gave it a clear own alternative for the failing economic policy of Colijn: it now possessed a powerful propaganda weapon. However, this was only the case from 1935. Before then the party had tried to find a policy which would reflect its socialist ideas. The somewhat surprising change in course represented by *Plan van de Arbeid* throws into even sharper contrast the earlier vagueness of economic ideas in the party leadership.(202) Moreover SDAP thinking was also determined by the fact that the party was still in isolation. Its desire to break out of this isolation and to be eventually considered as a coalition partner with middle class parties meant that it could not have the reputation of untrustworthiness on financial policy.

A still more important explanation for the monetary neutralism of the SDAP

Colijn breaks the guilder. From Vrijheid, Arbeid, Brood (NVV and SDAP), 3.10.1936.

leadership was probably the fact that the proponents of a devaluation had not succeeded in convincing the leadership that a reduction in the value of the guilder as an isolated measure would have sufficient positive effects on the Dutch economy to be worth taking the risk. In the course of 1934 Albarda more than once emphasised the point that a devaluation would have disadvantages, especially for the middle class and the workers. This was not just a general observation about the effects of a devaluation but was clearly tied in with the timing. He argued that the sterling countries had devalued at a time of falling prices whilst in 1934 raw material prices were rising once more.(203) Thus, the example of other countries did not seem relevant. The SDAP secretary, C. Woudenberg, expressed the dilemma as follows: "The danger should not be excluded that with a devaluation the existing problems would still remain and that it (the odium) will then come to fall on the head of the party."(204)

Finally, the personality of Albarda deserves consideration as a partial explanation. On the basis of his later conduct in London the historian, L. de Jong, condemned Albarda's inner weakness of character, which he described as "a lack of robustness".(205) Was it not a lack of nerve and drive which prevented the political leadership from agreeing on their position on the guilder at the crucial moment of July 1935? The impression that Albarda's position was one which came down to "Well, rather not" is confirmed many times in the internal party documents. It should be added that Albarda was apparently a complex man. Simple solutions for what he saw as an extremely complicated question – such as the monetary policy, did not lie in his character. It seems probable that a lack of economic insight also strengthened his hesitancy, despite all the efforts within the labour movement to construct a good economic position for an eventual decision. Albarda was a mechanical engineer with a limited and probably fairly traditional economic education, not an economist. Finally, the fact that Vorrink and Vliegen, both very important within the party, supported his position and that an economic expert of the weight of Dr. J. van den Tempel was opposed to devaluation, also contributed to the fact that he had little to fear from the pro-devaluation minority within the party.

The political parties had not really caused the Dutch government any great problems in its long struggle to maintain the gold standard. In the second chamber none of the spokesmen for the six largest parties had, even for a moment, advocated a devaluation of the guilder nor did any individual members break party discipline on this point. As has been shown, this did not mean that there were no proponents of devaluation among them nor that their number did not increase in the years and months before September 1936. However, it never came to the point where any of them openly criticised this one particular aspect of the government's monetary policy in the second chamber.

The explanation for the absence of such criticism, even on the part of individual members, lies partly in the phenomenon of the party discipline just mentioned. However, probably more important was the consideration that an open advocacy of devaluation on the part of one of the six major parties, or even a dissident splinter group of one of them, would be seen as a conscious political act which would undermine confidence in the guilder and make its devaluation in unpropitious circumstances ever more likely. This consideration clearly limited the freedom of action which the parties may have felt they had on this point. Finally, the point should be mentioned that many parties were fully and genuinely convinced that the government alone had the competence and the responsibility for determining policy on this difficult technical monetary question and should be left free to do so. This provides a further example of the generally observed division of powers between government and parliament in these years.

The freedom of expression which many members of the Second Chamber denied themselves was made use of by some members of the First Chamber: we have seen how individual members of the two largest parties (RKSP and SDAP) had come out openly in favour of devaluation. However, the First Chamber had considerably less political weight than the second. It was not the First Chamber but the Second which decided whether the government could find sufficient political support for its monetary policy. Dissident noises in the First Chamber could be relied upon having far less serious political or monetary consequences.

All of these considerations hold true to a greater or lesser degree for all the major parties. Nonetheless, there are a number of interesting differences in their respective positions. Before we briefly examine them again it is necessary once more to make the distinction between the five parties which supplied ministers for the Colijn cabinets on the one hand and the largest opposition party, the SDAP, on the other.

Without any shadow of a doubt, of the five coalition parties the ARP was the least inclined towards devaluation as a possible policy option: not a single statement in favour of devaluation was found which had been made by any of the prominent party members. It is true that the gold standard as such did not figure in the party's 'basic principles' but in its defence, use was made not only of social and juridic arguments but also of ethical and even biblical considerations.

The homogenity of ARP statements on this point can be partly explained by the absence of a large group of academically trained economists in its ranks and the large influence exercised by those it had, such as Nederbragt and even more importantly, Diepenhorst. However, more important would appear to be the dominant position of Colijn in 'his' ARP. Both as leader of the government, and as de facto leader of the party (a position which was readily accepted by Schouten who was the leader of the parliamentary party) his out-spoken anti-devaluationist opinions carried a great weight in the opinion forming within the ARP. Even so, there were limits even to his influence, as was illustrated on the *vaste lasten* question when Schouten and part of the parliamentary party had considered that too many concessions had been made to catholic sensitivities and they had voted against the government. But on the monetary question the ARP was undivided right to the end.

In all the four other 'government' parties were to be found both adherents and opponents to the gold standard. This applied least of all to the CHU, where pro-devaluationists were confined to F. de Vries, in the period late 1933/early 1934, and Lieftinck from April 1936. The absence of any searching discussion within the party can be explained from the fact the gold standard was not seen as an issue of principle but as a policy option like any other. Another consideration is the dominant position of ex-prime minister, ex-minister of finance, De Geer. Weighing up the pros and cons, De Geer remained opposed to devaluation right up to September 1936, even though he openly admitted to circumstances under which such a step would be acceptable. Nowhere has any evidence been found that in determining this position, which was barely discussed in the party, De Geer bent to any particular influence and, given his character, it is highly unlikely that he did: in splendid sovereign isolation he came to his insights from which he was later never to be budged. It was these insights which largely determined the position of the CHU on the devaluation question.

For both the liberal parties an important motive for supporting the government in its monetary policy was the desire, after long periods in opposition, not to put at risk their newly won status as coalition parties. Of the two, the VDB was the more closely identified with the government's monetary policy – a position not unassociated with the fact that P.J. Oud, after Colijn, was seen as its chief architect. After the fall of Marchant in the early summer of 1935 Oud assumed the dominant position within the party. The VDB's position as a government party and the prominent position of Oud explain why until the summer of 1935 pro-devaluation noises remained sporadic. Thereafter, the discussion within the party increased in intensity and the parliamentary party became deeply divided. However, this division was never brought into the open and again the much valued position of government party seems to have played a decisive role. Thus, despite the growing doubts within the party about the correctness of government policy, the cabinet faced no opposition from the side of the VDB.

The development within the other liberal party, the LSP, forms a noticeable contrast with the VDB in the sense that doubts about monetary policy were expressed very early on, whilst in the later period the discussion died away altogether. These doubts came from the economics professors in the party, especially those teaching in Rotterdam (N.J. Polak, G.M. Verrijn-Stuart). But, since none of these occupied top functions within the party, their political importance should not be overestimated. It was a completely different kettle of fish, however, with the pro-devaluationist member of parliament, H.D. Louwes, and the ambivalent position of the party leader, S.E.B. Bierema. It was their pronouncements in particular which prompted the executive to intervene towards the end of 1933. The upshot was that all discussion was virtually squashed although Louwes continued his activities outside the party. Within parliament, however, LSP spokesmen voiced no criticism of government monetary policy. The executive, thus, had achieved their goal – not to endanger their position as a government party and to prevent an open split within party ranks. The pro-devaluationists did not have sufficient political muscle to succesfully challenge the leadership on this point.

From the first, the RKSP was the most critical of the 'government' parties of cabinet policy but it is noticable that this never took the form of an outright condemnation of monetary policy. It is true that the RKSP was increasingly dissatisfied with other aspects of social and economic policy which culminated in Aalberse's speech in July 1935. When on that occasion he confronted the government with the choice between 'consistent' deflation and devaluation, he had not intended them to be seen, he explained in September 1935, as equal alternatives. On the contrary, he had wanted to make clear that if the cabinet refused to choose in favour of 'consistent' deflation, devaluation was the inevitable consequence.

How can we explain why Aalberse, neither on this occasion or later, made a frontal assault on the government's monetary policy even though the RKSP, unlike the liberal parties, felt no compunction to maintain faith with 'its own' cabinet? In the first place we have to mention the division within the RKSP itself. Although virtually everyone could line up behind a vague slogan like 'consistent' deflation, opponents and proponents of devaluation found themselves in a direct confrontation. It is true that the pro-devaluation camp increased in size over the years and embraced ever more prominent members (Steenberghe, the coming man Goseling, and ex-minister Verschuur) but Aalberse remained opposed right to the end. Even after his departure as leader of the parliamentary party, the anti-devaluationists apparently remained sufficiently strong to prevent a change in course. Another possibility is that the debacle of the Summer of 1935 made the party wary of risking another open confrontation with the government and thus of making any pro-devaluation noises. In any event the internal division within the RKSP, combined with a lack of daring to enter alone into a coalition with the SDAP, meant that the government was not confronted with any opposition from the RKSP in its monetary policy.

If an alternative to the gold standard policy of Colijn cabinets was to have been possible it would have required that the SDAP at least, as the largest opposition party, had chosen in favour of another monetary course. That it did not, meant that the cabinet faced no real danger on this point. This appeared more clearly during the cabinet crisis in the summer of 1935. What could have been more natural than that the RKSP and SDAP had found each other in an alternative cabinet programme which included a devaluation of the guilder. But although both parties included prominent proponents of a devaluation (in the SDAP one thinks of Drees and the NVV leaders Kupers and De la Bella) in the negotiations to form a new cabinet both were represented by opponents – Aalberse himself and Albarda. Add to that that both the other eventual coalition partners (CHU, VDB) were openly anti-devaluationist and it becomes clear that even had Aalberse succeeded in forming a new cabinet, it would not necessarily have countenanced devaluation. Unless that is, that devaluation had come about as a result of the speculation against the guilder. Albarda seems to have been banking on this.

Why did the socialist opposition party offer no opposition on monetary policy? Firstly, an important factor was that many prominent SDAP members, including Albarda, were not convinced about the positive effects of devaluation. Secondly, party-political considerations appear to have played a role. In general terms there was an awareness within the SDAP, as within the other parties, that open propaganda against the guilder would possibly provoke capital flight and would be seen as irresponsible (even, possibly, by its own supporters) but, more specifically taking, such a stance would widen the gulf between itself and the other political parties at the very time when its policy was aimed at closing it. Finally, it has to be noted that the choice for an alternative monetary policy would have been an act of daring and courage, neither of which qualities could be said to have characterised Albarda's political leadership. The alternative which the SDAP was to offer lay not in the monetary area but in the *Plan van de Arbeid.*

Notes

1. G. Puchinger, *Colijn en het einde van de Coalitie. II. De geschiedenis van de kabinetsformaties 1925-1929*, Kampen, 1980, 841.
2. P.J. Oud, *Het jongste verleden. Parlementaire geschiedenis van Nederland 1918-1940*, Vol.V, 1933-1937, Assen, 1950, 37.
3. Joh. de Vries, *Herinneringen en dagboek van Ernst Heldring (1871-1954)*, Groningen, 1970, 1129-1130.
4. A. Kuyper, *Ons Program*, with appendices, Amsterdam, 1879.
5. The subject of the gold standard is also entirely missing from the explanatory notes of H. de Wilde, *De Anti-revolutionaire Partij en haar Program van Beginselen*, Wageningen, 1903[2] and P.A. Diepenhorst, *Ons isolement, Practische toelichting van het program van beginselen der anti-revolutionaire partij*, Kampen, 1935.
6. H. Colijn, *Saevis tranquillus in undis. Toelichting op het anti-revolutionaire beginselprogram*, Amsterdam, 1934, par. 5, Geldbederf, 276-281. This paragraph was first published in *De Standaard*, 16.4.1932.
7. H. Colijn, *Saevis*, 277.
8. J.A. Nederbragt, *Korte lessen in staatsrecht en economie*, 2nd supplementary series, 's-Gravenhage, 1915, 284; J.A. Nederbragt, *Proeve eener theorie der economie naar christelijke belijdenis*, 's-Gravenhage, 1921, 247.
9. *Biografisch Woordenboek van Nederland*, 's-Gravenhage, 1979, 141-142.
10. P.A. Diepenhorst, *Grondbeginselen der Economie*, Zutphen, 1934[5], 231-234.
11. H. Colijn, *Saevis*, Article XIX *Program van beginselen*, 586-587.
12. P.A. Diepenhorst, *Stemmen des tijds, Maandschrift voor Christendom en cultuur*, Vol.23, No.1 (1934), 184-185.
13. Cited in *Cijfers en Feiten. Gids voor het politieke en sociale leven*, Vol.13, No.11, August 1933, 335.
14. *Ibid.*, Vol.5, No.9, June 1925, 261-262.
15. *Ibid.*, Vol.12, No.2, November 1931, 38. According to the christian-social periodical *Patrimonium*, 15.10.1931.
16. *Ibid.*, Vol.14, No.3, December 1933, 79-80; *De Standaard*, 21.11.1933.
17. *Ibid.*, Vol.16, No.8, May 1936, 227; *Nieuwe Provinciale Groninger Courant*, 2.4.1936.
18. *Ibid.*, Vol.15, No.1, October 1936, 20; *Patrimonium* 13.9.1934.
19. *Ibid.*, Vol.15, No.9, June 1935, 259; *De Maasbode*. As an exception *Cijfers en Feiten* took a quotation here from a roman-catholic paper.
20. Dr.J. Schouten, 1883-1963, became a member of the gemeenteraad, Rotterdam in 1916 and between 1922 and 1925 he was in charge of finance. From 1918-1956 he was AR party member of the second chamber and from 1945 party leader.
21. Oud, *Het jongste verleden*, Vol.IV, 1949, 150, 142.
22. *Handelingen Tweede Kamer* (HTK), 1931-1932, 124, 16.10.1931.
23. HTK, 1933-1934, 123, 6.11.1934. For the international economic and political activities of H. Colijn see also: G.J. van Roon, *Kleine landen in crisistijd. Van Oslostaten tot Benelux, 1930-1940*, Amsterdam/Brussel, 1985.
24. HTK, 1933-1934, 219, 7.11.1933.
25. HTK, 1934-1935, 193, 6.11.1934.
26. Documentatie Centrum voor het Nederlands Protestantisme, Vrije Universiteit, Archief A.R.-partij, A.R. kamerclubnotulen, 3.11.1934, 7.5.1935 and 10.7.1935.

27. HTK, 1935-1916, 2058, 9.6.1936.
28. H. Colijn, *De Financiën van het Rijk*, speech 1924.
29. H. Colijn, De economische toestand van Nederland, speech for Boaz, 4.3.1924, Amsterdam. Published by *De Standaard*, 13, 18.
30. HTK, 1931-1932, 304-305, 5.11.1933. Colijn also mentions here the striving towards a steady balance of payments as a means against inflation.
31. H. Colijn, *Wat kunnen wij doen en wat moeten wij laten om onze ingezonken volkswelvaart te verhogen?* Report of a speech for the Grote Club and the Industriele Club, Amsterdam, 26.1.1935, 14.
32. HTK, 1931-1934, 284, 10.11.1933. *Handelingen Eerste Kamer* (HEK) 1933-1934, 203, 8.2.1934.
33. Colijn, *Saevis*, 279.
34. HTK, 1931-1932, 2132-2136, 2151-2152, 20.4.1932.
35. HTK, 1934-1935, 2188, 2195, 2245, 19.7.1935.
36. HTK, 1935-1936, 26, 74 et seq., 95, 24.9.1934.
37. HEK, 1923-1924, 393 et seq., 30.4.1924.
38. HTK, 1933-1934, 284, 10.11.1933.
39. Speech, 13.4.1922 in *Geen vergeefs woord. Verzamelde Deputaten Redevoeringen*, Kampen, 1951, 252.
40. *Geen vergeefs woord*, 296. Speech 9.4.1931.
41. Oud, *Het jongste verleden*, Vol.IV, 179-185.
42. Algemene Rijksarchief (ARA), Archief H.W. Tilanus, inv. no. 133, minutes of fractie vergadering, 28.4.1933.
43. HTK, 1934-1935, 153, 7.11.1934.
44. HTK, 1934-1935, 154, 7.11.1934.
45. HTK, 1934-1935, 229, 9.11.1934.
46. ARA, Archief H.W. Tilanus, minutes of fractievergadering, 15.5.1935.
47. HTK, 1934-1935, 2128, 17.7.1935.
48. HTK, 1935-1936, 53-54, 26.9.1935.
49. HTK, 1935-1936, 64, 26.9.1935.
50. HTK, 1935-1936, 79, 27.9.1935.
51. HTK, 1935-1936, 82, 27.9.1935.
52. HTK, 1936-1937, 53, 30.9.1936.
53. ARA, Archief H.W. Tilanus, minutes of fractie vergadering, 2.10.1936.
54. Oud, *Het jongste verleden*, Vol.V, 326-327.
55. HTK, 1936-1937, 309, 11.11.1936.
56. HEK, 1934-1935, 145, 6.2.1935.
57. HTK, 1934-1935, 152, 7.11.1934.
58. HEK, 1934-1935, 145, 6.2.1935.
59. *Christelijk-Historische Unie. Jaarboekje*, 1937, 5-6.
60. J. Wieten, De relatie tussen het dagblad De Nederlander en de Christelijk-Historische Unie, *Christelijk-Historisch Tijdschrift*, Vol. 25, No. 5/6 (1980) 129-131. I would like to thank de heer Wieten for some details he supplied for the writing of this article.
61. S. van der Zee, *De Gouden Hoek van Buchenwald. Gesprekken met oud-gevangenen*, Alphen a/d Rijn, 1982, 77-78.
62. Aanpassing, *De Nederlander*, 26-10-1934 .
63. *De Nederlander*, 20.7.1935.
64. GAR, Archief G.E. van Walsum, inv. no. 176, P. Lieftinck to G.E. van Walsum, 21.7.1935.
65. *De Nederlander*, 20.7.1935.
66. Mr. Steenberghe spreekt, *Ibid.*, 21.6.1935.
67. GAR, Archief G.E. van Walsum, inv. no. 177, P. Lieftinck to the Commissie van Hoofdredactie of the *De Nederlander*, 3.4.1936. J. van Bruggen, De Christelijke-Historische Unie voor de oorlog, *Christelijk-Historisch Tijdschrift* Vol. 23, No. 2/3 (1978) 42, stated that the striving of Colijn to maintain the gold standard had the support of the Editorship of *De Nederlander*, to which at this time he belonged himself. Since at the same time he pointed to the great value that the editor of economic affairs attached to the judgement of Lieftinck (p. 41) it must be

assumed that this comment refers to the period before April 1936 and that in the writing of this article Van Bruggen had forgotten about Lieftinck's change in stance.

68. Laissez faire?, *De Nederlander*, 5.6.1936.
69. Internationale aanpassing van den gulden, *Ibid.*, 28.9.1936.
70. Kort overzicht van de jongste gebeurtenissen, *Ibidem.* 2.10.1936.
71. *De Vrijzinnig-Democraat*, 5.12.1931.
72. O. Vries, De Vrijzinnig-Democratische Bond als factor in de Nederlandse politiek (1917-1933), *Bijdragen en Mededelingen betreffende de Geschiedenis der Nederlanden*, Vol. LXXXVIII, 1973, 466.
73. H.J.L. Vonhoff, *Bewegend verleden. Een biografische visie op prof. mr. P.J. Oud*, Alphen a/d Rijn, 1969, 53.
74. *De Vrijzinnig-Democraat*, 19.4.1933.
75. *Ibid.*, 19.8.1933.
76. *Ibid.*, 2.12.1933.
77. *Ibid.*, 31.3.1934.
78. *Ibid.*, 31.3.1934.
79. Oud, *Het jongste verleden*, Vol.V, 140.
80. *De Vrijzinnig-Democraat*, 3.11.1934, 10.11.1934.
81. *Ibid.*, 1.12.1934.
82. ARA, Archief mr. H.P. Marchant, no. 283, margin comments on a note from P.J. Oud.
83. *Ibid.*, no. 413, *De devaluatie*, no date.
84. *De Vrijzinnig-Democraat*, 27.4.1935.
85. Studie- en Documentatiecentrum Nederlandse politieke partijen (SDNP), Rijks Universiteit Groningen, Archief J. Schilthuis, no. 3, minutes of fractievergadering 15.5.1935.
86. *Entente internationale des partis radicaux et des partis democratiques similaires* established 18.10.1924 in Boulogne sur Mer (France).
87. *De Vrijzinnig-Democraat*, 10.8.1935.
88. *Ibid.*, 17.8.1935.
89. SDNP, Archief Schilthuis, no. 3, minutes of party meeting 23.9.1935.
90. Gemeentearchief Amsterdam, Archief D. van Embden, not inventarised, *Rapport betreffende middelen, welke tot verruiming van de werkgelegenheid kunnen leiden.*
91. *De Vrijzinnig-Democraat*, 30.11.1935.
92. *Ibid.*, 18.4.1936.
93. *Ibid.*, 10.10.1936.
94. *Ibid.*, 3.10.1936.
95. *Ibid.*, 3.10.1936.
96. SDNP, Archief J. Schilthuis, no. 3, minutes of fractievergadering 29.9.1936.
97. Weekly organ of the Amsterdam section of the LSP.
98. *Het Liberale Weekblad*, 24.5.1933, 7.
99. *Ibid.*, 26.6.1933, 5.
100. *Ibid.*, 28.6.1933, 6.
101. *De Vrijheid*. Political weekly organ containing the official announcements of the LSP.
102. *De Vrijheid*, 19.9.1933, 3.
103. *Algemeen Nederlandsch Landbouwblad*, 7.12.1933, 1.
104. HTK, 1933-1934, 277, 8.11.1933.
105. *Het Liberale Weekblad*, 21.11.1933, 2.
106. *Ibidem.*
107. SDNP, VVD-collectie, no. 9, minutes of LSP hoofdbestuur, 9.12.1933.
108. *Ibidem.*
109. *Het Liberale Weekblad*, 20.12.1933, 6.
110. SDNP, VVD-collectie, minutes of LSP hoofdbestuur, 27.1.1934.
111. *Ibid.*, Minutes of LSP hoofdbestuur, 24.2.1934.
112. In the years 1934-35 *Het Liberale Weekblad* no longer directly referred to the devaluation question, *De Vrijheid* only occasionally.

113. Rijks Archief Groningen (RAG), archief H.D. Louwes, inv. no. 24, Introduction General Meeting K.N.L.C., October 1934.
114. *Ibid.*, Speech to the Groninger Boerenstand, Groningen, 18.6.1935, and a speech in Purmerend, 27.11.1935.
115. Oud, *Jongste Verleden*, Vol.V, 146.
116. *Ibid.*, 217.
117. De Vries, *Herinneringen en dagboek*, 1142.
118. HTK, 1935-1936, 328-330.
119. ARA, VVD archief, map 90, Copy of an address to the hoofdbestuur and the kamerfracties, 1.9.1934.
120. Universiteitsbibliotheek Utrecht, Archief P.H. Ritter, Letter from the Centrale Kiesvereniging Rijkskieskring, Utrecht, to the hoofdbestuur of the LSP.
121. *Het Liberale Weekblad*, 2.10.1936; *De Vrijheid*, 1.10.1936, 7.10.1936.
122. RAG, Archief Louwes, Speech given by H.D. Louwes to the General Meeting of the Drentsch Landbouwgenootschap, Assen, 28.11.1936.
123. Katholiek Documentatie Centrum, Nijmegen (KDC), Archief RKSP, (ARKSP) box III, minutes of the Partijraad, 24.5.1930, speech Mgr. W.H. Nolen; ARKSP, XI,1.0: H.Poels *De Moderne Wereld*, February 1931, 73-74.
124. E. Janssen, De Rooms-Katholieke Staatspartij en de krisis, 1930-1940, *Archief voor de geschiedenis van de Katholieke kerk in Nederland*, Vol.18, No.1 (1976) 53.
125. H. Hoefnagels s.j., *Een eeuw sociale problematiek. Van sociaal conflict naar strategische samenwerking*, Assen, 1957, 264.
126. C.H. Raaymakers s.j., *Economie en ethiek. Rede uitgesproken ter gelegenheid van de tweede dies natalis der R.K. Universiteit 31.5.1926*, Utrecht/Nijmegen, 1926, 17.
127. Oud, *Het jongste verleden*, Vol.IV, 143.
128. *Ibid.*, 156-157.
129. KDC, Archief Aalberse, file 369 g, *Nota inzake het economische regeringsbeleid.*
130. *Ibid.*, file 369 i, *Stellingen van A.J. Loerakker, 20.5.1932*, and *Stellingen van Max van Poll.*
131. *De R.K. Staatspartij*, Vol.I, No.11, 121.; H. van Hulst, A. Pleysier, A. Scheffer, *Het roode vaandel volgen wij*, 's-Gravenhage, 1969, 189.
132. KDC, Archief Aalberse, map 309, *Sociaal-ekonomisch urgentieprogram* 15.7.1933. *De R.K. Staatspartij*, Vol.II, No.8, 168-169.
133. KDC, Archief RKSP, box XV, inv. no. 136, minutes of the R.K. Kamerclub, 12.10.1933. F.J.M. Duynstee, De Katholieke Tweede Kamerfraktie na 1918 uit haar notulen, *Opstellen over recht en rechtsgeschiedenis, aangeboden aan prof. mr. B.H.D. Hermesdorf*, Deventer, 1965, 122.
134. Oud, *Het Jongste Verleden*, Vol.V, 130.
135. H.M. Hirschfeld, *Herinneringen uit de jaren 1933-1939*. Amsterdam/Brussel, 1959, 36.
136. *De R.K. Werkgever*, Vol.XII, No.18, 216 (prof.Kaag at the industrialisatiecongres, 1.3.1935); *De R.K. Staatspartij*, Vol.IV, No.6, 131-132.
137. Oud, *Het Jongste Verleden*, Vol.V, 134.
138. *De R.K. Staatspartij*, Vol.IV, No.6, 131-133.
139. KDC, Archief RKSP, box XV, inv. no. 137, minutes of the R.K. Kamerclub, 18.6.1935.
140. *Het Vaderland*, 18.6.1935. Summary of the afternoon and evening meetings of the second chamber, 17.7.1935, *Nieuwe Rotterdamsche Courant*, 18.7.1935.
141. HTK, 1934-1935, 2130-2136; Op verkenning uit, *De Volkskrant*, 18.7.1935.
142. Er is niets veranderd, *De Volkskrant*, 20.7.1935; De rollen omgekeerd, *NRC*, 20.7.1935.
143. HTK, 1934-1935, 2235; *De R.K. Staatspartij*, Vol.IV, No.8, 178.
144. Steenberghe triomfeert, *Dagblad van Noord-Brabant*, 25.7.1935.
145. *Ibidem.*
146. In een nationaal kabinet moet er plaats zijn voor sociaal-demokraten, *Limburgsche Koerier*, 25.7.1935.
147. *De R.K. Staatspartij*, Vol.IV, No.8, 177; *De Standaard*, 24.7.1935; *De Maasbode*, 25.7.1935; *De Nederlander*, 26.7.1935; *De Groene Amsterdammer*, 31.8.1935.

148. Een tweede kabinet Colijn? Eindelijke het roer om?, *De Tijd*, 30.7.1935; *De Volkskrant*, 29.7.1935; *De Maasbode* 30.7.1935.
149. Colijn geslaagd?, *De Maasbode*, 31.7.1935; Een nieuwe kabinet Colijn, *Het Vaderland*, 31.7.1935.
150. Een oplossing?, *De Morgen*, 1.8.1935; *De Tijd*, 6.8.1935; *De Groene Amsterdammer*, 17.8.1935.
151. *Maandschrift Economie*, Vol.I, No.1, (1935) 3.
152. *Ibid.*, Vol.I, No.3, 175.
153. KDC, Archief RKSP, box I, inv. no. 23, minutes of the Partijbestuur, 15-16.11.1935.
154. *Ibid.*, box VI, 7.1, inv. no. 75, *Aanschrijvingen van het Partijbestuur van 19.11.1935 aan de Kringbesturen*.
155. *Ibid.*, box I, inv. no. 23, minutes of the Partijbestuur, 24.1.1936.
156. *Ibid.*, box VI, 7.1, inv. no. 75, Notes written on jotting paper by Aalberse. *Ibid.*, box 1, inv. no. 23, minutes of the Partijbestuur, 24.1.1936.
157. *De R.K. Staatspartij*, Vol. V, No 2, 28.
158. KDC, Archief RKSP, box VI, inv. no. 76, speeches from the Landdag.
159. *Ibid.*, box VI, 7.0, inv. no. 76, Steenberghe to Goseling 10.1.1936.
160. *Ibid.*, box VI, inv. no. 76, speeches from the Landdag.
161. *Ibid.*, box XV, inv. no. 137, minutes of the R.K. Kamerclub, 11.3.1936. *Ibid.*, box II, minutes of the dagelijks bestuur, 9.5.1936.
162. Geen tijd te verliezen; Landdag der R.K. Staatspartij, *Volkskrant* 3.2.1936. Het effect van de Landdag, *Dagblad van Noord-Brabant* 5.2.1936.
163. KDC, Archief RKSP, box I, inv. no. 23, minutes of the Partijbestuur, 23.5.1936.
164. *Ibid.*, box XV, inv. no. 137, minutes of the R.K. Kamerclub, 5/11.3.1936. *Ibid.*, box VI, 7.1, inv. no. 75, notes written by Aalberse on jotting paper. Heerschouw, *De Tijd*, 11.2.1936 (evening paper). J.P. Gribling, *P.J.M. Aalberse, 1871-1948*, Utrecht, 1961, 430.
165. *Ibid.*, box VI, 7.1, inv. no. 75, notes by written by Aalberse on jotting paper.
166. Fijne manieren, *Eindhovensche en Meierijsche Courant*, 10.3.1936.
167. Gribling, *P.J.M. Aalberse*, 484.
168. KDC, Archief RKSP, box XV, inv. no. 138, minutes of the R.K. Kamerclub, 7.5.1936.
169. *Ibid.*, minutes of the R.K. Kamerclub, 22.5.1936. Het Vaste Lasten ontwerp, *R.K. Staatspartij*, Vol.V, No.3, 60. Op afbetaling?, *Ibid.*, Vol.V, No.6, 138.
170. *De R.K. Staatspartij*, Vol. V, No. 6, 6-7.
171 HTK, 1936-1937, 45-47; extra-number *De R.K. Staatspartij*, Vol.V, 2-8; KDC, Archief RKSP, box XV, inv. no. 138, minutes of the R.K. Kamerclub, 29.9.1936.
172 Extra-number *De R.K. Staatspartij*, Vol.V, 2-8, speech Goseling in the second chamber, 30.9.1936.
173. HTK, 1934-1935, 126, 6.11.1934.
174. See the letter from Albarda to the secretary of the SDAP, 19.5.1934. In this Albarda mentioned his impression "that recently in *Het Volk* more or less systematic propoganda has been made for 'devaluation' of the guilder" and concluded: "I find this not unthinkable. In this way, whether intentionally or not, a mood is nursed. Our party thus gets to carry the responsibility for an eventual devaluation without having decided to take on the responsibility in such a manner." Internationaal Instituut voor Sociale Geschiedenis (IISG), archief SDAP, 97, minutes of the Partijbestuur, 2.6.1934.
175. IISG, Archief SDAP 205, minutes of the Dagelijks Bestuur with diverse delegation, 7.3.1933. *Ibid.*, 3090, 88. cf. on the attitude of the commission also the minutes of the meeting of the Partijbestuur, 1.4.1933.
176. HTK, 1933-1934, 198, 7.11.1933. Albarda said the following: "If we ensure a sound financial policy, then there is no need to fear a catastrophic collapse of the currency. This does not mean that I do not think that the question of a managed devaluation does not deserve serious attention. In may opinion this question cannot be resolved satisfactorily by stating the dogma of the gold standard, as I think the government does too often. The acceptance of a limited devaluation is not in conflict with the gold standard system." To avoid any misunderstanding he immediately added: "Mark my words carefully, I am not advocating such a devaluation...." There then followed the demand for a better defence by the government of its own policies.

177. *Ibid.*, 283, 10.11.1933.
178. *Ibid.*, 198, 7.11.1933.
179. The other opponents of devaluation in the financial commission were: Mr. Dr. J. van den Bergh; Mr. J. Gerritsz; J. Oudegeest; G.J.A. Smit Jr; Dr. J van den Tempel; W.H. Vliegen; Dr. Ir. Th. van der Waerden; Dr. F.M. Wibaut. Those abstaining were: Z. Gulden Jr; Dr. K. Mendelsohn; Mr. S. Mok; Drs. W. Winbelt. Because of illness E. Kupers was not present at this meeting. IISG, F.M. Wibaut papers, 217 (with thanks to Rob Hartmans).
180. IISG, Archief SDAP, 97, meeting of partijbestuur 2.6.1934.
181. *Ibid.*, 1841. The letter was read out during a meeting of the Dagelijks Bestuur van de Algemene Raad, 6.9.1934.
182. *Devaluatie pro en contra. Rapporten uitgegeven in opdracht van de Algemene Raad uit NVV en SDAP*, Amsterdam 1935. Typically, the preface expressely stated that the decision to publish had been taken "in the first place in order to provide the modern labour movement with information", 3.
183. IISG, Archief SDAP, 101.
184. HTK, 1934-1935, 2106-2111, 17.7.1935; HTK, 1935-1936, 216-222, 7.11.1935, 293-298, 12.11.1935.
185. HEK, 1934-1935, 189, 7.2.1935.
186. IISG, Archief SDAP, 97.
187. IISG, Archive SDAP, 99, 101. See the meeting of the Partijbestuur of 6.10.1934 and 8.4.1935.
188. IISG, Archief SDAP, 101, 8.4.1935.
189. IISG, Archief SDAP, 211.
190. IISG, Archief SDAP 97, Partijbestuur, 2.6.1934. Drees expected no magic from a devaluation and wanted to see devaluation coupled with large-scale public works schemes to relieve unemployment. (De aanpassingspolitiek der regeering *De Sociaal-Democraat*, 23.6.1934). See also his lecture of May 1934, in *Devaluatie. Verslag van de vergadering van hoofdbesturen der bij het NVV aangesloten organisaties op 29/30.5.1934* Amsterdam 1934, 2-19, 44-49, and his article of early 1936, Devaluatie en economisch herstel in Nederland, in *De Socialistische Gids*, Vol.21, No.2 (1936) 81-95.
191. See especially Vliegen's statement in the second chamber, in HTK, 248, 13.11.1934, where he stated that he had resisted devaluation "with all power" within his own circle. This is not clear from the available internal articles.
192. See above, note 174.
193. IISG, Archief SDAP, 97, Partijbestuur, 2.6.1934.
194. IISG, Archief SDAP, 1841.
195. IISG, Archief SDAP, 3091.
196. HTK, 1934-1935, 131, 6.11.1934. In his second chamber speech Albarda demanded also on behalf of the SDAP "a positive step towards the lowering of *vaste lasten*". But it does not seem that they were truly enthusiastic.
197. IISG, Archief SDAP, 3091, Minutes of meeting of the SDAP-kamerfracties 29.7.1935.
198. IISG, Archief SDAP, 3091.
199. HTK, 1935-1936, 46, 25.9.1935.
200. HTK, 1936-1937, 41, 30.9.1936. See also *De Socialistische Gids*, Vol.21, No.10 (1936) 612 et seq.
201. For the changes in the SDAP in the 1930's see H.F. Cohen, Democratische socialisme in de jaren '30, P.W. Klein,G.B. Borger (eds.), *De jaren dertig. Aspecten van crisis en werkloosheid*, Amsterdam, 1979, 248-253; H. Verwey-Jonker, De ideologie van de SDAP 1930-1940, Jan Bank, Stef Temming (eds.), *Van brede visie tot smalle marge*, Alphen aan de Rijn, 1983, 13-30; Johan S. Wijne, Op weg naar de Partij van de Arbeid. Het beginselprogram van de SDAP van 1937 en het streven naar een democratisch-socialistische volkspartij, *Het vierde jaarboek van het democratisch socialisme*, Amsterdam, 1983, 148-175.
202. For the Plan van de Arbeid see especially John Jansen van Galen, Jan Nekkers, Dick Pels, J.P. Pronk, *Het Moet, het kan! Op voor het Plan! Vijfig jaar Plan van de Arbeid*, Amsterdam, 1985.
203 IISG, Archief SDAP, 97,99, Partijbestuur, 2.6.1934 and 6.10.1934.
204. IISG, Archief SDAP, 99, Partijbestuur, 6.10.1934.
205. L. de Jong, *Het Koninkrijk der Nederlanden in de Tweede Wereldoorlog*, Vol. 1, 's-Gravenhage, 1969, 691. In *Ibid.*, Vol.9, 1445, he speeks of "the eternal waverer Albarda".

CHAPTER SEVEN *

The Single Issue Pressure Groups

The unwillingness of established interest groups and political parties to throw their weight behind the pro-devaluationist cause was bound, sooner or later, to force opponents of the gold standard to seek alternative ways of translating their feelings into political pressure. Thus, the existence of such a group should in itself be no surprise. The timing of its formation, however, in the middle of 1933 is worthy of comment. Looked at one way, its formation could be considered as coming late in the day since more than a year and a half had elapsed since the devaluation of sterling had knocked away one of the last props of Dutch prosperity. This time lapse helps to illustrate the impact of events in the Spring of 1933, particularly the devaluation of the dollar and the collapse of the World Economic conference in London, in changing the attitudes among a small but important cross-section of informed opinion in the Netherlands. It also demonstrates that any possible counter-factual model which presupposes an earlier devaluation of the guilder would be fundamentally a-historic in this aspect. On the other hand, working from the assumption that devaluation was not really considered as a policy option until early 1933, the formation of such a group could be considered early. The numbing effects of the heterogeneity within interest groups and the impact of government responsibility on the attitudes of political parties had yet fully to reveal themselves in the context of the decision-making process concerning the gold standard. In this respect the change in government and the hope that the new cabinet might consider a change in policy would seem to have been decisive factors.

There was less reason to expect those opposed to devaluation to bother to form any group at all. The standpoint of the government was precisely what they wanted as far as the desirability of maintaining the gold standard was concerned and the established forums of organised political pressure acquiesced, at least in public, in that decision. The fact that such a group was formed stemmed purely and simply from the transformation of the pro-devaluationists from a private, informal lobby into a public, organised pressure group towards the end of 1934.

This chapter attempts to trace the development of both groups and the tactics they employed from the very partial archive sources which have survived.

* Dr. Schoorl was responsible for the sections dealing with the pro-devaluation lobby and professor Griffiths was responsible for the rest.

THE PRO-DEVALUATION COALITION

By the middle of 1934 (i.e. almost a year before the Belgian devaluation) many people were convinced that it would not be possible to maintain the gold standard much longer at its gold parity of just over 0.6 milligrammes to the guilder. Among those was the Amsterdammer A.F. Bronsing, a director of the Steamship Company 'Nederland'. He had made a bet predicting the imminent demise of the guilder with the wife of one of his fellow directors, D.A. Delprat. When in August 1934 the gold guilder still stood unbowed, he had to admit defeat and sent her a strongbox filled with chocolate "golden coins" and a four couplet poem in which, despite his loss, he stood by his prediction that the guilder would fall (of which the concluding lines are quoted below).

Some day, when specie's price will rise
More than remembered, oh what prize!
That we have erred, we recognize.
New life to guilder's strength and size.
how WISE.
(A.F. Bronsing, 1934)(1)

Bronsing was a prominent representative of a sector of the economy whose international competitiveness had been particularly handicapped by an overvalued guilder. But in other sectors of industry and trade too, as well as in the economic *hogescholen* and economics faculties, more and more doubts were being voiced about the reliability and efficiency of the gold standard.(2)

Towards the end of June 1933 some of these groups and individuals came together. Bronsing's anger had been raised by two editorials in the liberal daily *De Telegraaf*, denouncing the ideas of Sir Henry Deterding (see pp 35-36), under the headings 'A plea for inflation' and 'Colijn or Deterding? Deterding at the head of the inflationists'. On 26 and 29 June his own two letters to the editor were published and for the next two days his letterbox was overflowing with reactions. Among these there was a letter from the Rotterdam economics professor F. de Vries, who, together with his colleague Nico J. Polak, sent a draft of the petition they were contemplating sending to the government. Their initiative was aimed at representatives of the academic and business communities.

The reactions of a number of rather well known professors were negative: H.W.C. Bordewijk, W.A. Bonger, P.A. Diepenhorst, D. van Embden, H. Frijda and W.C. Mees. Perhaps surprisingly they were joined by the director of the Rotterdam shipping company *Philippus van Ommeren*, W.H. de Monchy, and by the president of the General Association of Bulb Growers, Krelage. The telegram from the Amsterdam professor of business economics, Limperg, was rather amusing: "Returning from abroad find circulating letter exchange medium stop consider mailing dangerous stop new unrest is awakened stop concept arguments are weapon in hands of devaluationists stop have otherwise opinion that in these days nothing should happen without consulting Nederlandsche Bank = Limperg." Had he misunderstood the intention of the authors? Or had they somewhat veiled their intentions, in seeking the broadest possible support?

At any rate, twenty eight prominent adherents signed an address to the prime minister on 19 July. Most came from the business community but there were also 8 professors and 2 politicians.(3) The five page address was balanced and analytical in tone. Of course this was to be expected in an initiative stemming from the academic community, behind which a mixed group of adherents had rallied. In the light of subsequent events, however, its judgement cannot be denied a certain predictive value. Three alternative economic policies were sketched out: a straight forward maintenance of the gold standard, an immediate, managed devaluation and an unmanageable depreciation in the future.

In theory, the first policy option could be realised through a combination of measures of external protectionism and internal support. But the financing of the support would lead to either unbearable extra taxation or to equally unbearable pressure on the budget, making this policy mix unworkable in practice. The only possibility left open was a combination of expenditure cuts and forced price reductions on a scale unheard of in the Netherlands. To implement such a policy the government would have to extend its controls "to wage regulations, obligations from current loans, profit margins of producers and retailers, rents of houses and shops, as well as life insurance, pensions and savings banks obligations, etc.".

The petition was careful to state that the second alternative of a managed and limited devaluation, was not supported unconditionally by all the undersigned. However, "they are all of the same opinion that given the able bank management and the healthy banking institutions enjoyed by the Netherlands a devaluation managed and controlled by the powerful government is in no way such a disaster for Dutch society as the press repeatedly wants us to believe". According to an (undisclosed) computation for a devaluation of 20 per cent, the cost of living would scarcely have to rise (this would partly be financed by the means no longer necessary for the support of business). On the other hand, there would be large gains for the competitiveness of export industries. The danger of foreign counter-measures was considered to be very small.

The third alternative supposing an unmanaged devaluation or depreciation as the result of insufficient support for the guilder, was starkly sketched as a horrifying picture of shrinking national capital, shrinking productive capacity and loss of international markets.

In this form, the address was certainly a good example of tactical reasoning. It was not an unambiguous plea for lowering the guilder's gold parity since it left open the possibility, in principle, of maintaining the exchange rate at the existing level. Its accent lay not on the impossibility of such a policy, but rather on its inconsistency. After all, the functioning of a gold standard presupposes a smoothly working price mechanism. Any interference with this mechanism was repellent to someone like Colijn. To quote a statement of his from this period:

"All day long, from early morning till sometimes two thirty at night, we do nothing but regulate (...) I wish I could limit that to one tenth".(4)

The conclusion of the address also contained a request for an audience with the government. Possibly its granting was helped by contacts between Trip of *De Nederlandsche Bank* and Ernst Heldring, Bronsing's neighbour in the *Scheepvaarthuis* (then the home of many shipping companies, now a monument of the Amsterdam School of brick architecture).(5) On 30 August Colijn, accompanied by his finance minister P.J. Oud and Trip, received four of the addressees: the Rotterdam professors F. de Vries and J. Goudriaan, Bronsing and the banker H.F. van Leeuwen.

Only a short summary of the two hours discussion is preserved in the papers of the NVWG. The government took seriously the arguments of the address but it stood by its adopted policy. Colijn's main economic argument was that not so much unbalanced exchange rates, but primarily the existing high tariff barriers were the causes of the economic problems. Next to, or rather above these considerations, ethical reasoning played an important role: devaluation is "debt forsaking", it is immoral.

According to Bronsing's memory, Colijn was practically the only spokesman on the side of the government and de Vries on the visitors' side. But in an interruption Bronsing introduced into the argument the threat of competition by cheap Japanese imports. Colijn objected that these were made by people going barefoot. Against this argument Bronsing claims to have asked: "Your excellency, do you mean as a minister that we should rather walk barefooted than leave the gold standard?". Colijn's concluding remarks are remembered by Bronsing as follows:

> "Gentlemen, I have heard your opinion, but what do you want? By reason of your arguments, you want us to take the responsibility for going off gold. Well the government will not do so. But if you continue your propaganda against the gold guilder and money is running – as he said literally – out of the country, then the government has no choice, it will turn off the tap and then we are off the gold guilder. Now you must know what you will do.
> And so we left him. And I found that very, very well spoken. I must say in that meeting it struck me that of the three men on the other side – the other two had hardly anything to say – Colijn was very well informed. But he had, so to speak, a certain heaviness of heart to take the responsibility for debt forsaking. And I can understand that, I can even respect that. And so we then left."

Both parties agreed to reconsider each other's arguments and with the government's promise of a second audience, they parted.

The government's policy remained unchanged. The economic situation did not improve. And the increasing frustration among the signatories of the address was canalised during the autumn through much 'confidential' correspondence with professor Polak. Moreover, the public debate grew more and more fierce. A cartoon by L. Raemaekers in *De Telegraaf* with the caption 'Inflation tosh' and depicting the colleagues J. Goudriaan and N.J. Polak as 'inflationists', provoked a furious letter to the editor from Goudriaan. He referred to various scientific publications by Polak, Verrijn Stuart and himself. To this the editorial response was: What is the use to the general public of professorial discussions about devaluation, appreciation, reflation, inflation, and deflation? A cartoonist has the right to sum this up as 'Inflation tosh'. You would do better to produce for us a more understandable terminology!(6)

In December the core of signatories of the July address started preparing a second. In a meeting of 16 December its line of argument was mapped out: an unambigious plea in favour of devaluation, with special reference to the economic problems of the Dutch East Indies, and an emphasis on the positive moral aspect of devaluation. On 5 January 1934 the second address, comprising 8 pages and a large appendix, was dispatched to the government by professor Polak.(7)

It started by referring to the audience with Colijn on 30 August 1933 and by pointing to the apparent willingness of the government to have a second discussion. The drafters by no means considered devaluation to be a panacea but saw it rather as a necessary precondition for economic recovery. This was elucidated on three points: a comparison between the recent economic development of the Netherlands and of other countries, the development anticipated should no devaluation occur and finally, an evaluation of the arguments against devaluation.

On the first point, the address pointed to the generally more favourable development of prices and of goods and shares, the better balance of imports and exports, and the much nicer employment figures in those countries which had already devalued. These statements were supported by the 42 page appendix, prepared by dr. J.G. Stridiron. (See pp 175-179 for a more detailed presentation of these arguments and their rebuttal by Trip and Verschuur).

On the second point, the address stressed the practical impossibility of drastically lowering wages and prices: "Then automatically the dualistic policy will be followed which is now being practised by the Dutch government: by lowering civil servants' salaries, by cutting employment benefits, by indirect pressure on the unions in protected industries it tries to bring about a lower cost level, but, simultaneously, by crisis levies and taxation measures it is driving up many prices." Here the old argument, presented in the first address, of inconsistency in the official policy can be recognised.

The second address ended by refuting a number of old and new arguments against devaluation. In the first place the moral argument was put forward. It was not devaluation which was morally objectionable but the enormous shift of fortunes between holders of guilder assets and liabilities which had resulted from government policy. The gross injustice of the increased real burden for debtors could best be relieved through 'mint correction'. (This is the first instance where I noted this word as a euphemism for the ominously charged notion of devaluation – E.S.)

As in the first address, it was stressed "that the monetary policy recommended by the undersigned does not at all have the aim of carrying our country upon the road of an uncontrolled inflation". The threat of counter-measures by other countries, mentioned but minimised before, was now linked to the expected price reduction not only of Dutch exports but those of the Dutch East Indies as well. It was now claimed that for countries with already depreciated currencies, these sectors which had benefitted from increased exports had more than outweighed those in which reductions had taken place as a result of increased trade barriers.

Equally, the possibility of repraisals had also been used as an argument against devaluation in the context of the capital market: the possible threat to the role of Amsterdam as an international financial centre and the risk of capital flight. Against the first it was argued that the interests of Amsterdam were scarcely served by an "overstressed currency". Against the second, that it would be easy to counteract capital movements by the immediate use of the revalued gold stock in as an equalisation fund.

The first address still left open the option of maintaining the gold standard through a policy of drastic cuts and lowering of prices. In the second, devaluation was advocated as a necessary precondition for any viable economic policy. Hesitant signatories of the first address had either defected or had been converted: all 24 addressees (20 old and 4 new names) were of one opinion. The most notable new members of the group were M.P.L. Steenberghe, the later minister of economic affairs, and the Tilburg professor E.G.J. Gimbrère.

The latter published his pamphlet 'The Netherlands' Monetary Policy' on 1 February 1934.(8) So it became clear that there was a public discussion going on in which the 'devaluationists' not only addressed themselves to the government but also to the Dutch people. And, in turn, they were subject to attacks and insinuations in the press. But their increased activity and homogeneity, though provoking study and refutation within the government, did not lead to a prolongation of the dialogue: a second audience never came.

Colijn's summary reactions upon Gimbrère were in line with his reasoning during the July audience. Where Gimbrère attributed the weakened Dutch competitiveness to the devaluation of the pound, he annotated: "The usual misunderstanding. Our exports are not too expensive but their outlet is made impossible by the quota system." And upon the increased export figures of the 'silver countries', Japan and China: "Not because of the currency, but because their growing development had made them into industrial nations." At Gimbrère's remark that "the striving for autarky is the defense against the gold attacks from abroad", he only wrote "Mis" (wide of the mark). Gimbrère's final sentence, concluding a passage about the high costs of protection, read as follows: "No, here it is indeed far from clear." Colijn's rejoinder was: "But very much darker if we abandon the guilder now, with a (floating) debt of hundreds of millions and a rate of interest much too high."(9)

THE DUTCH ASSOCIATION FOR VALUE STABLE MONEY (NVWG)

In spite of the piling of arguments on both sides, it soon became clear that no real dialogue could be carried on with the government. So, in February, the addressees had become convinced that they would have to turn their attention to the public at large since alone they would not be able to turn the government's policy one millimeter in their desired direction. They correctly supposed that the money question would hold public attention for a longer period so they pleaded the foundation of a "durable organisation". Yet the plans did not materialise until May and it was not until the middle of September that the organisers came out into the open with a public appeal for the foundation of a "Dutch Association for Value Stable Money, in the sense of money with stable purchasing power" on 20 October in Hotel Krasnapolsky in Amsterdam.(10)

From the 49 names under the appeal it is apparent that during the spring and summer months the movement had acquired broader support from the academic and business worlds and, to a lesser extent, from politics. When trying to classify the names by political colour one comes across many Roman Catholics, liberals and socialists, but hardly any protestants (whether CHU or ARP). So the letter from professor C.F. Gerretson, the (protestant) historian of Royal Dutch Shell, to the lawyer W.J.L. van Es as one of the organisers, was rather exceptional. Regarding the possibility of financial support from Sir Henry Deterding he wrote on 20 September: "A good relationship with Sir Henry is very desirable, if only from the financial point of view."(11) In the same letter he made a remark about "a certain contact commission", whose petition Deterding considered signing. This gives the impression that various groups were still active in combating the official monetary policy. Efforts to bring these together may also account for the long preparation period of the *Nederlandsche Vereeniging voor Waardevast Geld*, NVWG, (Dutch Association for Value Stable Money), from February to October 1934. It wanted to be neutral "not representing any political or religious persuasion" but, above all, once founded, it wanted to be respectable: "Nothing is farther from us than opposition against our Government as such."(12) But, before describing the NVWG's activities it might be useful to examine who took part and who did not.

The authors of the NVWG's founding appeal had considered "in normal times the foundation of an association of a purely academic character would have been preferable". But, under the existing circumstances they claimed the double objective of bringing home to the public the necessity of having money with stable purchasing power and of unifying, as far as possible, the many plans which had been constructed to that end. The names of the Association's proposed committee members were written on a piece of jotting paper by Polak, arranged first by the division of Social and Economic Group, and subsequently by the criterion of 'Political' Group (apparently not the same as political party).(13) This gave the following picture:

Social and Economic Group

Industry:	(name of J. Goudriaan crossed out) G.A. Kessler, D. Dresden – yet another person from a different branch of the metal working industry!
Agriculture:	M.P. van der Weyden, H.D. Louwes.
'Intelligentia':	N.J. Polak, H. Bogaardt, C.A. Verrijn Stuart, E.C.G. Gimbrère, J. Goudriaan, J.W. Mathijsen (who had not signed the appeal).
Trade Unions:	P.J.S. Serrarens (not in appeal), J. Brautigam.
Trade, Shipping, and Banking:	???
Dutch E. Indies:	(no entry).

Political Group

Unknown:	Goudriaan, Dresden
Roman catholic:	Bogaardt, Gimbrère, Serrarens, van der Weyden
Socialist:	Brautigam, Mathijsen
Liberal:	Polak, Stuart, Kessler, Louwes
Orthodox Protestant:	??

It was not the empty line for the Dutch East Indies, but the absence of any names in the very last category of all – orthodox-protestant - which could account in advance for the failure of the NVGM as a pressure group. Moreover, it is worth noting that of the earlier deputation to the government three of its four members no longer played an active part. The name of professor F. de Vries was already missing from the public appeal. A.F. Bronsing, who was often abroad, considered it "rubbish" to found an association for value stable money without any unanimity among the founders about the content of this notion. Bronsing's explanation for the withdrawal of H.F. van Leeuwen was that Colijn had threatened to cross out the name the name of the Twentsche Bank, of which he was president, in the prospectus of a public loan if he continued to spread his devaluationist ideas.(14) Both men, however, had signed the founding appeal.

The wording to the prime objective of the Association had the smell of compromise. It wanted to spread the insight in the importance of "a value stable exchange medium with as much as possible stable purchasing power".(15) To this end, the means envisaged were the swaying of public opinion, possibly through an own journal, the influencing of government and parliament and, finally, scientific study.

The NVWG was run by a Daily Committee of five members chosen from the General Committee, which numbered a maximum of 21. In practice, most of the work was done by the president N.J. Polak and the secretary H. Bogaardt, a lawyer from The Hague whose office also became the Association's address.(16) It was also possible to found local or regional committees but only five of these came into being.(17) Finally there was a 'study circle' which rapidly came to number 70 members. The first number of the journal *Waardevast Geld* appeared in January 1935.(18)

One month after the founding meeting Polak wrote a letter to his fellow committee members which illustrates how carefully he wanted to operate in all respects: "My attention has been drawn to the fact that it may not be tactical to put the NVWG, which is odious in many eyes, under the presidency of someone who by his name is recognisable as being of Jewish descent." But there is no indication that his proposal to switch with the vice-president, C.A. Verrijn Stuart, received any serious consideration.

Towards the end of 1934 much attention was given to broadening the base of the committee, with special attention paid to the economic and social rank and file behind the proposed candidates. Thus, the manufacturer dr. G.C.A. van Dorp was asked to join the daily or executive committee because of the "auxiliary troops of the Dutch Employers Association".(19) Another notable member was the later president of the central bank, dr. M.W. Holtrop, who worked at the time with the giant iron foundry *Hoogovens*. It seems likely that he was recruited through the cooperation of G.A. Kessler, one of the firm's directors.

So, by the end of 1934 the board of the NVWG was constituted by an executive committee of eighteen: professor N.J. Polak as president, professor C.A. Verrijn Stuart (the father) as vice-president, H. Bogaardt as secretary-treasurer, and the ordinary members J. Brautigam, prof. D. Dresden, dr. G.C.A. van Dorp. professor E.C.G. Grimbrère, professor J. Goudriaan, dr. M.W. Holtrop, J. Hudig, G.A. Kessler, Harry ter Kuile, J.W. Mathijsen, Justus Meijer (who edited *Waardevast Geld* with professor G.M. Verrijn Stuart (the son) and professor Gimbrère), dr. J. Oortwijn Botjes, D.F. Pont, P.J.S. Serrarens and M.P. van der Weyden.

A short lived discussion arose over the possible admission of opponents of devaluation. This had been prompted by the application for membership by the roman catholic politician C.P.M. Romme, but it died down very quickly as only a few anti-devaluationists were willing to join. Miss E.C. van Dorp replied to the founding appeal that, being in favour of gold value stable money, she did not want to become a member.(20) Among those who did join – 360 names soon after the founding, 750 a year later – were professor J. Tinbergen and the post-war minister of foreign affairs, D.U. Stikker. The latter immediately applied for membership of the study circle to deepen his insight in monetary matters.(21)

The NVWG was not very wealthy. Even for the payment of the minimum membership fee of Dfl. 2.50 many members needed to be reminded. Yet early in 1935 there existed a growing organisation with a journal of its own and an increasing number of influential members.

The events of the early months of 1935 seemed to bring the NVWG tantalisingly close to their goal. The Belgian devaluation on 30 March portended

Leap in the dark. This cartoon illustrates how the NVWG visualized the consequences of devaluation of the different nations.

a worsening of the Dutch competitive position and there were few who could have drawn much comfort from the victory of the Dutch national team's victory over the Belgians by 4 : 2 on the football field the same day. The fall of the Belgian franc served to stir Steenberghe, who had signed the group's second address to the government and who had become minister of economic affairs in June 1934, into action. His failure to sway the cabinet prompted his resignation and seriously weakened the government's position. Then, in July, Colijn stumbled into a confrontation with parliament and submitted his cabinet's resignation. For a few days an alternative coalition and an alternative policy became a very real possibility, but the moment was lost. All these events are described in greater detail elsewhere in this book. The question we will examine now is how did the NVWG react to these opportunities?

The Belgian devaluation gave the NVWG the opportunity to beat the big drum about "being legally and morally committed to other countries". Bogaardt wrote a letter to the editor of the roman catholic daily *De Maasbode* printed on April 11 under the title of 'Monetary Agreements?'. This contribution was also spread as a leaflet by the Association. In it he scrutinised the legal foundations of the gold bloc: "If Belgium broke the arrangement then that country is to blame and we may reproach it for breach of promise." Inside parliament it was argued by Colijn and Oud that the Netherlands was absolutely free to maintain or leave the gold standard. Was this compatible, he asked, with the stubborn defense of the gold parity outside both chambers? His final question was whether the agreements between the gold countries' central banks ran parallel to those of their governments.

The NVWG executive committee also addressed itself directly to Colijn on 12 April. In a 10 page letter they urged the government to "to alter the foundation of our monetary system following the large majority of other countries". In an argumentation with a distinctly Keynesian flavour they pointed to the favourable effects of devaluation upon unemployed labour and capital, as well as its positive consequences for public finance. A change in policy was equally desirable for social reasons "because the demoralising evil of unemployment will become less through devaluation".

Unfortunately, their conclusion was rather far-sighted: "Now the undersigned still have the feeling that a devaluation of the guilder carried out by this government can still be executed in a controlled manner. The situation will become much worse if after a prolonged exhaustion of business the Netherlands will become so weak that it is finally pushed off the gold standard. Your excellency is already facing this possibility, but apparently also awaiting it with a certain fatalism." The committee did not want to express itself on the question whether the guilder should float down or devalue by a fixed percentage.(22)

In the middle of June, by which time the immediate prospect of change had receded, Van Dorp wrote to the secretary, Bogaardt, doubting whether a devaluation of 20 or 25 per cent, as proposed by Steenberghe and the Tilburg professor A.H. Kaag, would be sufficient. But Bogaardt's reply concentrated on an examination of the political situation. "July and August are ill months for political crises to which no political party will wholeheartedly cooperate. On the other hand, the counter-pressure (i.e. anti-devaluationist? E.S.) has considerably gained strength during the last two months. Taken together this makes me anxious that all kinds of uncontrolled factors will disturb the public insight in monetary matters."(23)

Professor Grimbrère was pessimistic and optimistic in turn. At the end of June he wrote to the secretary: "Still no blessing rests upon our labour." But, in August, when Colijn's reconstructed cabinet was lining up for a new parliamentary year, he proclaimed: "The harvest is ripe! I hear there is a majority in the second chamber for devaluation but, no-one dares to bell the cat. People are waiting for the moment when the Netherlands is pushed off the gold base. Then no one is responsible for the 'fait accompli', least of all the newly acting government."

One month later he had a setback to report. There had been a (further undisclosed) plan of a number of industrial entrepreneurs, together employing 50.000 people, to sign a petition to the second chamber demanding a change of economic policy. Otherwise, they would close down their business. However, they had dropped the idea because of... "their dependency on the government".

In November Bogaardt sent him his own appraisal of the political situation :

"To me the political atmosphere seems tenser than ever. I have my doubts whether Holland will be still just ahead of France in devaluing or whether ... Holland will be the last after having suffered all the disadvantages."(24)

From October 1935 to (at least) March 1936, twice monthly, an anonymous pamphlet was circulated under the title 'The Patriotic Villain, a mirror to ministers, M.P.'s, bankers and the press'. The title was derived from Colijn's disdainful nickname for the devaluationists 'unpatriotic villains'. Although its arguments were about the same as those of the NVWG, the tone of the pamphlet was much sharper. The Association even found it necessary to disavow any relationship: "To dispel any doubt the committee of the NVWG wants to declare that it entertains no relationship with this pamphlet. We say, to dispel any doubt, because our association has always carried out its action openly, so an anonymous action would entirely fall outside its line of conduct."(25)

If the actions of the NVWG towards the attainment of its prime goal were unsuccesful, even less spectacular were the activities of the study circle. It had a low frequency of meeting as is shown by the adoption of the minutes of 1 June 1936. Officially, there were four 'study cores', some of which were further subdivided:

1. a. Improvement of the metallic standard;
   b. Raw materials currency; subdivided into study groups for the systems of Goudriaan, J. Dijt and W.C. Mees.
2. a. Price level standard;
   b. Cost of living standard;
   c. Wage level standard.
3. Neutral money.
4. Free money.

One should not be surprised that the executive committee did not wait for the ideal currency to emerge from the study circle and decided to send yet another address to the government in May 1936. It collected 232 signatures under a call for "mint correction". The one page appeal was sent to Colijn on 11 May: "Unemployment here is at an unknown high level and shows an alarmingly increasing tendency (...) The ability of workers is lost in idleness (...) A balanced budget is unattainable as long as deflation leads to lower tax receipts."(26)

Simultaneously the plan arose within the NVWG to organise a broader movement with a narrower objective. On 9 May the 'Committee for Currency Correction' gathered in Utrecht.

THE COMMITTEE FOR DEVALUATION

Not currency or mint correction but, *devaluation*, that aim should be mentioned in the name of the action committee. This was decided during the founding meeting. Soon the committee numbered fifteen names: for the larger part entrepreneurs like A.H. van Heek (Enschede) W.C. Hudig (Rotterdam) and E.J. van Puyenbroek (Goirle). Gimbrère, Polak and C.A. Verrijn Stuart were the only professors. The younger Verrijn Stuart had already expressed his hesitations before the first meeting. To Bogaardt he wrote about the limitations imposed upon him by his "position as public servant": "As you know, I make no secret of my opinion. But there is a difference between this free speech and an action which has as its direct consequence the fall of the present government." (27)

A few large companies provided financial support, so the committee could rapidly dispose of a 'propaganda fund' of almost Dfl. 10,000. Its first advertisments were inserted in *Algemeen Handelsblad, NRC, De Maasbode,* and *Het Volk* on 18 and 19 May. These attracted many notifications of adhesion, especially from smaller entrepreneurs (among them a number of tree nurseries) and from Dutchmen abroad.(28)

The series of advertisments offered to the papers in June and July was formulated in a more aggresive and provocative tone than hitherto used by the NVWG and they also had a more 'political' message. Probably responsible for these texts were the president of the new committee, E.D. van Walree, and its secretary, W.J.L. van Es. "The Belgian Example" (retail prices risen by 9.2% after devaluation, unemployment reduced by 40%); "The Fairy-tale of Adaptation" (Once there was a snail who thought he could equal a grasshopper; no fairy-tale but, the sad truth); "All those who fish in troubled waters are defending the untarnished guilder. They are right: a consistently executed adaptation policy strikes at the roots of our society and opens the best prospects for all *un-Dutch* movements."

From the difficulties in placing these advertisements it may be concluded that the troubled relationship of the devaluationists with the press had little changed since Goudriaan had voiced his anger with *De Telegraaf*. This paper and *De Standaard* refused to take any advertisement, the (also anti-revolutionary) *De Rotterdammer* the second and later ones. More friendly were the roman catholic and socialist press and at first also the liberal papers. Still, the committee had to operate carefully in catholic circles, as was pointed out by a one letter-writer: the RKSP should take care not to drive the catholic adherents of the gold standard into Colijn's arms at the elections.(29)

To overcome the limitations of accessibility to the press, in June the committee also started to stick bills and posters with a 'Call to the Dutch Nation' in Amsterdam, The Hague, Rotterdam and Groningen. The latter was the home of the committee member P. Dijkhuis, who had in vain offered his article 'Mint correction' to the Groningen newspapers. This article, expressing his joy about the conversion of the former minister T.J. Verschuur to the devalutionist camp, was later printed and distributed by the committee as a leaflet.

As a result of the adhesions received, the committee could now add a list of 605 signatures under the text of the address of May 1936 and this was sent to the government on 10 July. The next activity was to be the organisation of a conference in The Hague in October. Steenberghe, and the professors Polak, Goudriaan and G. Gonggrijp would speak in favour of devaluation. Professor Bordewijk was invited to defend the gold standard. And although Bogaardt and Polak had both joined the devaluation committee, the former had also tried to revitalise the NVWG with the following reasoning:

"The adhesion we received so far both for devaluation and for value stable money, is badly shrinking. A symptom is the alarming number of resignations from our association. In my opinion this dwindling is due to:
a. the fermentation of Europe (political aspects, communism and fascism, the Far East etc.);
b. the Dutch stock exchange gains on American stock, which are nicely stimulating our rentier mentality;
c. resignation c.q. ostrich-policy;
d. the confused national political situation, which no human being can understand."(30)

It was his proposal to Polak to organise a "decent" demonstration in The Hague coinciding with the committee's conference.

By the beginning of September Polak himself had come to the conclusion that at the next elections he wanted to acquire political influence, "if necessary through our own list". In the committee he was supported by Goudriaan but opposed by C.A. Verrijn Stuart and van Es. The meeting decided to defer any decision on the matter.(31)

And then, at the end of September, it was all no longer necessary.

Since the Netherlands left the gold standard only because France and Switzerland had done so, it cannot be said that the actions of the NVWG had accelerated the Dutch devaluation by even one hour. As to the immediate events, the reservation of the conference room in The Hague could be cancelled. But the distribution of Goudriaan's pamphlet 'What is your plan?' (a reprint of two of his articles) to all members of parliament was carried out by the NVWG.

In October Bogaardt thought, in an optimistic vein, that it would be a useful task for the study circle to determine the correct devaluation percentage. A year later, he was of the same opinion. He wrote to professor J. van Gelderen: "Now that the era behind us has been closed off on 26 September, 1936, the search for the ideal value stable money can increasingly bear the scientific stamp which this endeavour deserves."(32) A number of its members wanted to turn the Association into a society for "active business cycle policy" and a detailed action programme to this end was developed in 1939. This turn prompted Polak's comment that without his "safety valves" the NVWG was in danger of becoming "a convoy of the SDAP and related politicians and political (sub)groups."(33) The Association remained in existence till 1943.

THE ANTI-DEVALUATIONIST GROUP

The establishment of the Dutch Association for Value Stable Money in October 1934 acted as a catalyst for the formation and organisation of a group in favour of maintaining adherence to the gold standard. The initiative stemmed from the Groningen economics professor H.W.C. Bordewijk who wrote to a number of sympathisers on 1 November suggesting a meeting "without it having the character of a counter-action".(34) In top secrecy the fifteen founder members of the Anti-devaluationist group met on 17 November in Amsterdam to deliberate upon the most effective course it could take. Consensus emerged quite quickly that it should not become a public pressure group: firstly because it would endow the NVWG with too much status and secondly because it would be "grist to their mill" and merely provoke further action and publicity. It should be an "invisible force". Of course, if it was too invisible there would not be much point either and it was agreed that more anti-devaluationist articles were necessary – popular articles, to inform the public and to avoid the danger of the pro-devaluationist cause becoming sentimentalised, and academic articles, designed to knock the pro-devaluation professors from the pedestals of esteem which they enjoyed in the publics' eyes. Finally, it was agreed to send an address to the government and the professors Bordewijk, de Jong, Lieftinck and Limperg (in consultation with the bankers J.W. Beyen and H.A. van Nierop) were charged with preparing a draft for consideration at the next meeting.(35)

When the group next met (with five new members present) there were not one but two texts for discussion – one short, one long. Although the authors declared a willingness to compromise, the meeting was still confronted with a dilemma. If the object of the exercise was to furnish the government with an arsenal of arguments obviously the longer text would be the most appropriate but, if the idea was to obtain a large number of important signatures the shorter the text the better. The inherent danger of a longer text was immediately and eloquently illustrated when the chairman of the Amsterdam chamber of commerce, G.H. Crone, suggested working from Bordewijk's longer text and removing all points of contention. Limperg intervened with a statement that he and others had objections to using Bordewijk's text at all. A proposal to send two texts was defeated but the meeting took the point, amending the shorter de Jong/Limperg text. It was further agreed not to go public and seek declarations of support but that potential supporters (of high individual standing) would be approached individually.(36) The address argued that the (temporary) advantages of a devaluation would be far outweighed by the longer-term disadvantages and that the "return to normal circumstances" would be delayed even further. Export industries, it was admitted, might benefit if their costs rose less than the guilder had fallen, but even that depended upon the reaction abroad in the form of protectionism and the price response of Dutch competitors. On the other hand, all businesses which depended primarily upon the domestic market would have to cope with the effects of higher cost imports without any compensatory price advantage. Given the distortions created by devaluation, the economies of the gold countries, once they had become competitive again, would be in a far healthier position. Moreover, devaluation was always accompanied by a national and international shock effect "and, on past experience, nothing undermines confidence in the economic and financial field more than monetary experiments". Domestically this would take the form of difficulty in financing the national debt, capital flight and gold hoarding; internationally it would strengthen autarkic tendencies and delay the restoration of normal trade relationships. Despite everything which had happened, nobody had conceived a better means of restoring international monetary stability than the gold standard. The last point it made was on the subject of the devaluation – *vaste lasten* controversy. Here it argued, tellingly, that the devaluationists could not have it both ways. If devaluation were to effect a reduction in the real weight of all forms of debt and debt charges domestic price levels would have to rise (or else there would be no effect as all) but the devaluationists kept emphasising that prices would rise only little, if at all! Besides, if domestic prices should rise, so too would nominal wages. "What would be saved on *vaste lasten* would be spent again on wages" and where would be the improvement in profitability then? It was left to the government itself to decide if and when it wished to publish the address and the list of names of those who had signed it.(37)

Who would compose such an address and who would sign it? The answer to the first question is simple – a few economic professors and a larger number of bankers and financiers. Of the 26 members which constituted the group in January 1935 five were academic economists (all of professional rank) and no less than twelve had been recruited from the top of the banking and financial world. The answer to the second question is equally simple – the members of the group and those known personally to them, though professional economists were made a special target group. Thus, of the 63 signatories of the address, fifteen were academics (though only twelve were economists). Banking and financial circles with fifteen signatories, however, still constituted the largest single group. Efforts to broaden the representatives of the address had been noticeably successful in two areas at least: shipping contributed four signatures and industrialists, who were not represented in the group at all, seven. All 63 names have been analysed and classified below on the same basis as Polak had tried to do with the executive members of the NVWG (see p 146).

Intelligentia: H.W.C. Bordewijk (Groningen), I.B. Cohen (Groningen), H. Frijda (Amsterdam), P. Lieftinck (Rotterdam) T. Limperg (Amsterdam), (GROUP MEMBERS) J.H. Broeke (Leiden), D. van Blom (Leiden), E.C. van Dorp (private economist), D. van Embden (Amsterdam), A.C. Josephus Jitta (Delft), R. Kranenburg (Leiden), E.M. Meijers (Leiden), C. Raaymakers (Nijmegen), B.M. Telders (Leiden), J.G.C. Volmer (Delft).

Shipping Trade and Banking:	J.W. Beyen (Banking), G.H. Crone (Trade), F.H. Fentener van Vlissingen (Trade), J.E. Gerzon (Retail trade), T. Greidanus, P. Hofstede de Groot, A.M. de Jong, D. Crena de Jongh, T. Ligthart, K.P. van de Mandele (Banking), J.L.C. van Meerwijk (Insurance), R. Mees, H.A. van Nierop (Banking), A. Plate (Shipping), A.A. van Sandick, A.R. Zimmerman (Banking), (GROUP MEMBERS) D.G. van Beuningen (Trade), W.A. Engelbrecht (Shipping), J.W. Niemeijer (Insurance), A. Pierson (Banking), B.E. Ruys (Shipping), C. Smeets (Trade), W. Willems (Financial bulletin) W.B.K. Verster, W. van der Storm (Shipping).
Industry:	NO GROUP MEMBERS, H.P. Gelderman (Textiles), L. Hamburger (Chemicals), G. Heineken (Brewing), H.I. Keus (Engineering), G.E. ter Kuile (Textiles), C.H. Teschmacher(Shipbuilding), S. van Zwanenberg (Food-processing).
Agriculture:	NO GROUP MEMBERS E. Welderen Baron Rengers.
Dutch East Indies:	J.C.E. Baron van Lijnden (GROUP MEMBER).
Others:	J.H. Bast, T.J. Engelberts (Lawyer), C. Kool (Police), W.J. van de Woestijne (Economics student, Amsterdam) (GROUP MEMBERS) G. van den Bergh (Politics), G.H.A. Grosheide, H.J. Hellema (Lawyer), W.W. van der Meulen (Historian, teacher), D.W.D.A. Schut (Lawyer).
Not known:	G . Mesdag, (GROUP MEMBER) F.F. Beukema, J.W. Dekker, A.E. Duijnstee, A.H. Baron van Hardenbroek van Ammerstel.

The petition was to have been handed over to Colijn on 9 February immediately after the group had had an opportunity to meet and elect a delegation. But, because Colijn could only manage 4 February, Bordewijk had had to select a delegation himself. As he explained to the meeting, he had done so by selecting those most active in recruiting new signatories – Van Nierop, Van der Mandele and, from the Amsterdamsche Bank, Hofstede de Groot. It is noticable that none of the six who had drafted the original texts, apart from himself, had been included, nor, it transpired, had they been consulted. Limperg objected by letter to the entire way the question had been handled, mentioning in passing that he did not think that the group should have a permanent character.(38) Later he was to object to the group discussing anything falling outside the narrow definition of the gold standard or to undertaking joint initiatives which did not have the endorsement of each individual member.(39)

Having mangaged, without tearing itself apart, to compose and deliver an address to the government, the group was forced to consider what to do next. The first step it took was to reaffirm its closed character; any extension of its membership was to be by invitation only.(40) But then what? This was a question which was to rack the group throughout its existence. If it were to remain an 'invisible force' then the only target for its pressure had to be the cabinet or the Netherlands Bank since they at least could be relied upon to keep its existance undisclosed. This, in turn, presupposed that a consensus could be reached on the message which it wanted to transmit. But, this was rendered virtually impossible by the fact that the only thing holding the group together was 'no devaluation'. As soon as it came to any discussion of the measures necessary to prevent a devaluation ever occuring, that consensus would evaporate. To illustrate this it is worth quoting a number of examples. In May 1935 it was decided to entrust Keus, Van Lijnden, Plate and Zimmerman with drafting an address to the government drawing attention to the need for a reduction in wage disparities (i.e. to lower wages in local government and public services) as a contribution towards making the economy more competitive and thus reducing the danger of a devaluation.(41) This was the final straw for Limperg, who resigned his membership, but the proposal was also fiercely resisted by Van der Woestijne and Frijda, both of whom had missed the previous discussion and who viewed the draft as too one-sided in its emphasis on wage-cuts. Indeed, Frijda was of the opinion that "this draft could just as easily have been written by a devaluationist to demonstrate the consequences of maintaining the gold standard". Van Sandinck and Fentener van Vlissingen too opposed the draft, though for different reasons, whilst de Jong wondered why the government needed such an address anyway: what it advocated was precisely what it was trying to do. The draft was referred back to its authors.(42) By July, when the re-draft was discussed, it was considered that the urgency had passed and it was decided instead to send a short, less controversial note drafted by de Jong in its stead.(43) In October, the same thing happenend again. Zimmerman and Keus were mandated to prepare a draft report on wage differentials(44) which again stranded on the twin objections of those who could not agree with the conclusions and those who could see little point in telling the government what it already knew. That note was not sent either.(45) This lack of consensus, it was realised, would also hamstring the group's ability to present itself as a group to the outside world. But even on this point there was no consensus. So, if it could not agree on any substantial message and if it could not agree to present itself openly as an anti-devaluationist bulwork, what could it agree to do? The following paragraphs will attempt to follow in more detail the discussions on the group's role and to trace the steps taken.

The issue first arose at the meeting on 6 April. It was less than a week after the devaluation of the Belgian franc and the guilder was caught up in the eddy of the shock wave of speculation against the gold bloc currencies. In the five days before the meeting took place the Netherlands bank had lost gold reserves worth Dfl. 106 million. Those present were divided over whether the situation was bad enough to warrent some immediate response or not, with a further subdivision among the former over what that response should be. One thing which it soon became clear they could not do was to come out into the open and reveal to the World the backing which existed in the Netherlands for the gold standard. This may seem strange but it must be remembered that the only tangible proof of this backing was the address to the government and, leaving aside the question whether it was suitable for the occasion, they had left it to the government to decide if and when to publish it. The group could hardly pre-empt that right, especially since the government did not consider events so bad as to warrent publication. So, if the group wanted to make a statement, and not everybody did, it would have to start from scratch. Another approach was to get the government to issue an official statement of support for the guilder but with parliament not in session some felt that it would do more harm than good. Finally, and this approach was agreed, Trip could try to persuade his fellow 'gold-bloc' Central Bank presidents to make a joint declaration at their meeting in Basel. When Bordewijk phoned him he was initially sceptical over the value of such a declaration but agreed to suggest it to his collegues. He reserved his own position (In the event Trip made a statement alone declaring that the guilder had been succesfully defended and, somewhat inconsistently, followed this up by announcing a further 1 per cent hike in the prime interest rate – a move which the 'invisible force' had not considered).

The group then moved on to consider a memorandum from Van Lijnden, entitled 'Necessity for Information In and About the Press', in which he emphasised the need to counter devaluationist propaganda. To do that effectively, he argued, the group also needed to be well informed about what was being said in the press, both domestic and foreign. What he proposed was that the group establish a small bureau to survey the press and to be staffed by "a competent young economist with practical experience as a journalist, supported by a steno-typist" who, under the direction of a small committee, would be able to respond immediately if the need arose and who would prepare a constant stream of counter-propaganda. The problem with Van Lijnden's proposal was firstly, that it would be expensive and secondly, that it would break the group's 'invisibility'. Instead, a compromise was reached. A 'fire-watch' of three members was created (Ligthart, Van Sandick and to be recruited, G. Verwey from the *Nederlandsche Handel-maatschappij*) which would point out the dangers and initiate appropriate counter-measures by individual group members.(46)

The stress on individual initiative remained until September 1935. Once again the guilder had come under heavy speculative pressure through fear that the cabinet might again fall on its budget legislation. Van Lijnden repeated his view that "systematic press propoganda" was necessary, hammering at the negative consequences of devaluation in Belgium and the U.K. This time he had better luck. Van Nierop and Hofstede de Groot offered to utilise the services of the statistical department of the *Amsterdamsche Bank*, which collected press information and had its own press contacts, to achieve the goal. The group, as such, would not be mentioned,(47) nor, it transpired, would the Bank: the news items were sent to the Dutch national press agency, A.P.N. and distributed anonymously.(48)

In January 1936 Van de Mandele drew the group's attention to the potential danger of the *Landdag* organised by the RKSP at which Steenberghe was scheduled to appear (see pp 118-119). "We have to be ready to fight again, perhaps on a larger scale than before. Someone has to take care of the antidote (lit. counter-poison)." Bordewijk responded by suggesting that this reopened the question of whether to go public, adding that the passive reaction of the government to the group's activities to date warrented a possible reassessment of its role. But that still left the problem, "it is the negative that unites us". It was agreed for the time-being to alert the 'fire-watch'.(49) It was with some degree of satisfaction that the membership next met. The *Landdag* had not been as bad as feared. De Jong noted that if Steenberghe's intention had been to mobilise a mass movement for devaluation it had been a "virtually complete fiasco", whilst the NVWG also appeared to be completely bogged down. In these circumstances he considered that going public would be counter-productive. On the other hand, Zimmerman asked when such a step would be appropriate. Parliament's position was weak and if left too long the move could come too late. "If devaluation comes it is a matter of Saturday to Monday, in complete secrecy. It is doubtful whether resistance is still possible." Nonetheless, it was agreed that the group should try to agree a report which sketched the measures necessary for economic recovery whilst on the gold standard.(50)

That report, which would probably anyway have enjoyed the same fate as most of the others, was never discussed. This was partly because of the preparation time involved and partly because events swept (if that's the appropriate word) the group in a new direction. Before then, however, there took place a painful, and inconclusive re-examination of its own identity and purpose. Two events prompted this discussion. The first was a speech made by Gelissen in the First Chamber on 11 March 1936 in which he had suggested that further efforts towards industrialisation or work creation were doomed to failure unless the weight of costs and fixed changes were reduced either by *aanpassing* (deflation) or devaluation. This implied, he stated, that something had to be done but did not mean that he favoured devaluation. He then added, "that I am not opposed in principle; should it prove necessary I would not hesitate to do it but I do not find it necessary at the moment!"(51) The second was the news of Lieftinck's defection to the pro-devaluationist camp, not because he no longer believed that the gold standard was the optimal term solution to the Netherlands' problems, but because the increased international tension made the realisation of the necessary conditions for its maintenance impossible (see p 102). Until April 1936 the group's membership had been relatively stable. Only two resignations had taken place and neither had been because of a disagreement with its goals. Beyen had resigned in April 1935 to take up a post with the Bank of International Settlements in Basel and was replaced by H.I. Keus from the engineering firm *Heemaf*, Limperg, as we have already seen, resigned a month later (I suspect because he didn't really like the company -RTG). Three other new members had been recruited: E.E. Menten from the bank *Heldring en*

Pierson, A.N. Molenaar, secretary of the employers' association VNW and Verwey. Lieftinck was the first turn-coat.

In examining Gelissen's speech, Bordewijk made the distinction between an 'opportunist' or a 'principled' belief in the gold standard. He characterised Gelissen's comments as an example of the former – adding that if that was all the people believed in the danger for the guilder was great. By contrast, the Group represented those who defended the guilder from a 'principled conviction'. But did it? Lieftinck had been a member for virtually a year and a half and his conduct was a 'warning' to the group. Griedanus pointed out that Frijda's postion was not really one of principle either (Frijda was not there to reply). So it was that the one point which had unified the group turned out not to be a unity at all. But, of course, that was not the only disunity. A further split, which had been evident from the beginning, was on the measures considered necessary to preserve the gold standard. Thus, alongside 'opportunists' and 'fundamentalists' we also have 'deflationists' and 'reflationists'; all in the same club. It was Keus who first mentioned the unmentionable.

"Mister Keus said that before we discuss a possible replacement for the vacancy left by Lieftinck it is necessary to put the question whether a purge of the group is not necessary." He went on to explain that the continued necessity to come to compromises was robbing the movement of its momentum. In this he was supported by Zimmerman, who pointed out that if the group were to go public it had to do more than merely proclaim the beauty of the gold standard; it had to come out with concrete proposals for measures necessary to make its maintenance possible. But there was never any unanimity on that point. It is noticeable that both men had been involved in the preparation of the two 'wages reports', the latter written by them alone, which had been set aside for lack of consensus. However, the only support they received was from Molenaar, who wanted a number of 'articles of faith' drawn up to which all would be expected to adhere. No one else was willing to go so far. Van de Woestijne, who was obviously one of the targets of these attacks, argued that the fact that 'birds of different plumage' were represented in the group was one of its strengths. Without it, it would become an employers' club. Van Sandick added in passing that the NVWG was not united in their end-goals either. The blood letting was postponed.(52)

Lieftinck was replaced by two new members, W. Suermondt and the ship-owner and chairman of the Rotterdam chamber of commerce, W.A. Engelbrecht. It was just as well that there had been more than one replacement because the next meeting was informed of Frijda's resignation – prompted by a disillusion with the progress of the government's deflationary policy. The group decided to invite the director of the textile concern *Koninklijk Stoomweverij Nijvendal*, G. van der Meulen, and the financial journalist, W. Willems, to join (both later accepted). It was also decided to send Colijn a short personal letter informing him of the defections and warning him that disenchantment with his policies was eroding the support for the gold standard. Of more immediate concern, however, was the increasing activity of the NVWG in the form of advertisements placed in the press calling for adherents to the views expressed therein. It was decided that the time had arrived for the group to unfurl its banner in public by publishing a short declaration in the press. Bordewijk agreed to draft an appropriate text for the next meeting whilst Van Nierop agreed in the meantime to prepare an article attacking the pro-devaluationists' arguments.(53)

The need for such action was underlined by the NVWG's further escalation of action by pasting posters in the streets of the major cities. The draft text was not available so the only decision taken was that names of the group's members would appear underneath.(54) In July, the text was ready. Two months had elapsed and the urgency had passed. It was decided to keep it in reserve until a more suitable moment and to use the intervening time to assemble as many signatories as possible, with the emphasis again on the quality of the names. The manifesto read:

> The campaign for devaluation of the currency which had recently been conducted in this country has prompted the undersigned, from a strongly held conviction, to a word of protest. Devaluation means a deliberate reduction in the value of the guilder. The undersigned consider such a measure in conflict with the true interests of the Dutch people. They are convinced that devaluation is a totally inappropriate means for combatting the malaise and its consequences. A deliberate reduction in the value of the Dutch guilder, as wanted by the advocates of devaluation, would not attack the causes of the malaise. The relief possibly afforded to some firms from such a measure would only be temporary and, certainly in a small country as ours, not long-lasting in view of the fact that such a reduction in the value of the guilder would undoubtedly result in price rises at home,so that the devaluation strongly would push up the cost of living and, in all probability, unleash a violent wage struggle.(55)

Holidays intervened and it was not until 19 September that the group met again. Its membership, since the recruitment of Van der Meulen and Willems, had been further extended with the addition of the banker A.B. Henny, A.E. Duijnstee and J.J. Montijn, Director of the *Moluksche Handelsvennootschap*, with interests in rubber plantations in the Dutch East Indies. The summer too had brought a further defection, C. Kool, head of the police force in Leeuwarden. More heartening was the news that no less than 78 signatories had been collected for the manifesto. There was no pressure for its immediate publication, even though the vulnerability of the French franc was extensively discussed. The last word on what was the last agenda point was uttered by Van Lynden: "We can keep the powder of our publication dry for a while and wait for the correct moment."(56)

A week later the guilder had fallen. It had happened as Zimmerman had said it would – from Saturday to Monday, with no opportunity for resistance. The

Anti-Devaluationist Group had failed utterly in its primary aim. For some it was seen as the end of the road: the group no longer had any purpose and could best be disbanded. But there were stouter hearts among them who felt that, more than ever, the country needed the vigilance of a group such as they – a group which could forge new alliances now that the gulf of 'devaluation or not' had been eliminated, a group dedicated to the elimination of inflationist policies, a group driven by a new consensus, a Commission for Monetary Policy. And so, indeed, it came to pass.

When comparing the pro- and anti-devaluationists it is important to bear in mind their very different natures. From September 1934 onwards, with the creation of the NVWG, the pro-devaluationists formed an open, public political pressure group, whilst the very existence of the anti-devaluationists, relying on personal contacts for recruitment, remained clothed in secrecy to the very end. This means that the fact that the membership of the NVWG at one point numbered more than 700 or that it collected more than 800 signatures for the petitions of May and July 1936 cannot be compared with the 20 + members of the anti-devaluationist group or the 60 or 70 signatures it succeeded in collecting and then used as an indicator of the support enjoyed by either side. Indeed, when one considers how many potential signatories there were in the Netherlands (1,300,000 signed the 1923 petition against the government's plans to modernise the navy) the number 800 is not very large and it attests to the failure of the NVWG to capture the public imagination. This is possibly because it had retained its 'academic' character and relatively low political profile for too long. When it changed tactics in May 1935, it was already too late. Moreover, the intensification of pressure may possibly have lost it support – one member of the anti-devaluationists drew a parallel between the 'street propoganda' of the pro-devaluationists and that of the fascist NSB, a comparison which may have occured to others. However, if devaluationists failed to mobilise mass-support, the anti-devaluationists did not even bother to try.

Ironically, neither group had much success in winning the ear of the government either. This is not really surprising as far as the NVWG was concerned. Its very existence, every move and utterance it made constituted a threat to the policy of maintaining the gold standard. All the more reason, therefore, to have expected the government to have cossetted the anti-devaluationist group. But in a way its existence too was a condemnation of government policy. If *aanpassing* was working the group should not be necessary and, as some members perceived early on, articles and statements defending the gold standard were virtually admissions that there was something to defend against! Moreover, the policy prescriptions which the anti-devaluationists had to offer implied a criticism of Colijn and his cabinet. Little wonder that Bordewijk often complained of the government's coolness towards himself and disinterest in the group's message.

A final point worth making is this. The creation of a single issue pressure group may overcome the problem of hetrogeneity which often hamstrung the established interest groups in establishing a standpoint on the devaluation question. However the desire of a single issue pressure group to demonstrate broad support introduced a new element of hetrogeneity which limited its own freedom of action. This was clearly illustrated in the anti-devaluationist case, but it also existed with the NVWG. Although there was talk of new alignments once the divisive issue of 'devalue or not' had been resolved, it is instructive to see the direction in which each group, shorn of dissidents, was to develop – the pro-devaluationists towards supporting an active counter-cyclical policy, the anti-devaluationists towards monetary conservatism. The battle for the gold standard is long gone but, perhaps the value of a study of these two streams lies in the fact they formed the beginning of a dichotomy which has divided economic thinking ever since.

Notes

1. In 1984 dr. E. Schoorl had an interview with Mr. Bronsing, then aged 94, which added this and other information that derived from archive sources.
2. P. de Rooy, *Werklozenzorg en werkloosheidsbestrijding*, Amsterdam, 1978, 137, quotes an interesting letter, written by the leading roman catholic politician Kortenhorst to the prime minister Colijn, 8.7.1933: "I cannot withhold from you the information that in leading circles of our catholic community the opinion is gaining ground that the gold standard will become a disaster for our economic life".
3. *Address Aan zijn Excellentie den Minister van Koloniën, voorzitter van den ministerraad*, 19.7.1933; signed by the businessmen: S. van den Bergh (Unilever), D. Bolderhey, (Handelsvereeniging, Amsterdam), A.F. Bronsing (Stoomvaartmaatschappij Nederland), W.J.L. van Es (lawyer), A.H. and J.H. van Heek (G.J. van Heek en Zonen), H.C. Hintzen (R. Mees and Zn.), H. ter Kuile (Nico ter Kuile en Zonen), H.F. van Leeuwen (Twentsche Bank), W.F. van Leeuwen (Ned. Gist- and Spiritusfabriek), L.H. van Lennep (Van Eeghen and Co.), Dr. A.F. Philips (Philips' Gloeilampenfabriek), Dr. L.F.H. Regout (Industrialist), U.J. Reinders (Reinders' Olie- and Veevoederfabriek), E.L.C. Schiff (Rubberfabriek, Vredestein), L. Stokvis (R.S. Stokvis and Zn.'s Handelmij), the professors, G. Gonggrijp, J. Goudriaan jr., N.J. Polak, G.M. Verrijn Stuart, F. de Vries, J. Wisselink, all from the Handelshogeschool, Rotterdam, J.A. Veraart, Technische Hogeschool, Delft, C.A. Verrijn Stuart, Utrecht, and R. van Genechten, privaat-docent, Utrecht, Dr. S.E.B. Bierema from the second and J.Bs. Westerdijk from the first chamber.
4. H. Colijn in a lecture to Amsterdam entrepreneurs, 1935; quoted by H. de Vries, Colijn en de Nederlandse economisten, *Exercities in ons verleden*, Assen, 1981, 111.
5. A.F. Bronsing's recollection of Heldring's mediation and of the audience with Colijn were told by him in 1984.
6. Algemeen Rijksarchief (ARA), Archive of Nederlandse Vereeniging voor Waardevast Geld (ANVWG), box 9, Newspaper cutting *De Telegraaf*, November, 1933.
7. ARA, Ministerraad, ingekomen stukken, 307, 13d. Address to the Minister-president, 5.1.1934.
8. E.H.J. Gimbrère, *Nederland's Monetaire Politiek*, Tilburg, 1934, 48, pamphlet consisting of reprinted articles from the newspapers *Dagblad voor Noord-Brabant* and *De Maasbode*, November 1933 and January 1934. I express my thanks to prof. H. Visser for the opportunity to consult Colijn's copy with his annotations.
9. *Ibid.*, 17, 36, 45, 48.
10. ARA, ANVWG, one page leaflet, L.S., *Ondergeteekenden zijn voornemens...*, dated middle of September 1934; with Polak's private address as contact address.

11. ARA, ANVWG, box 5, C. Gerretson to J.W.L. van Es, 20.9.1934, copy sent by Gerretson to Polak.
12. Art. 2, Statutes of the NVWG, *Waardevast Geld*, January 1935.
13. ARA, ANVWG, box 8, Note by Polak.
14. As told by Bronsing in 1984.
15. Art. 2, Statutes of the NVWG.
16. Most correspondence by far was conducted by Polak and Bogaardt, Goudriaan and Gimbrère were also quite prolific writers.
17. Of these sub-committees, the regional one for West NoordBrabant was by far the most active. Its papers are contained in the NVWG's archives.
18. The NVWG archives have no complete set of its journal. I consulted the one at the Amsterdam University Library.
19. Correspondence of secretary NVWG (arranged alphabetically), box 5.
20. ARA, ANVWG, box 8, Miss E.C. van Dorp, Bloemendaal, 10.10.1934.
21. *Ibid.*, D.U. Stikker, Leiden, 24.10.1934.
22. ARA, ANVWG, box 4, April 1935, Copy of address.
23. ARA, ANVWG, box 5, Van Dorp to Bogaardt, Bogaardt's reply.
24. *Ibid.*, Bogaardt to Gimbrère.
25. ARA, ANVWG, October 1935-March 1936, *De Vaderlandslievende Schobber; spiegel voor ministers, kamerleden en pers*; comment in *Waardvast Geld*, 11.11.1935.
26. ARA, Ministerraad, ingekomen stukken, 318, 188, address NVWG to His Excellency dr. H. Colijn.
27. ARA, ANVWG, box 5, G.M. Verrijn Stuart to Bogaardt.
28. ARA, ANVWG, box 4, Reactions to newspaper advertisements, May/June 1936.
29. ARA, ANVWG, box 9, Newspaper cutting.
30. ARA, ANVWG, box 8, Bogaardt to Polak, August 1936.
31. ARA, ANVWG, box 15, Minutes of the Dagelijks Bestuur.
32. ARA, ANVWG, box 6, Bogaardt to Van Gelderen, October 1937.
33. ARA, ANVWG, box 7, Polak to Bogaardt, 1939.
34. Archief De Nederlandsche Bank (ADNB), Monetaire politiek binnenland II, Dossier Handhaving gouden standaard October 1934-November 1936, Circular from Bordewijk, 1.11.1934. Although the initiative was obviously not unwelcome to the government. I have been unable to find any evidence that they set it up. Nor does it seem likely that the initiative was prompted by Trip since he received his circular in the same way as the rest. He replied that he felt it unwise to attend himself since should the involvement of the Netherland's Bank become known, it would provide a propoganda weapon for the opposition. *Ibid.*, Letter Trip to Bordewijk, 2.11.1934.
35. *Ibid.*, Dossier Notulen vergaderingen Group van Anti-devaluïsten, minutes meeting, 17.11.1934.
36. *Ibid.*, minutes of meeting, 22.12.1934. Copies of the draft texts have not been found.
37. ARA, Ministerie van Financiën, General Thesaurie (199) – Nederlandse Monetaire Politiek. Devaluatie. Address of the Anti-devaluationist Group, 9.2.1935.
38. ADNB, Notulen vergaderingen Groep van Anti-devaluisten, minutes of meeting,9.2.1935.
39. *Ibid.*, minutes of meeting, 18.5.1935.
40. *Ibid.*, minutes of meeting, 9.2.1935.
41. *Ibid.*, minutes of meeting, 18.5.1935.
42. *Ibid.*, minutes of meeting, 15.6.1935.
43. *Ibid.*, minutes of meeting, 6.7.1935.
44. *Ibid.*, minutes of meeting, 26.10.1935.
45. *Ibid.*, minutes of meeting, 23.11.1935.
46. *Ibid.*, minutes of meeting, 6.4.1935.
47. *Ibid.*, minutes of meeting, 21.9.1935.
48. *Ibid.*, minutes of meeting, 26.10.1935.
49. *Ibid.*, minutes of meeting, 28.1.1936.

50. *Handelingen van de Eerste Kamer*, 1935/1936, 453, 11.3.1936.
51. ADNB, Notulen vergaderingen Groep van Anti-devaluïsten, minutes of meeting, 28.2.1936.
52. *Ibid.*, minutes of meeting, 6.4.1936.
53. *Ibid.*, minutes of meeting, 16.5.1936.
54. *Ibid.*, minutes of meeting, 13.6.1936.
55. *Ibid.*, minutes of meeting, 4.7.1936.
56. *Ibid.*, minutes of meeting, 19.9.1936.

CHAPTER EIGHT

The Policy Makers

Once a government has determined its overall economic strategy it is disinclined to submit it repeatedly to internal scrutiny. It confines its attention to formulating the optimal policy for achieving its goals within the framework defined. What others may consider a viable policy option has become for the government, from that moment on, an immutable constant; an act of faith. This seems to have been the case as far as the question of adherence to the gold standard was concerned. The question was simply not a topic for discussion. The fact that this decision meant that increasingly after 1931 the nominal price level in the Netherlands showed all the signs of being uncompetitive was a problem which had to be solved in other ways. That was what policy-makers were for. The extent of expenditure cuts, the extent of civil servants' salary cuts, which taxes to increase and by how much, the scope, scale and form of protectionist measures – these were the issues which absorbed the time of the various cabinets in the 1930's. The question of the gold standard did not, at least, not if it could be avoided.

Occasionally, however, a fundamental re-examination of an article of faith cannot be avoided and, whatever the inclination of the majority in cabinet, that very item which had previously been considered sacrosanct has to be placed on the political agenda. One way in which this can occur is as a result of outside pressure. But, as we have seen, there was very little effective organised pressure since none of the nationally organised interest groups or major political parties came out openly against the maintenance of the gold standard. The exception was the single-issue pressure group formed under professor Polak whose adherents were sufficiently influential to evoke a response – at least in its early stages. Another way in which this can occur is through a statement from one of the government's own advisory bodies though in the 1930's this was unlikely since most of the items upon which advice was requested were themselves determined by the government .... and why ask advice on what has already been decided? There was, however, one moment when it appeared that the cabinet might be given advice, like it or not, and that was when the newly constituted Economic Council seemed about to speak out on the question of the gold standard. But it decided to gag itself and the moment was lost. Again, it is possible that one of the cabinet's own members may break ranks, even to the extent of making the whole question a resignation issue. This is not something which happens often and when it does the potential damage, especially to a coalition cabinet, means that the threat has to be taken seriously just as it was in April 1935 when the minister of economic affairs, M.P.L. Steenberghe, wrote his 'Note Concerning the Problem of the Gold Standard for the Netherlands'. Finally, a government may be forced to reconsider its position when it becomes clear that that position either has already become, or seems imminently likely to become, politically or economically untenable. This situation arose twice in the course of the 1930's; once when the Colijn cabinet resigned in July 1935, and again after the devaluation of the French franc and the Swiss franc in September 1936. On the second occasion the cabinet bowed before the inevitable and abandoned the gold standard.

These events form the core of this chapter, since they allow us to get close to the logic and reasoning used by policy-makers in determining their positions at the moment when a real chance existed that that position might be changed – however small in practice that chance may have turned out to have been. The reasoning used on such occasions may well have differed from that employed on a more public platform, where considerations of maintaining international and domestic confidence undoubtedly weighed much more heavily. As Colijn once commented to E. Heldring: "If I ever devalue and meeting you on the way to the second chamber you ask me about my plans, then even if I am planning within the hour to present the necessary measures to the chamber, I would deny any such intention."(1)

THE IMPACT OF THE STERLING DEVALUATION

When the news of the sterling devaluation broke it had caught virtually everyone unprepared. Yet, within the department of trade and industry the reaction was calm. H.M. Hirschfeld, the secretary-general in the department wrote to his minister, T.J. Verschuur, acknowledging that the sterling depreciation would have more serious consequences for the economy than had those of the franc and the mark in the 1920's. On the other hand, he disparaged those who would immediately scream for protection – the economy had made its way through previous difficulties without government intervention and would presumably be able to do so again. The only exception he was prepared to consider was the specific case of shipping, since freight-rates were traditionally expressed in sterling and the industry was already facing a situation where a quarter of the fleet was laid up. Apart from that, he felt that the best industry could do was to prune back its costs, including wages, and that in this central and local government should itself set an example. There was no thought given to the idea that the Netherlands should follow the British lead.(2) This was the advice which Verschuur passed on to the rest of cabinet.(3)

Meanwhile, within the *Rijkscommissie voor Werkverruiming* (Government Commission for Work Creation) the idea had been floated of setting up a special commission to investigate the effects of the sterling devaluation on the economy and to examine the possibility for a 'holy peace' – whereby entrepreneurs would forego profits if workers would accept wage cuts.(4) The cabinet had agreed to this and on 12 October a special meeting of leading civil servants and representatives of the national employers' associations and trade unions met to consider the various ways in which industry could be supported in the wake of the new situation. Although the minister-president, Ruys de Beerenbrouck, stated at the outset that the purpose of the meeting was to consider the broadest panoply of possible measures, Verschuur immediately made it plain what he considered its main purpose to be. Virtually half of his opening address was devoted to the sacrosanct nature of the guilder's gold parity and the rest, having described how the upper classes had already suffered from the depression, to asserting that it was time for the working classes to do their bit by accepting wage cuts. Not surprisingly, this one-sided interpretation of the issues soured the whole atmosphere; the labour representatives were not prepared to discuss wage cuts at all and if they were, they wanted to be given a complete insight into companies financial records – an idea equally stridently resisted by employers.(5) Verschuur had been considering giving the commission permanent status. Draft legislation had been drawn up and J.B. Kan, ex-minister of home affairs and agriculture 1926-29, had been found prepared to take over its chairmanship, but nothing came of the idea. As far as the documentation in the archives is concerned, the cause would seem to lie in a disagreement over the exact representation of the national organisations on the committee, but more probably it lay in the fact that the committee seemed unlikely to come up with the 'advice' Verschuur wanted.(6)

The Dutch Central Bank took a much less phlegmatic view of the immediate consequences of the sterling devaluation than did the government since at the time it was holding £10,860,000 of its gold and foreign exchange reserves in the form of sterling assets, worth just over Dfl. 130 million at the pre-devaluation rate. Towards the end of August 1931, as international speculation against sterling was gaining momentum, the Bank's President, G. Vissering, and its Governor, P.J.C. Tetrode, visited London to discuss the situation with the Deputy Governor of the Bank of England, Sir E.M. Harvey. At the start of that meeting Vissering handed over an Aide-Memoire, which quite frankly expressed the opinion that unless something was done to allay the unease felt among the Board of Commissaries, they were likely to demand that the Banks' sterling holdings be very considerably reduced. It was pointed out that approximately £9,000,000 of these holdings had been accumulated in 1925/26 against the export of gold which had been used to boost sterling's gold cover immediately after the restoration of the gold standard "although the rate of exchange of the Florin did not afford any reason for the exportation of gold". Vissering then requested whether the Bank of England would guarantee that the Netherlands Bank's present sterling holdings "could always be converted back into gold at a reasonable rate of exchange, for example; on the basis of the Bank of England's selling price for gold". Such an undertaking, he argued, would probably be sufficient to allow the managing board of the Netherlands Bank to forestall any move to liquidate the Bank's sterling reserves.(8) Harvey had replied to this by pointing out that the new British government had pledged itself to maintaining the gold parity of sterling and that the Bank of England had reached an agreement with the government to utilise *all* its gold reserves in defence of sterling, even if that meant that the domestic circulation become entirely fiduciary (i.e. with no gold backing at all). He also added that the government was prepared to mobilise the country's foreign assets for the support of sterling and mentioned, confidentially, that the government was about to conclude a loan agreement worth about £80,000,000 which would be used for the same end. If, in these circumstances, he concluded, the Netherlands Bank wanted to liquidate its own sterling assets, it would be paid out in gold "to the last penny". Vissering had replied that this was not his intention: the Directors of the Bank, he explained, had sufficient confidence in sterling; what he wanted was a declaration "that at any time and in any circumstances" the Netherlands Bank would be able to exchange its sterling reserves for gold at the rate of exchange already determined, since such a declaration would enable him to still the fears of the Board of Commissaries. Harvey replied that no bank could give such an undertaking, since if the Bank had indeed exhausted its reserves such a statement would place the Netherlands Bank in a preferential position, and this he could not do.(8) Three days after the meeting Harvey telegrammed Vissering, drawing his attention to the international loans concluded by the British government, adding: "I trust this announcement will serve to abolish all doubts as to the safety of foreign funds in London."(9) The next communication which Vissering received from Harvey was a telegram sent on 20 September, which began: "I regret to inform you that the Bank of England are compelled to suspend the sale of gold in accordance with their obligation under the Gold Standard act 1925." (10)

Between the interview with Harvey and the abandonment of the gold standard by the United Kingdom, the Netherlands Bank had kept its reserve of sterling intact. Indeed, it had even purchased small amounts of sterling on the Amsterdam exchange! Vissering now pointed to two items in his earlier conversation with Harvey on asking whether the Bank of England was willing to guarantee the Dutch sterling reserves at the old exchange rate – the pledge that the Bank of England was prepared to sacrifice its entire stock of gold in sterling's defence and the statement that the Netherlands Bank could withdraw its sterling assets at any time and obtain its gold value in full.(11) That was not the interpretation which Harvey put on the interview however. He claimed that his statement implied that the Netherlands Bank would always be at liberty to exchange its sterling assets for gold and that would still apply when the temporary gold embargo was lifted but, he pointed out, he had explicitly refused to guarantee the gold value of those sterling assets.(12) Vissering replied simply, "I regret to say that we cannot share your views as to the question concerned."(13) A few days later he resigned, ostensibly for reasons of ill-health, and it was left to his successor Dr. L.J.A. Trip to clear up the mess, since sterling's immediate decline on the foreign exchange markets had the effect of wiping millions off the gold/guilder value of the Bank's sterling assets.

Trip attempted to push the Dutch claims along the lines already set out by Vissering. He wrote to Montague Norman, governor of the Bank of England, pointing out that the assurance that sterling would be defended down to the last ounce of gold had been a major factor in the Netherlands Bank's decision not to liquidate its sterling holdings. Yet when sterling began its depreciation the Bank of England's own weekly returns showed that the institution still held gold reserves worth £130,000,000. "For these reasons the Netherlands Bank feels that it is entitled to claim that the Bank of England should make an arrangement by which the Netherlands Bank will be safe-guarded against losses which it would otherwise suffer as a result of the depreciation of the £."(14) It was to no avail, Trip then attempted to enlist the direct help of the Government to exercise political pressure on the British Government on behalf of the Netherlands Bank. That too, failed. The minister of foreign affairs, F. Beelaerts van Blockland concluded that there could be no question of an official claim for restitution by the Dutch government since such a claim had no judicial basis and, for the same reason, the government should be wary of taking any aggressive stance on the matter. As far as he could guage from the documentation, the Bank of England had never guaranteed the value of the Netherlands Bank's sterling assets and had even invited the Netherlands Bank, in August, to withdraw those assets there and then.(15) Trip did, however, manage to persuade the government to allow the Dutch ambassador in London to hand over a memorandum from the Netherlands Bank to the British Goverment.(16) The reply was polite but final, "His Majesty's Government in the United Kingdom greatly regret the loss suffered by the Netherlands Bank as the result of the suspension of the gold standard by this country, but, after the fullest and most sympathetic consideration of all the circumstances of the case, they find it impossible to accord any preferential treatment to the sterling assets of the Netherlands Bank."(17) A final suggestion made by Trip to take the Bank's claim to the International Court of Justice in The Hague, was firmly quashed by the ministry of foreign affairs.(18)

THE DOLLAR DEVALUATION

Whilst the Netherlands Bank was exploring every avenue in an effort to recoup its sterling losses, the incident had done little to undermine the attractiveness of the Netherlands as a harbour for foreign capital. The value of official gold and foreign currency reserves rose from Dfl. 931,000,000 in September 1931, to a record level of Dfl. 1,106,000,000 in January 1933, and this despite the fact that virtually all the economic indicators were falling and that the problems of balancing central government expenditure were growing. 'In the Kingdom of the blind....'. In 1933 that was to come to an end.

In February 1933 Ruys de Beerenbrouck's cabinet lost a crucial budgetary vote in Parliament and had called for an early general election to be held on 26 April but it was not until a full month later that Colijn's new five party cabinet was officially installed in office. It was not the most propitious time to be without an effective government because on 19 April the United States, whilst holding the largest gold reserves of any country in the world, announced that it was abandoning the gold standard. A wave of speculation broke over the guilder, costing the Netherlands Bank Dfl. 100,000,000 of its gold reserves between the date of the dollar devaluation and the end of the first week in May. Trip urged Colijn that the only factor which could stem the flood was an early announcement of a cabinet committed to "sanitising" public expenditure.(19) However, neither the announcement of a strong cabinet, nor the unwavering support by Colijn at the World Economic Conference in London for an "untarnished" guilder, nor the announcement on 30 June of the monetary agreement among those countries still adhering to the gold standard, served to stem the nervousness about the postion of the guilder or to put an end to the ebbing away of reserves. By July 1933 the value of Dutch gold and foreign exchange reserves had fallen to Dfl. 811,000,000 , at which point foreign confidence was restored – for a while at least. Although that still left reserves well above what they had been until virtually the middle of 1931, the sheer scale of currency movements and the political vacuum in which they had taken place had caught most policy-makers completely unprepared. In view of this it is perhaps easier to understand why there was little sympathy, not only for speculators (naturally), but even for the most mannered pro-devaluation publicists, who were seen as providing the fuel for such speculation.

The next two paragraphs will be devoted to an analysis of two initiatives which found their origins in these stormy months, designed to persuade the government to change its course by agreeing to devalue the guilder. Before doing so, however, it is worth perhaps just illustrating the mild paranoia pervading the atmosphere of decision making. All three examples stem from July 1933, the same month in which the first "pro-devaluation" petition was sent and the month in which the Economic Council agreed to deliberate upon the devaluation question. First of all, J. Westerman Holstijn, one of the directors of the Netherlands Bank, wrote to P.J. Oud, the new minister of finance, asking whether there were not some judicial or constitutional way of taking action against those making propaganda in favour of devaluation (he was thinking about Sir Henry Deterding!! – see pp 35-36), or even those spreading rumours about devaluation. The fact that this was taken seriously, for a moment at least, was evidenced by the concept answer in the margin. "The matter has been discussed with Mr. Fruin from Justice and it appears that this is not possible under criminal law, and besides it would be a sign of weakness vis-à-vis the guilder."(20) Civil servants working in the Dutch East Indies were not to be so lucky. The fact that they were public employees made the task here much easier. Trip wrote to Oud stating that by openly making propaganda in favour of devaluation, or by at least making it known that such a step would not be unwelcome, they were creating unrest and undermining government policy. What he wanted was a warning sent that the government's patience was limited. In this case Oud agreed and such a warning was indeed issued.(21) Meanwhile, the ministry of foreign affairs had found another scape-goat in German (i.e. Jewish) refugees and an investigation was set up to discover whether they were indeed speculating and which measures could be taken against them. Here at least, common-sense prevailed.(22)

THE ECONOMIC COUNCIL

The Economic Council was a brain-child of Verschuur conceived with the purpose of furnishing the ministry of economic affairs with independent (and useful) advice on matters of policy. It was not as though the ministry was without a forum for testing policy initiatives before they actually took on concrete form. Indeed, it was littered with advisory organs – some devoted to particular aspects of policy, others representing particular strata of economic interests – but none seemed to work (or, were allowed to work) in a satisfactory manner. The Economic Council was designed to be different. Its membership was to be individually recruited on the basis of demonstrated qualities of economic excellence from the industrial and academic world and the compass of its deliberations was to be all embracing. The legislation setting up the council was introduced before Parliament in July 1932, though it was not until June 1933 that the Council, with its fifteen members, was officially installed.(23)

At its second meeting on 8 July 1933 professor H.A. Kaag proposed that the Council should discuss the question of the exchange rate, firstly, because he considered that it was necessary that the council should try to form a concensus on the issue and secondly, because it affected so many other aspects of its future deliberations. This was immediately opposed by the chairman, professor I.P. de Vooys, who argued that the government had requested no advice on the matter and that although the Council was free to give advice on its own initiative, it should not do so lightly; especially on a question "over which there should be no division in the country and (over which) great discipline should exist, whereby the words of those in whom the people have trust should be followed". On the other hand, professor F. de Vries could not see how the question could be avoided if the Council was to discuss economic policy and economic issues in general. Nor did he agree that it was an issue for discipline and solidarity. "What is involved here is a question where dogma has no place. It is a difficult, scientific question which must be seriously discussed." That discussion, he argued, could best be prepared for by installing a small sub-commission. This suggestion seemed to find general backing, though the general treasurer at the ministry of finance, Dr. A. van Doornick, urged that a distinction be made between the Council discussing an issue for its own enlightenment and discussing an issue with the aim of advising the government. "If the Council agrees with the government then the advice is not necessary; in the other event would not the advice of the Council have the result not that the government would alter policy but only that a conflict would exist." In the end it was agreed to form a committee comprising Trip, Heldring, Van Doorninck, De Vries and Kaag which was to have completed its work, if possible, before October.(24)

Trip, who had missed the meeting, was apoplectic when he heard the news. He wrote to Hirschfeld urging that the entire discussion should be stopped, adding that "if the Economic Council has nothing better to do than to begin such dubious and, in the view of the established policy of the government and the Netherlands Bank, totally useless and damaging discussion, then I fear that that institution is taking the wrong path and that for me at least in the long run there can be no place."(25) He wrote in a similar vein to Heldring, urging him to approach the ministers concerned to obtain a clarification on the question of the competence of the Council. The way it was going, he felt, held the risk that the Council would be "smothered in the crib". It could only discredit itself by discussing questions which had already been decided, and its time would be better employed looking at what policy the government should follow after the setback of the World Economic Conference.(26) Trip's efforts to silence the discussion there and then, however, failed. Hirschfeld replied that he had discussed the question with Verschuur and that the latter considered that the government did not value an advice on the question of whether or not to maintain the gold standard, asked for or not. Verschuur had suggested that the Council could, valuably, consider what measures the government should take in the interests of the economy and thus give extra support to the decision which had been taken. In the process, it was possible that a difference of opinion could emerge "over the consequences of that decision, or, possibly better expressed, the consequences of the wrong decisions which had been taken abroad, but such a difference of opinion could clarify issues". Anyway, the advice of the council had not been asked for, and if it gave the government that advice, Verschuur would merely take cognicance of it. It was always possible, of course, that the Council would decide that the sub-commitee's study was only intended for the information of its own members.(27) Trip received somewhat better news from Heldring, who declared that whilst he, himself, was not of the opinion that the question should never be discussed, he did consider a discussion at that moment "highly inopportune and dangerous" and he pledged his co-operation in helping to defer such a discussion until a more suitable time!(28)

Nothing has been found about what went on in that sub-committee, but it did have an in-built anti-devaluationist majority in the persons of Trip, Heldring and Van Doorninck, with Kaag and De Vries against. The report it eventually produced was certainly comprehensive....but, did it really take nine months to prepare? The fact that it did not eventually appear until March 1934 was obviously a result with which Trip and Heldring would have been pleased, but whether they deliberately stalled proceedings can only be guessed at. The real surprise in the report, however, was not the timing of its appearance but what it had to say on the contentious gold standard question. The sub-committee reported that it had decided to keep its deliberation on monetary policy secret because of the "psychological and political implications". It was further unanimously agreed to withold from criticising government policy (general economic, military and financial) in anticipation of the measures to be taken by the cabinet and a majority (viz. presumably Trip, Heldring and Van Doorninck) were of the opinion that such criticism would weaken the position not only of the goverment but of the Council itself.(29)

When the fruits of this work, such as they were, were presented to the Council meeting in full session, they were accepted with remarkable aquiescence. Only the socialist professor Bonger recorded a dissident note, though he did so with a fervour which made up for the silence of the rest, pleading for social organisation to forestall the danger of anarchy, arguing against the stress on wage-cutting etc. However, as far as devaluation was concerned, he stated that he had nothing to add to what he had said at the previous meeting, which is unfortunate for the historian because what he had said then had not been minuted.(30)

If the members of the Council had thought that by avoiding controversy they were likely to win the confidence of the government, they were doomed to be sadly disappointed. More and more major legislation passed them by and they were often left with the task of fine-tuning rather than making policy.

THE PRO-DEVALUATION LOBBY

In July 1933 the first 'pro-devaluation' address was sent by Professor Polak to the government. It argued that the government's decision at the London Conference to maintain the gold standard meant that it had to find other ways to cope with the impact of a relatively high Dutch price level – import barriers or subsidies financed from increased consumer levies or taxation would only serve to raise costs even further, whilst subsidies financed through increased borrowing would also be inflationary. The address was sceptical over the chances that a deflationary policy would be successful in closing the gap. However, before going on to urge that the government should go ahead and devalue, it somewhat confusingly stated: "A number of the undersigned expect good from the abandonment of the current gold price of the guilder, others among them preferred the above-mentioned measures (i.e. domestic deflation-RTG) though they do not conceal from themselves that these will bring with them large, possibly insurmountable, problems. But the undersigned are unanimous in the opinion that both possibilities are the only alternatives to maintain the level of Dutch business and thus of our national welfare." The remainder of the address went on to argue that a modest devaluation would stimulate business profitability and enable the cost of agricultural support programmes to be reduced without major impact on domestic price levels (because only prices for imported goods would rise and that, because of retail margins, domestic prices for those need not rise as fast).(31) The address had requested a meeting of the delegation with representatives of the government; a request which, perhaps in the view of the influential list of signatories, was granted. Colijn requested Oud and Trip also to be present. Archival research to date has only uncovered a written record of Trip's reflections on the address. Trip was, in the first place, perplexed as to whether the document did indeed represent a plea to abandon the gold standard since, as appeared from the text itself, some of the signatories quite clearly preferred to stay on gold at the existing parity. How many and who were they he asked?(32) Moving into the arguments put forward in favour of devaluation, he argued that the high price and wage level in the Netherlands was not the only reason for the difficulties faced by business. Even if the gap were eliminated, enterprise had still the general recession in World trade to deal with. It was true that that problem, in turn, was aggravated by currency depreciation elsewhere, but the answer to that was for those countries to return to gold. Nor did he consider that the process of deflation would involve a large (and impossible) task for the government – "When the government puts its finances in order and stops working against deflation by artificially holding up the wages and salaries of personnel in government service and allows the public to pay prices for the services rendered, then deflation can, for the rest, be left to enterprise itself." Moreover, he felt that the address underestimated the dangers inherent in a devaluation. He did not consider that a return to gold at a lower parity was possible but that the exchange rate would have to be left more or less to its own lot (perhaps eventually to be stabilised). In such circumstances a *small* depreciation was unlikely to be the result. Domestic prices would rise significantly. "It is true that the same quantum of exports at the same foreign price would give a higher return in guilders than before. But, firstly it is the question whether foreigners will not make themselves master of a large part of this export premium and, in addition, the danger for repraisal measures from abroad is not as the addressees would have it."(33)

The two sides met at the end of August. The pro-devaluation camp represented by the Rotterdam professors J. Goudriaan and F. de Vries, by A.F. Bronsing, one of the directors of the shipping company *Stoomvaart Maatschappij Nederland* and by H.F. van Leeuwen, director of the *Twentsche Bank*. Perhaps not surprisingly the two sides began and ended the meeting poles apart. The only concession which Colijn was prepared to make to the pro-devaluation case was that the shipping industry, where freight rates were expressed universally in sterling, might well benefit from a lower guilder exchange rate. F. de Vries' argument that the whole world was heading in the direction of an international currency system in which central banks would be responsible for exchange-rate management, that trade would be reduced to a minimum and that in these circumstances the conditions for a restoration of the gold standard would never return, failed to make any impact at all. That was about the only new standpoint advanced and for the rest the meeting seemed to have consisted of the reiteration of existing stances. Colijn ended the proceedings by announcing that "the gentlemen did not succeed in convincing him that the government's standpoint was wrong or that the Netherlands or the Dutch East Indies would be better off were the gold standard to be abandoned". He did offer to meet them again after a time "without in any way giving the impression that his opinion could be changed in that time".(34)

In January 1934 the pro-devaluation group sent a second petition to the government. It was a much more substantial document than the first and, apart from reiterating the familiar arguments and attempting to rebut the possible counter-arguments, it was accompanied by an extensive statistical appendix comparing the performance of 'gold' and 'non-gold' countries.(35) It was answered by two separate memoranda – one from Verschuur(36) and one from Trip, accompanied by a separate statistical commentary.(37) It is worth dwelling on the statistical data used to support the pro-devaluation case partly because, at a purely academic level, it illustrates the difficulties in proving the argument one way or the other, but more importantly because it is possible that the onslaught of Trip and Verschuur may have destroyed whatever lingering credibility the pro-devaluationists may have had in government circles.

Two general points were made by both. In the first place, whatever the results of the comparison, it was doubtful whether the difference in development could be attributed simply to differences in the external value of the currency – differences in developments before 1929 or 1931, differences in foreign trade regimes and differences in economic structures also played a role. In the second place, both were sceptical about the arbitrary and inconsistent choice of countries represented in the comparisons made (each table lists underneath the countries represented in the 'gold' and 'non-gold' groups).

The first point which the pro-devaluationists made was that despite the greater decline in wholesale prices experienced by the 'gold countries', retail prices had fallen by a lesser extent and that the disparity between the two was greater than in the 'non-gold' countries. This was, according to them, an indication of the greater internal dislocation in the economies of the former (see table 8.1).

This attracted a barrage of criticism from both Trip and Verschuur. The 'arithmetic average' took no account of the relative importance of the various economies and the addition or subtraction of a country to the group could easily change the whole picture. The wholesale price indices themselves had different weightings which made comparison between them difficult (see table 8.2).

Neither made the point that the Dutch index was as good as useless even for measuring changes within the Netherlands, let alone for purposes of international comparison.(38) More tellingly, they pointed out that the 'retail price index' was not a retail price index at all but a cost of living index. Aside from the problems of comparability, the cost of living index included a heavy

TABLE 8.1
INDICES OF WHOLESALE AND RETAIL PRICES, 1927-29 = 100, Arithmetic Average
(wp = Wholesale Prices, rp = Retail Prices)

	1929		1930		1931		1932		i-vi 1933	
	wp	rp	wp	rp	wp	rp	wp	rp	wp	rp
Non-Gold Countries *	97.76	99.05	86.81	93.03	77.55	85.05	77.61	83.10	76.60	81.32
Gold Countries **	97.59	101.58	85.42	100.02	74.11	89.31	64.85	81.67	57.95	80.79
Netherlands	97.06	99.83	79.97	95.66	66.30	89.84	54.00	83.71	48.55	81.75

* England, Sweden, Norway, Denmark, Finland, India, Australia, Japan, New Zealand, S.Africa (after 1932)

** Netherlands, Belgium, France, Switzerland, Italy, Czechoslovakia, Poland, Romania, Dutch East Indies, S. Africa

weighting of items such as rents and energy which not only did not figure in the wholesale price indices but which were also relatively slow to adjust.

A further point made by the pro-devaluationists was that the exports of the 'gold countries', measured in value terms, had fallen faster than those of 'non-gold countries' countries and that the former had failed to experience any up-turn in 1933. The data was expressed in terms of national currency valuations and also as an index, after correction, for price fluctuations using the national wholesale price index (see table 8.3).(39)

Again, protests were made about the use of arithmetic averages. Portugal, which did not appear in any other of the calculations, accounted for 0.3 per cent of European exports and received the same weight as England, which accounted for 22.6 per cent. Why include it at all? Perhaps because in 1932 its index for exports in national currency was 84.1 compared with the 'non-gold' index of 64.9. Moreover, the comparison in national currency was almost bound to show a divergence since every gold-dollar earned, for example by England, after devaluation earned 30 – 40 per cent more pounds. The correction for domestic price fluctuations hit the problem of the comparability of the wholesale price indices. What was required, and what Trip supplied, was a comparison of what those exports earned in hard currency – i.e. gold. (see table 8.4 the data for the Netherlands has been supplied by the author).(40) The result no longer supported the pro-devaluation case!

TABLE 8.2
THE WEIGHTINGS OF COMPONENTS IN CERTAIN WHOLESALE PRICE INDICES, per cent.

	England	Sweden	Netherlands	Belgium	France
Food	37.9	45.2	58.3	13.3	44.3
Minerals and Metals	19	12.8	12.5 22.6 17.8		
Textiles	19	16.9	6.2	16.4	13.3
Various	24.1	25.1	23.0	52.3	24.6

TABLE 8.3
VALUE OF EXPORTS, 1927-29 av = 100. Arithmetic Average.

	National Currencies					National Currencies deflated by WP				
	1929	1930	1931	1932	I-VI 1933	1929	1930	1931	1932	I-VI 1933
Non Gold Countries *	101.4	82.7	68.5	64.9	65.5	103.0	95.2	84.1	83.0	85.4
Gold Countries **	99.6	83.3	63.8	41.9	36.3	102.9	96.7	85.4	63.5	61.1
Netherlands	101.6	87.8	67.0	43.2	36.8	104.7	109.8	101.0	80.0	75.7

* England, Sweden, Norway, Denmark, Finland, India, Australia, Japan, New Zealand, S. Africa (after 1932), Argentina, Mexico, Portugal.

** Netherlands, Belgium, France, Switzerland, Italy, Tjechoslowakia, Poland, Dutch East Indies, S. Africa.

The pro-devaluationists also attempted a comparison of the export performance of both groups (albeit redefined yet again) on the basis of the volume of exports, but that fell so flat on its face that it is not even worth giving the figures. What they did was to list the quantities of a number of export products in 1927-29, 1932 and i-vi 1933. The percentage change of each product was calculated. These percentage changes were then added up and divided by the number of products (i.e. an arithmetic average). So, for Sweden, hides and leather declined by 12.6 per cent whilst iron and steel declined by 25 per cent. These two products together (there were others!) would yield a decline of 18.8 per cent by the method used. But, hides and leather only represented 0.1 per cent of exports in the base year whilst iron and steel represented 76.7 per cent! No further comment was required.

The final point which the pro-devaluationists sought to make was that unemployment in the 'gold countries', which had been lower at the start of the crisis than in the group which were to form the 'non-gold' countries, had exceeded it by the first half of 1933 and that the position of the Netherlands was particularly unfavourable. The way in which this was illustrated was to express actual employment as a percentage of the active population (see table 8.5).

The first query was, what exactly was unemployment? For England, Belgium

TABLE 8.4
TRIP'S CALCULATIONS OF THE VALUE OF EXPORTS, 1927-29 av = 100, Arithmetic Average.

	National Currencies					Gold Value				
	1929	1930	1931	1932	1933	1929	1930	1931	1932	1933
Non Gold Countries *			67.1	63.1			55.4		41.9	
Gold Countries *			65.4	42.1				45.4	42.1	
Netherlands	103.4	90.8	71.1	49.0	45.4	103.4	90.8	71.1	49.0	45.4

* It is not clear which countries have been included in each group.

TABLE 8.5
EMPLOYMENT AS PERCENTAGE OF THE ACTIVE POPULATION, 1927-29 av = 100, Arithmetic Average.

	1929	1930	1931	1932	1933 (I-VI)
Non Gold Countries *	97.4	96.8	94.1	93.6	93.1
Gold Countries **	99.6	99.1	97.6	94.3	92.6
Netherlands	99.1	98.7	97.2	91.5	98.4

* England, Sweden, Norway, Denmark.
** Netherlands, France, Belgium, Czechoslovakia.

and the Netherlands (till 1931), it was those without work who had been insured against unemployment, for Sweden it was those reported unemployed by trade unions, for Norway, Czechoslovakia and The Netherlands (from 1932 onwards) it was those registered with employment bureaus, for France it was all those seeking work. And what was the active population? The German source used worked on the basis of the active population in 1920 or 1921 multiplied by the population increase which had occurred between then and 1931. Furthermore Trip had located errors in the English and Dutch figures (41) and, after correcting for these and substituting Switzerland for Czechoslovakia in the 'gold countries', he then presented his own calculations (see table 8.6).

All of this led Verschuur to conclude that although the address was not shown to be wrong, the statistical material employed had not survived the critique and that the situation in the first six months of 1933 did not represent the end phase by which the effects of currency depreciation could be said to have worked themselves out. Overall he felt that the address was too concerned with the needs for industry and took too little account of the interests of the population as a whole. Trip's conclusion was more of less the same. What the cabinet made of this remains unrecorded. On the copy of the address in the cabinet's archive, Colijn's secretary had drawn his attention to the fact that the addressees had offered a verbal exposition of the arguments. Did he want to take up the offer? "No" Colijn had scrawled, "verbal exposition, in my view, cannot bring any change. On both sides the subject has been exhausted" (in Dutch 'doodgepraat'). And, exhausted it appears to have remained. Neither the third

TABLE 8.6
TRIP'S CALCULATION OF EMPLOYMENT AS A PERCENTAGE OF THE ACTIVE POPULATION, 1927-29 av = 100, Arithmetic Average.

	1929	1930	1931	1932	1933 (I-VI)
Non Gold Countries	97.4	96.8	95.3	93.6	
Gold Countries			98.4	96.6	
Netherlands	99.1	98.7	97.2	95.2	94.1

address sent in April 1935 nor the two petitions in May and July 1936 attracted any written rebuttal which could have formed the basis for an eventual discussion.

THE STEENBERGHE RESIGNATION

In April 1934 Verschuur had resigned as Minister of Economic Affairs for reasons of ill-health. His successor was the ex-chairman of the Roman Catholic Employee Association, M.P.L. Steenberghe, himself one of the signatories of the 1934 pro-devaluation petition who had apparently agreed, on accepting the position, not to press for a change in government monetary policy unless external circumstances altered.(42) The suspension of the Gold Standard by Belgium on March 30th 1935 and the subsequent devaluation of the Belgian franc by 28 per cent provided just such a change in external circumstances!

Steenberghe instructed Hirschfeld to prepare a cabinet memorandum on the problem of maintaining the gold standard.(43) The memorandum focused on two major issues – the likely implications of the Belgian devaluation for the Dutch economy and the necessity for a devaluation in the context of Dutch economic policy. On the first issue, it was pointed out that 77 per cent of imports from Belgium were competing in sectors of the Dutch economy which enjoyed no protection whatsoever and that the metal, glass, chemical and textile industries in particular would be likely to experience intense Belgium competition. At the same time Dutch exports to Belgium would also undergo a loss in competitiveness and this would primarily affect agriculture (which accounted for over half of Dutch exports) iron, radios, rayon, fine pottery etc. Moreover the increased Belgium competition in third markets would have serious negative consequences for the machinery industry and for transit carriers.

It was not possible, the memorandum argued, to meet this challenge by a further dose of deflation since any possible gains in reducing domestic price levels could be overturned by further currency depreciation elsewhere. Moreover, the stage had been reached where the effects of further cuts in government spending were being increasingly eroded by the increased budgetary claims of unemployment benefits and measures of industrial support. Now was the time to put the question of the continuation of the gold standard firmly on the political agenda.

On the negative side it was admitted that a devaluation would push up the costs of imported raw materials but, it was argued, since raw materials comprised no more than half of total production costs, industry would benefit, on balance from the new situation. The impact on the cost of living, and thus the potential trigger for increased wage demands, was unlikely to be muted by a reduction in retail margins (evident in other countries which had devalued) and it could be even further reduced by a change in agricultural policy. On this second point, calculations had been made which showed that a 25 per cent devaluation would yield a net income of Dfl. 41,000,000 to the Agriculture Crisis Fund, turning the anticipated deficit of Dfl. 19,200,000 for 1935 into a surplus of Dfl. 22,700,000.(44) This surplus could be used to stabilise bread prices, to abolish levies on meat and to reduce the tax on sugar. A second possible negative consequence was the risk of repraisals against Dutch exports. It was claimed that the effect of these was likely to be small and that, anyway, even if export volume did not increase, exports themselves would become more profitable. Finally the memorandum discussed the possible financial consequences. It argued that no country which had devalued had found credit difficult to obtain, that any financial difficulties were usually temporary and that the Netherlands, with its healthy financial structure, was less likely to experience such problems than countries which had been forced off the Gold Standard.

Colijn's reply was, not unexpectedly, entirely negative.(45) He doubted whether exports would increase at all (a claim which Steenberghe had not made). He considered that any gains in profitability expressed in 'new guilders' would be eroded by higher wages and the latter would be inevitable given the equally inevitable rise in the cost of living. After tackling some of the more specific points in Steenberghe's note, he went on to conclude that "sacrificing of the gold standard by The Netherlands means sacrificing every fixed point in the monetary confusion". He pointed out that he had not come to this conclusion "from considerations of international decency – I am in agreement with the compilor of the note that we don't have to get worked up about that – but from the fact that it will unleash a run on the various currencies downwards, whilst no one can predict how far this depreciation must go, before international stability is restored". He proposed that the Belgian 'experiment' should be closely followed and that it should be decided to depreciate, it should not be done immediately after a run on the guilder but at a time when the decision could be freely made – not that he was personally prepared to take part in that decision.

Oud was equally dismissive(46) though whilst Colijn seemed to lay his stress on the dangers of international monetary chaos Oud's argument emphasised the risk of domestic monetary chaos. He felt that the first result of a devaluation or depreciation would be an "enormous" flight of capital which could only be stemmed by the introduction of exchange control and without which "we would half bleed to death". That exchange-control would itself form an enormous burden for trade. Furthermore, the exchange rate would plummet and if an attempt were made to control it through an equalisation fund, it would end in the exhaustion of all metallic (i.e. gold) reserves. The result would be inflationary. Meanwhile, the capital flight would create difficulties in funding the floating debt, the government would have to resort to the printing press which, again, would be inflationary. All of this would make the hoped for advantages of a devaluation illusory. Import prices would also rise and he doubted whether the middle-class would be willing to reduce their trading margins. The result would be that the cost of living would rise, and, with it, wages. Any temporary advantage to exports would also be immediately annulled through reprisal measures abroad.

The matter came to cabinet in June 1935. Against the combined opposition of Colijn and Oud. Steenberghe had little chance. Colijn's suggestion that an ongoing study into the Belgian experience be instigated was rejected by Steenberghe "out of hand".(47) Apparently isolated in cabinet, he had little choice but to resign. To Heldring whom he bumped into afterwards, he confided, "Purely a fundamental difference of opinion".(48)

THE CABINET CRISIS JULY 1935

Steenberghe's resignation was not the only symptom of the fact that Colijn's administration was approaching something akin to a mid-term crisis. Only a month earlier the Minister of Education, H.P. Marchant had been dropped from his post and replaced by J.R. Slotemaker de Bruïne.(49) The month before, in April, the elections for provincial office had shown a disquieting fall in support for all but one of the five parties represented in government compared with the general elections of 1933 and, more disturbingly, an alarmingly high level of support for the fascist NSB.(50)

In July 1935, the government began the parliamentary defence of a supplementary round of expenditure cuts. The original budget estimates for 1935 had envisaged a deficit of Dfl. 92 million and parliament had approved a series of

Meeting of the cabinet. Photo: Historisch Documentatiecentrum voor het Nederlands Protestantisme.

measures designed to trim the figure back to Dfl. 30 million. However, in April the government had done its sums again and had calculated that without corrective action the deficit for the year would approach Dfl. 75 million and the measures proposed were intended to eliminate that deficit entirely. In parliament the proposals ran into a storm of protest from both the socialist opposition and the catholics. It was the criticism of the latter which prompted Colijn to risk a show-down. In his speech he asked: "Do people still have confidence in the general policy of the government; yes or no? I consider that such an answer must be given ..." At least that was what the stenographer recorded. Later, Colijn added the following words: "... by dropping undermining criticism." The difference was an important one since without the addition Colijn's speech could be interpreted as a demand for a vote of confidence, a highly unusual practice in Dutch parliamentary democracy. Whether Colijn had intended to demand a vote of confidence or not did not really matter, the RKSP leader, Aalberse, thought that he had and declared that his party had no intention of voting for the government. These exchanges had transformed a difficult parliamentary situation into a crisis. If the government were to demand a vote of confidence (and there were those among its supporters who did not want to see such an unusual procedure employed) it would undoubtedly lose. But having seemingly countenanced such a move, could it now go back and simply request a vote on the budgetry legislation itself? On the evening of 23 July Colijn announced before parliament that his interpretation of a vote which had not taken place on a motion which had not been tabled was that the cabinet could not command a parliamentary majority. He suspended the debate until he had consulted the Queen about what to do next.(51) There was little doubt that the political uncertainty would place the guilder under immediate and severe speculative pressure.

Trip was in hospital with a kidney stone. On that same evening the Netherlands Bank directors J.F. de Beaufort and J. Westerman Holstijn had discussed policy options over the telephone with Oud. They had agreed that it would be premature to announce a 1 or 2 per cent hike in the discount rate first thing the next morning since such a move would be more likely to provoke panic than to allay it.(52) Panic, however, is what there was. By 11.30 am the next day the bank had already lost 2000 kgs of gold and 125,000,000 French francs (worth approx. Dfl. 17,700,000) and it was decided to raise the discount rate from 3 to 5 per cent.(53) By the evening the Bank had lost gold and foreign exchange reserves worth Dfl. 62,116,000. During the course of the day Trip had been in telephone contact with Colijn. Colijn had asked if Trip considered that the guilder could be successfully defended should the cabinet resign and should a drawn-out cabinet crisis follow – to which Trip had replied, no. To the question whether the guilder could be defended if the cabinet attempted to hang on and came out with a declaration in parliament pledging commitment to the gold standard, Trip merely replied that it was worth trying. Later, at the hospital, Trip, de Beaufort and Westerman Holstijn had discussed how much gold the Bank should be prepared to sacrifice in defence of the guilder and had decided that a line should be drawn when reserves reached Dfl. 500,000,000. Together they then drafted an official death-knell for the Dutch gold standard.

> 'The political development, which is generally known, has led to such a large and continous capital flight, that the Directors have come to the conviction that it can no longer bind itself to its declaration of 1925. They have therefore asked the government to suspend its provisions. They were in complete agreement with this and agreed that the Bank should no longer consider itself bound by the declaration. In conjunction with this the government has announced a general prohibition on the export of gold. It follows from this that the link between the guilder and gold has been broken.
> The Bank will forthwith concentrate its attention towards the domestic price level and will work towards, as far as possible, preventing a rise in domestic prices through means of its credit and discount policy. This however does not mean that the Bank will cease to follow carefully the course of exchange rates and, if the occasion demands it, to intervene in this area.'

De Beaufort and Westerman Holstijn then met with Colijn and Oud. They said that what was urgently needed was some "reassuring news" from the government. "What reassuring news?" asked Colijn rhetorically. De Beaufort then went on to state that the Netherlands Bank did not feel that it was responsible to allow its gold reserves to drain away to satisfy the demand for flight capital and that after a certain point, it would request the governments approval to abandon the Gold standard. The ministers agreed, though "they regretted that a government, that had wanted to maintain the Gold Standard should have to be the one to take the decision whilst those who were actually responsible for it should be able to declare themselves innocent". Colijn did ask, however, for a "drastic increase" in the discount rate to which De Beaufort replied affirmitively, should it prove necessary.(54) It only remained to see whether the Dfl. 500,000,000 barrier would be reached before a resolution of the political crisis could restore the expected calm to the market.

On 25 July, Colijn tendered his cabinet's resignation and the following day, amid the uncertainty over who was to be charged with forming a new coalition, a renewed wave of selling hit the guilder. The Netherlands Bank announced a further one per cent rise in the discount rate, bringing it to 6 per cent but nonetheless over Dfl. 47,000,000 of gold and foreign exchange reserves were lost. Two more days at that rate and the battle for the guilder would be lost. Meanwhile, Aalberse had been appointed with the task of forming a broadly-based 'parliamentary' cabinet – a virtually impossible task but one which was also dangerously time-consuming. In the event the money market was relatively calm. It was a Saturday and the rise in discount rates had also played a contributory role. In the course of the day Aalberse handed back his mandate and on Sunday 28 July Colijn was called upon to reconstruct an 'extra-parliamentary' cabinet. The announcement served to stem the tide of speculation and

TABLE 8.7
MUTATIONS IN THE GOLD AND FOREIGN EXCHANGE POSITION OF THE NETHERLANDS BANK (guilders)

	Gold Loss	Loss of French Francs	Total Loss	Value of Gold * f/e Reserves
Monday 22 July				688,468,000
Tuesday 23 July	875,000	3,144,000	4,019,000	
Wednesday 24 July	26,905,000	35,211,000	62,116,000	
Thursday 25 July	20,772,000	7,423,000	28,195,000	
Friday 26 July	28,179,000	19,378,000	47,557,000	
Saturday 27 July	2,734,000	7,596,000	10,330,000	
	79,465,000	72,752,000	152,217,000	
Gold Purchases			+ 14,140,000	
Adjustment for Acc. Procedures *			+ 7,593,000	
Monday 29 July				557,984,000

* Namely that gold was sold including a profit margin but was inventorised minus that margin.

Source: Arch. DNB, Dossier: Monetaire politiek binnenland, De moeilijkheden in Juli/Augustus 1935, Goudverliezen 23-27 July 1935 dd. 31.7.1935

when on 30 July he had completed his task the crisis had been brought to an end. But what if the Monday had arrived with the political situation unresolved? The Netherlands Bank holdings of gold and foreign exchange reserves were Dfl. 58,000,000 away from the guilder's trip-wire of Dfl. 500,000,000. Another day like 24 July would have been sufficient to push the guilder over the edge. Instead it was to take another fourteen months!

TOWARDS THE ABANDONMENT OF THE GOLD STANDARD

The July cabinet crisis had brought home to the government not only how close it had come to actually doing the unthinkable but it should also have forced home the message of how woefully unprepared it had been with respect to following an effective exchange-rate policy should it have been forced to abandon the gold standard. Although the formation of a new Colijn cabinet had removed the immediate cause of the panic, confidence in the guilder remained fragile at its best. Whilst in public speeches and utterances government ministers attempted to put a brave face on things behind the scenes contingency planning began in earnest.

In August Westerman Holstijn drafted some thoughts on the basis of the draft announcement of the abandonment of the gold standard.(55) He considered that a devaluation would be a disaster for the Dutch people (those who were savers and those salary earners who would lose out as a result of rising prices) that it would not solve the problems with which business was confronted nor the problems of government finance. Thus the government should dc everything in its power to resist a devaluation and should that prove impossible, it should be advised to keep the devaluation as small as possible. He felt that if the Netherlands Bank should be forced to suspend gold payments, it should not announce a depreciation but leave that to the government "if gold payments are stopped, this does not mean that the guilder *must* be devalued (margin comment by Trip "in my opinion untrue"). The guilder is after all *not overvalued* (margin comment by Trip "in my opinion untrue"). The exchange rate can easily maintain its gold value (other than in the case of capital flight on a large scale caused by panic)." Should the government decide to suspend support for the guilder, he felt that the resulting depreciation could be small or even neglegible. Should the government indeed decide to devalue by fixed percentage, then the guilder should be held at that rate. However his own opinion was that the possibility existed that temporary suspension of gold-payments could be followed by a return to the gold standard at the old rate; an opinion which, judging from his margin comments (there are more – RTG) Trip did not share.(56) On the back of an envelope Trip jotted the following thoughts "I am firmly convinced that if gold payments are suspended it will result in a guilder *depreciation*. It cannot be doubted that this depreciation will be permanent since after a depreciation no further deflationary measures will be pushed through. Depreciation means, at least temporarily, the end of the deflation. This must lead to a *devaluation*."(57)

A few days later, the Bank had completed its work on a draft Royal Decree for the abandonment of the Gold Standard. It announced that the guilder would be traded until further notice at a price of Dfl. 2196.67 per kg (it had been Dfl. 2928.29 implying a devaluation of 25 per cent). The 'profit' accruing on existing reserves would be placed in an exchange equalisation fund(58) under the supervision of the minister of finance to be used by the Bank to neutralise speculative or other influences on the exchange rate. The explanatory text, which was to form the basis for the governments defense of the legislation, explained that the figure of 25 per cent had been chosen "because it is of the opinion that this percentage, in the light of the price deflation and of the depreciation or devaluation observed in other countries, does not provide any occasion for the accusation of exchange-rate competition".(59)

Oud responded to this proposal by calling upon the Royal Commissioner to the Netherlands Bank, professor G.W..J. Bruins, to prepare a separate memorandum on the future policy to be followed in the event of abandoning the gold standard. It differed from the semi-official Bank version both in respect of the size of the depreciation envisaged and on the need to return to a fixed gold parity. As far as the former was concerned Bruins argued for a level of depreciation between that of the Belgian franc and that of sterling, i.e. between 28 and 40 per cent. He argued that it had already become clear that the Belgian devaluation had been insufficient to restore equilibrium and that the authorities had erred on the side of conservatism because they were still wary of the experience in the 20's when the franc had been reduced to 1/7 of its previous parity. On the other hand it was not necessary to follow sterling all the way since the currency had quite clearly been overvalued before 1931 and because the Netherlands had made some progress in reducing nominal prices and costs. Exactly where, between the two, the guilder should aim for he refused to say. However, he was firm on the point that whatever level was *temporarily* chosen (and he recommended linking the guilder to sterling) the Dutch should retain the freedom to correct the exchange rate in the future. Even if there were a partial return to the gold standard, the Netherlands should not follow suit. By way of further argument against fixing a new gold parity he pointed to the experience of the United States where, he felt, the 'gold profits' resulting from a devaluation had fuelled an unhealthy degree of money creation. Where his advice did agree with the Bank's vision was on the need to introduce an exchange-equalisation fund for managing the exchange rate.(60)

Trip's reaction to Bruins observations began by suggesting that he seemed to expect only good to flow from a devaluation and that the note itself constituted a plea in favour of devaluation. He accepted the point that the guilder did not need to depreciate as far as sterling but he did not think it needed to depreciate as far as the Belgian franc either. Where Trip did change his position, however, was in conceding that a new gold parity should not be fixed immediately, not because he sympathised with Bruin's main argument of keeping a degree of freedom of action but because of the danger that new paper money might be issued against the revalued gold reserves.(61)

At this point Trip and Oud together must have agreed to the main outlines of policy to be followed in the event of a guilder devaluation; namely a lower level of depreciation than 28 or even 25 per cent, the creation of an exchange equalisation fund and a managed float of the guilder tying it to sterling.(62)

The contingency planning for managing a guilder devaluation appears to have been completed by the end of 1935, but nothing further untoward happened which made it seem likely that they would be called upon until September 1936.(63) On Thursday 24 September, Jaques Rueff informed Colijn and Oud, on behalf of the French government, of his country's plans to announce France's abandonment of the gold standard the following evening. The cabinet decided not to follow suit. The domestic price inflation which had occured in France and the lack of confidence in bourgeois circles with the Popular Front government found no counterpart in the Netherlands and it was felt that the Netherlands Bank could cope with the anticipated backlash of speculation. Besides, there was no indication that Switzerland planned any change in its currency either. However, in the course of Saturday 26 September the news was received that the Swiss government had abandoned the gold standard leaving the Netherlands utterly alone.

That evening a hastily convened cabinet meeting took place, with Trip alsc in attendance, which lasted to after midnight. The image later painted was that Trip and Oud had had the greatest difficulty in convincing Colijn that it was futile even to attempt to defend the guilder. Oud wrote later: "The motive behind his position can only add to his reputation. The motive was no other than one of decency. I do not believe that any decision affected him so badly as this one. We met from the evening ... until after midnight before the die was cast. Several times Colijn posed the question... whether hanging on was really impossible."(64) That may be true: I have seen no account of the meeting. Certainly it is a version which did Colijn's political reputation no harm at all but it does not really square with Colijn's statement in April 1935 that considerations of international decency played no role in his defence of the gold standard (see p 180) or with his apparently easy concession to devalue the guilder should gold reserves fall too far in July 1935 (see p 183). Besides there were plenty of other things which the cabinet had to decide that night such as the target rate for the new parity, the exact size of the equalisation fund and the wording of all official statements. It is worth noting that when the guilder devalued in 1949, the cabinet met for two days and the main item for debate was whether to devalue by 25 or by 30 per cent.

On Sunday 27 September the morning papers announced that the guilder was no longer tied to gold.

THE 'FLOATING' GUILDER : AN EPILOGUE

The decision to suspend the gold standard marked a change both in the content and the form of Dutch policy towards exchange rate management. The move was backed by two measures – a ban imposed on the private export of gold and the establishment of an exchange equalisation fund (*valuta-egalisatiefonds*) to manage the external value of the currency. The first of these measures was largely of psychological importance and once it had become clear that the government had no intention of taxing or otherwise penalising the windfall profits accruing to gold holders, the measures were relaxed and finally abandoned altogether (in June 1937 and August 1938 respectively).(65) The second measure marked a distinct break with previous monetary policy. The responsibility for managing the exchange rate was removed from the Central Bank and transferred to the Fund, directly responsible to the ministry of finance. The primary reason for this change was that such a fund could operate in complete secrecy – changes in the distribution of its portfolio between gold, foreign exchange and domestic currency and the margins of currency fluctuation within which it was prepared to operate were carefully concealed to discourage speculation. With this in mind the Dutch Equalisation Fund was set up with Dfl. 300,000,000 in Treasury Bills at its disposal.(66)

Although the government resisted any inclination to quickly re-allign the guilder to a new gold parity, its public statements that it intended to allow the guilder to find its "natural level" (67) were completely untrue. From the outset the fund was issued with clear and unambiguous operating instructions: the maximum depreciation tolerated was 24-25 per cent, the minimum 20-20.5 per cent with a target level of 22 per cent.(68) There was no return to the gold standard but there was no 'free float' either. In effect the guilder was on a sterling/dollar standard operated with wider margins than before and for the first two years of its operation the activities of the Fund were largely directed at resisting pressure for an upward revaluation in the guilder's market value.(69) The new arrangements, however, did not automatically bring an end to the devaluation question within the Dutch cabinet.

In June 1937, following general elections, Colijn had formed his fourth inter-war cabinet. In it the Anti-Revolutionary, J.A. de Wilde, took over the portfolio for the ministry of finance and M.P.L. Steenberghe was brought back to a newly reconstituted ministry of economic affairs. At the same time, exchange rates ceased to be the exclusive preserve of the ministry of finance and was brought under a seperate financial committee of cabinet, presumably reflecting a recognition of the wider context within which the exchange-rate issue had to be seen. At its first meeting in June 1937 the Committee had decided that in the event of a divergence in the dollar:sterling rate, the guilder would follow sterling,(70) though it should be borne in mind that it was expected at the time that the dollar would depreciate and so the measure has to be seen as one designed to limit the fall in the guilders value. In the event, the dollar depreciation did not materialise and indeed, a year later as the political environment in Europe deteriorated further and the Czechoslovak crisis threatened to push Europe over the brink into war, it was sterling which appeared to be the most likely candidate for speculation and depreciative pressure.

In July 1938 the English authorities had already begun to relax their support of the prevailing dollar:sterling rate. The financial committee responded by deciding to follow sterling downwards until it implied a guilder devaluation of 22 per cent but to go no further. Once that point had been reached, the guilder was to be linked to a new dollar parity and sterling was then to be allowed to find its own level against the guilder.(71) That point had been reached two months later with the result that a gap began to open up between the guilder and sterling of the order of 4 per cent. Not surprisingly it was Steenberghe who sounded the alarm. In a somewhat tempered memo to Colijn he pointed out that the government had pledged itself to maintaining a competitive price level and he asked how long the new situation could be tolerated. To his fellow catholic ministerial colleagues he expressed himself more forcefully, "If in the near future we do not want to be forced into introducing a new deflationary policy with all the wretched consequences thereof, not least in respect to unemployment and political extremism, then it is necessary to grasp the situation speedily!"(72) To date we have found no record of the financial committee meeting where the question was discussed but, one thing is certain, namely that Steenberghe failed to deflect the government from the course already decided upon. The fear of fuelling inflation at a time when the rearmament boom was beginning to force up raw material prices, the need to hold down the domestic cost of the governments war stockpiling policy, the scarcely veiled threat from the United

States that if too many countries followed sterling America would cease supporting the dollar (73) and the fact that in January 1939 the British authorities again moved to stabilise the exchange rate of the pound may all have contributed to the decision.

In September 1939, after the outbreak of the Second World War, the financial committee was called together again, on the initiative of Steenberghe, to discuss the exchange-rate question. The British, it must be remembered, had allowed sterling once again to fall sharply. However the committee decided that there was no reason for the Dutch to follow suit. The minutes recorded, with a certain grim satisfaction, "It is worth noting that minister Steenberghe made it clear that he had abandoned his earlier standpoint with regard to the desirability of lowering the value of the guilder to encourage Dutch exports. The minister emphasised that under the current circumstances he considers the question of exports to be of low priority and that (he considers) it as an interest for the Netherlands that the guilder be kept at such a level that the Netherlands does not need to pay too much for its imports."(74)

Notes

1. Joh. de Vries, *Herinneringen en dagboek van Ernst Heldring (1871-1954)*, Groningen, 1970, Vol 2, 1093.
2. Ministerie van Economische Zaken (MEZ), Archief Handel en Nijverheid (AHN), 736/8, Hirschfeld to Verschuur, 26.9.1931.
3. *Ibid.*, Verschuur to Ruys de Beerenbrouck, 3.10.1931.
4. MEZ, AHN, 734/16, minutes of meeting held at Min. Binn. Zaken en Landbouw with representatives of the Rijkscommissie voor Werkverruiming, 7.10.1931.
5. *Ibid.*, minutes of the meeting of the Crisis Commissie, 12.10.1931.
6. For someone for whom external advice seemed almost anathema, Verschuur was surprisingly resourceful in experimenting in the creation of advisory platforms – the Economic Council was also his idea.
7. Algemene Rijksarchief (ARA), Ministerie van Financiën, Generale Thesaurie (MF,GT), 656 (Nederlandsche Bank), Dosssier: Pondenverlies 1931/1932. *Afschrift van een Aide Memoire, overgelegd door Mr. G. Vissering en Mr. P.J.C. Tetrode, resp. President en Directeur van De Nederlandsche Bank, bij hun bezoek aan den Deputy-Governor van de Bank of England Sir Ernest Musgrave Harvey, op 26 Augustus 1931.*
8. *Ibid. Afschrift van een resumé van het verhandelde bij gelegenheid van het Bezoek van Mr. G. Vissering en Mr P.J.C. Tetrode bij den Deputy Governor van de Bank of England. Sir Ernest Musgrave Harvey. op 26 Augustus 1931.*
9. *Ibid. Afschrift van een telegram van den Deputy-Governor van de Bank of England aan den President van De Nederlandsche Bank dd 29 Augustus 1931.*
10. *Ibid. Afschrift van een telegram van den Deputy-Governor van de Bank of England aan den President van de Nederlandsche Bank dd 20 September 1931.*
11. *Ibid. Afschrift van een brief dd 21 September 1931 van President Vissering aan Deputy-Governor Sir Ernest Harvey.*
12. *Ibid. Afschrift van een schrijven van den Deputy-Governor van de Bank of England aan den President van De Nederlandsche Bank dd 25 September 1931.*
13. *Ibid. Afschrift van een schrijven van den President van De Nederlandsche Bank aan den Deputy-Governor van de Bank of England dd 1 Oktober.*

14. *Ibid. Afschrift van een brief dd 27 Oktober 1931 van President Trip aan Governor Norman.*
15. *Ibid.*, Letter Ministry of Foreign Affairs to Ministry of Finance, 4.1.1932.
16. *Ibid.*, Copy of Memorandum, 21.1.1932.
17. *Ibid.*, Copy of reply from Foreign Office, 22.3.1932.
18. *Ibid.*, Letter Secretary Netherlands Bank to Min. Fin., 3.8.1932, Letter Min. For. Aff. to Min. Fin., 9.9.1932.
19. Archive of De Nederlandsche Bank (ADNB), Handhaving van den gouden standaard Mei/Juni 1933, Trip to Colijn, 9.5.1933.
20. ARA, MF, GT 656.37 Positie Nederlandsche Gulden, Westerman Holstijn to Oud,7.7.1933.
21. *Ibid.* Trip to Oud, 14.7.1933.
22. *Ibid.* Letters Secretaris-Generaal Min. For. Aff. to Min. Fin.,8.7.1933; Min. Fin. to Dir. DNB, 14.7.1933. The following passage from the last letter was never sent but it gives a good flavour of the prevailing atmosphere. "The Letter of the Procurator General justifies stubborn action. Since although it only involves little people, they spread rumours which are very damaging, also through their plausibility for the public in other countries. There is no single reason any longer to offer these elements hospitality if they engage in speculation. Criminal proceedings cannot be persued in most cases for lack of evidence, but deportation as foreigners (dangerous for public order, Art 12 Foreigners Law) is certainly possible as, in some cases, is the refusal to extend residents permits. It must be put to an end!".
23. Represented on the Council were: D. Beaufort (commissioner at the Netherlands Bank) H. Bijleveld (chairman of the Government insurance bank) Professor W.A. Bongers (University of Amsterdam) Professor G.W. Bruins (Director of the Dutch Clearing Institute) Professor P.A. Diepenhorst (Free University Amsterdam) A. Groothoff (Director of Biliton Mij, a tin mining company) E. Heldring (shipping magnate) Professor H.A. Kaag (Catholic Economic Highschool, Tilburg) H. van Manen (Director of Dutch Nationalised Railways) F.E. Posthuma (Director of insurance company, Centraal Beheer) J.A. Stokdijk (Director of Stokdijk and Co. international fruit and vegetable traders) L.J.A. Trip (President of the Netherlands Bank) Professor I.P. de Vooys (Technical Highschool, Delft and Director of the artificial fibre conglomerate AKU) Professor F. de Vries (Trade Highschool Rotterdam) C.J.M. Welter (ex-minister of colonies 1925/26 and chairman of the governments budget cutting commission) Its secretary was P. Lieftinck (then working for the Ministry of Finance.)
24. MEZ, AHN, 1560/4, minutes of the Economischen Raad, 8.7.1933.
25. ARA, MF, GT, Dossier entitled Economische Raad 1933, Correspondence attached to copy of the minutes of the second meeting, Trip to Hirschfeld,12.7.1933.
26. De Vries, *Herinneringen en dagboek*, Vol.III, Utrecht, 1970, 1607.
27. ARA, MF, GT, Dossier Economische Raad 1933, Hirschfeld to Trip, 14.7.1933.
28. De Vries, *Herinneringen en dagboek*, 1608.
29. MEZ, AHN, 1000/4, *Rapport van de Commissie uit den Economischen Raad, ingesteld ter voorbereiding van de behandeling van het algemeen economisch beleid der Regering*, 21.3.1934.
30. MEZ, AHN, 1560/5, *Notulen 11de vergadering van den Economischen Raad* 24.3.1934 He described Trip's Aide-Memoire which had presumably been leaked in the following terms, "Mr. Trip's aide memoire makes the speaker think of the old ship's doctor who wants to know nothing of modern things and just goes on prescribing castor oil – in this case wage cuts.".
31. A copy of the Address is to be found in ARA, MF, GT, 199, Nederlandsche Politiek, Dossier Devaluatie.
32. In his pencil comments on his copy of the address he noted that one of the signatories, Dr. A.F. Philips had written only two months earlier in his annual report "we must trust that the Netherlands Bank will continue following the policy of maintaining the gold standard", ADBN, Dossier: Handhaving gouden standaard Juli/Aug 1933.
33. *Ibid., Nota naar aanleiding van het Adres, door Prof. dr. J.J. Polak en 27 anderen onder dagtekening van 19 Juli 1933 gericht tot den Minister van Kolonien, Voorzitter van de Ministerraad, inzake de Nederlandsche geldpolitiek* , 1.8.1933. A number of these points were further worked out in a somewhat less

cryptic formulation, *Opmerkingen naar aanleiding van het adres van de Heren S. van den Bergh c.s. dd 19 Juli 1933 aan den Voorzitter van den Ministerraad.*

34. *Ibid.*, Report from Trip of the meeting held 30 August 1933.
35. A copy of the petition is to be found in ARA, Ministerraad, Ingekomen stukken, 307, 13d.
36. *Ibid., Enige aantekeningen betreffende 'Adres inzake devaluatie dd 5 Januari 1934* no date, covering letter dated 21.2.1934.
37. ARA, MF, GT, 199 (Nederlandsche Monetaire Politiek) Dossier: Devaluatie *Tweede Adres aan den Minister President inzake den Gouden Standaard dd 5 Januari 1934* dd. Jan 1934 and *Feiten over devaluatiepolitiek* n.d.
38. It was an unweighted average of 48 import price observations related to foodstuffs, raw materials and semi-manufacturers. The new index, compiled in 1936, did provide a better indication of internal price developments but the difficulties in international comparison still remained. For the record, it would have shown the following price movements 1929 = 98.16, 1930 88.22, 1931 75.12, 1932 63.60, 1933 61.93, *Maandschrift van het Centraal Bureau voor de Statistiek* Vol. 30, No. 8 (1936) 1218-1219.
39. They also included a series deflated by the retail price index but the less said about that the better.
40. Derived from the League of Nations, *Review of World Trade Geneva* various years.
41. In the Dutch case no allowance had been made for the change in the definition with result that the jump was artificially high.
42. P.J. Oud, *Het jongste verleden*, Assen, 1968, Vol. V, 134; P. de Rooy, *Werklozenzorg en werkloosheidbestrijding 1917-1940. Landelijk en Amsterdams beleid*, Amsterdam, 1979, 138. If this was indeed the case, Steenberghe was certainly true to his word. In September 1934 he prepared a note for the cabinet on the economic policy outlook for the Netherlands in which devaluation as a policy option was not mentioned once. MEZ, AHN, 759/15, *Nota voor den Ministerraad inz. econ. politiek*, 4.9.1934.
43. The text of the note, Nota betreffende het probleem van de Gouden Standaard voor Nederland, 9.4.1935, is reproduced in H.M. Hirschfeld, *Herinneringen uit de jaren 1933-1939*, Amsterdam, 1959, 135-218.
44. Calculations had also been made to cover the possibility of a 40 per cent devaluation. This showed a net increase in the Fund's revenue of fl.50,000,000 and a disposable surplus for 1935 of fl.31,600,000. MEZ, Particuliere stukken van de Heer Hirschfeld, Dossier 37, *Nota Crisis accountant dienst*, 25.3.1935. It is worth noting that this document predates the Belgian devaluation by five days!
45. The text of the note, Nota van den voorzitter van den Raad van Ministers, 15.4.1935, is reproduced in Hirschfeld, *Herinneringen*, 219-226.
46. ARA, MF, GT, 199, Nederlandsche Monetair Politiek. Dossier Devaluatie, *Opmerkingen van den Minister van Financien naar aanleiding van de nota 'Het probleem van den gouden standaard voor Nederland'*, no date.
47. MEZ, Particuliere stukken van de Heer Hirschfeld, 36, Hirschfeld to Gelissen, 22.6.1936.
48. De Vries, *Herinneringen en dagboek*, Vol. II, 1122.
49. This was a typically Dutch affair, Marchant had been one of the leading lights of the Liberal Democratic VDB. In December 1934 he was secretly baptised into the Catholic Church, but not secretly enough! Since in some circles of his own party, Catholics belonged to the Catholic Party, he lost the support of his parliamentary fraction and was subsequently and unceremoniously dropped from the cabinet.
50. In the 1935 provincial elections the fascist NSB attracted 7.9 per cent of the popular vote.
51. This account is drawn from Oud, *Het jongste verleden* Vol. 5, 207-224.
52. ADNB, Dossier: Monetaire politiek binnenland, De moeilijkheden in Juli/Aug 1935, Note of telephone conversation 9.15 Wednesday 24 July 1935.
53. *Ibid.*, Note of telephone conversation Wednesday 24 July 1935.
54. *Ibid.*, Handwritten report beginning, "Dir de Beaufort, Mr Westerman Holstijn hebben 24 Juli na het sluiten van de Bank in Den Haag met den President de toestand besproken".

55. Trip had earlier redrafted this, with a few essentially cosmetic adjustments. ADNB, Monetaire politiek binnenland II, Dossier: Handhaving gouden standaard, Aug/Sept 1935, Concept draft announcement, 15.8.1935.
56. *Ibid.*, Westerman Holstijn to Trip, 21.8.1935.
57. *Ibid.*, Note Trip, 5.9.1935.
58. It is worth noting that the Netherlands Bank wanted at least fl.15,486,148 of the sterling losses outstanding on 31.3.1935 to be written off and wanted the possibility left open that the rest of the losses should be repaid.
59. ADNB, Monetaire politiek binnenland II, Dossier: Handhaving gouden standaard, Aug/Sept 1935, Draft text of legislation and 'Memorie van Toelichting' sent to Colijn and Oud 10.9.1935.
60. ADNB, Monetaire politiek binnenland II, *Aantekeningen nopens de te volgen gedragslijn ingeval Nederland genoopt mocht zijn de goudafgifte te staken* , 9.11.1935. It seems clear that Bruins was not aware before hand of the thinking of the Netherlands Bank.
61. ARA, MF, GT, 199, Gouduitvoer verbod, Trip to Bruins, 12.12.1935.
62. No account of the agreement was found either in the archives of the Ministry of Finance nor in the Netherlands Bank but nor was anything else of substance relating to the entire question, I can only concur with the substance of Professor Joh. de Vries' explanation to me that the reason why there is nothing more after 1935 was that there was nothing left to decide.
63. This account has been based on Oud, *Het jongste verleden* Vol. V, 375-382 and J. Bieshuizen and E. Werkman, *De magere jaren. Nederland in crisis tijd, 1929-1939*, Leiden, 1968, 68-71.
64. Oud in *Een groot vaderlander*, 137.
65. G.J.M. Vlak, *Het Nederlandsche Valuta-egalisatiefonds, 1936-1940* , Assen, 1967, 46.
66. *Ibid.*, 56.
67. *Ibid.*, 79-81.
68. *Ibid.*, 64-65.
69. *Ibid.*, 66-147.
70. ADNB, Egalisatiefonds portefeuille 1, Map 4 Algemene Zaken, minutes of the first meeting of the Financial Committee, 26.6.1937.
71. *Ibid.*, minutes of the meeting of the Financial Committee, 21.9.1938.
72. MEZ, Particulier archief van M.P.L. Steenberghe, Map 49, Both letters dated 25.11.1938.
73. ADNB, Egalisatiefonds, portefeuille 1, map 1, algemene zaken, *Kort verslag van het besprokene tijdens een bezoek van Mr. Cochra, eerste Secretaris der Amerikaansche Ambassade te Parijs, aan den Minister van Financiën*, 4.1.1939.
74. ADNB Egalisatiefonds, portefeuille 1, map 4, algemene zaken, minutes of the meeting of the Financial Committee, 6.9.1939.

CHAPTER NINE

Belgium, France, Switzerland and the End of the Gold Standard

This chapter seeks to set the Dutch 1936 devaluation into the context of the respective defections of the other 'gold bloc' countries. Perhaps the first point to make is that in reality the gold bloc was a 'bloc' in name only, comprising a hotch-potch of countries whose one basic common factor was that their currencies were still linked to gold. It was hastily created in the light of the debacle of the 1933 World Economic Conference, by which time it had become clear to all that the defection from the gold standard of countries such as the U.K. was not to be just a temporary one. The gold bloc, strictly speaking, consisted of the Netherlands, France, Belgium/Luxembourg, Switzerland, Italy, Poland and the Free City of Danzig. This present study, however, will concentrate on the first four cases, the others even at the time not being regarded as fully-fledged members.

An important element linking France, the Netherlands, Belgium(1) and Switzerland when the gold bloc was formed was that all were holding historically large gold stocks. In retrospect, this was something of a mixed blessing. Massive gold holdings deprived the respective governments of these countries of an easy way to justify the abandonment of the gold standard. Even for Belgium, whose whole banking system came near to collapse in 1935, gold cover never fell below 56 per cent of obligations.

In addition to this, France and Belgium had already experienced in the 1920's considerable price inflation and currency depreciation, with much of the population (especially savers) being personally traumatised by the experience. Indeed, in the late 1920's both countries rather helped to institutionalise a certain level of inflation by stabilising their currencies at relatively low gold parities.(2) By the 1930's, however, both nations had grown highly sensitive to the least hint of inflation. A determination to avoid a return to upward spiralling prices was certainly a strong motive for them in clinging onto the gold standard. For Switzerland and the Netherlands this did not apply to the same extent of course, although much Swiss investment abroad had been hit by the foreign exchange turmoils of the previous decade since a substantial part of it had been held in local currencies.

The gold bloc consisted largely of countries who had the inclination but more crucially perhaps, the means, to maintain their current gold parities. They saw themselves as holding the ring – keeping the international economic system intact while for various reasons other nations temporarily strayed from the 'true' path. On the other hand, it must be admitted that there had been an element of glee when the mighty pound had fallen in 1931. Still, it was at first confidently expected that the U.K.'s temporary exchange rate advantage would soon be wiped out by rising domestic prices. The Depression, however, had a dampening effect on world prices and the anticipated price surge did not materialise. Still more unfortunately for the gold bloc countries their situation continuously worsened. After the initial sterling devaluation emulated by a large number of other economies and accompanied by a rise in protectionism, further depreciations followed – and then in 1933 the Americans devalued too. The pre-1931 gold standard seemed further away than ever. The formal creation of the gold bloc was a closing of ranks in the face of this adversity.

The various members of the gold bloc promised each other assistance in order to protect their existing gold parities. In theory, they had reached 'complete agreement' as to how this was to be done and, indeed, they sought to expand trade considerably amongst themselves. In practice though, the gold bloc had no organisation and little cohesion.(4) Moreover, differences between members outweighed similarities. Although the various gold bloc currencies were all overvalued in relation to sterling, they were overvalued to different degrees. Furthermore, economic policies followed by members were not compatible, the most obvious problem involving trade. In this respect France was usually painted as the chief obstacle in the way of increased trade within the group. This, however, ignored the fact that even the smaller economies strongly protected their own domestic interests. For example, the weekend immediately prior to Belgium's devaluation, senior Belgian ministers travelled to Paris in a well-publicised attempt to wring last-minute trade concessions from the French. The Belgians returned, claiming their overtures had been bluntly rejected with the French unwilling to pay the price for holding the gold bloc together. Sources in France hotly disputed this, particularly resenting the rather transparent Belgian ploy to blame the French for the Belgian devaluation. What can be stated in support of the French is that the politically strong, although domestically-oriented, agricultural sector in Belgium seriously hampered Belgian trade negotiators. Indeed, the latter were often sent into committee rooms with the unrealistic instruction to gain new markets for industrial products, while at the same time giving no agricultural concessions in return. This was naturally a block on Belgo-Dutch trade relations too. Interestingly, the much vaunted 1932 Ouchy Agreement, which involved mutual staged tariff reductions between the two countries, excluded agricultural produce. It also did little to address the more central problem of quotas.(5)

In fact trade within the gold bloc fell rather than increased. In 1933, Dutch exports to France, Belgium and Switzerland represented 26.4 per cent of its total exports, but in 1934 this proportion fell to 22.1 per cent and in 1935 to 20.2 per cent. Where, indeed, was the incentive to buy goods from other (high cost) gold bloc countries?

BELGIUM

At this point it might be interesting to consider in some depth the devaluation of the Belgian franc. Firstly, this Southern neighbour was an as equally small and trade-dependent country as the Netherlands with historically much in common. Secondly, the Belgians devalued a full year before France, the Netherlands and Switzerland and so followed a somewhat maverick course. Confining our comparison for the moment, what can help to explain why Belgium chose to abandon its gold parity in March 1935 and the Dutch chose not to do so?

Looking first to industrial production figures (fig. 9.1), we see that Belgian production fell from a relatively high level in 1928-29 to a low one in 1932-34. The steep fall in Belgian industrial production relative to that in the Netherlands is indeed noteworthy and will be returned to presently. Nevertheless, the extent of the Belgian industrial slump during the Depression still does not seem, of itself, to provide sufficient basis for its unilateral decision to abandon its existing gold parity. Moreover, one could introduce compensating items such as the greater Dutch reliance on agricultural exports. Klein(6) for one has made much of the relative size of the Dutch agricultural sector and its depressing effect on the Dutch economy.

Turning to general trade figures, by 1934 export value had fallen to 43 per cent of its 1929 level in Belgium, whereas in the Netherlands it had fallen to 37 per cent. In both Belgium and the Netherlands the trade deficit actually improved during the Depression and gold stocks remained high. Looking at domestic price evolution it appears that Belgium may have been slightly more successful at deflating – at least in respect to 1929. The difference was small, however, and it could not really be argued in terms of price evolution alone that the deflationary process in Belgium had come to a natural end. Lastly, the unemployment figures as given by Mitchell(7) suggest levels were consistently higher in the Netherlands than in Belgium.

The above infers that one has to look beyond the main economic indicators for an explanation. Now, one clear way in which the Belgian economy differed from that of the Netherlands – or France and Switzerland for that matter, was in its banking structure. The overwhelming majority of all Belgian banks were so-called 'mixed' banks. These differed from pure deposit banks since in addition to the normal, short-term range of banking activities, they also provided substantial long-term loans to industry and accumulated large investment portfolios. A comparative analysis of bank balance sheets during the interwar years is difficult enough on a national basis and so an international approach must be subject to still more reservations. Nevertheless, Table 9.1 is offered as an indication of banking policies in the countries involved.

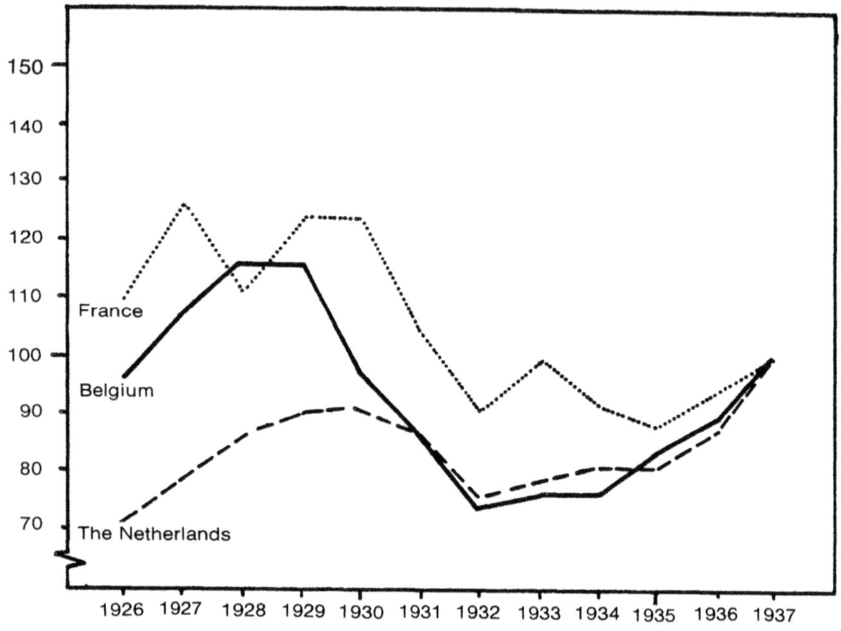

Figure 9.1. Industrial Production Indices for Belgium, France and the Netherlands, 1926-1937. Source: B.R. Mitchell, European Historical Statistics (London, 1980) p. 376 and Table 1.3 above.

The most obvious difference was the tendency of the Belgian banks (the figures exclude financial holding companies) to hold a larger proportion of their assets in the least liquid form (loans and securities). Their investment portfolios were relatively much greater than those of their neighbouring counterparts. Moreover, it should be pointed out that the investment portfolio of Dutch banks largely consisted of government securities, whilst in Belgium there was an overwhelming preference for industrial holdings. Dutch banks lacked the historical lineage of those in Belgium and indeed had evolved separately from Dutch industry. Nevertheless, during the inflationary boom that followed the First World War (and to an extent in the years immediately preceeding the war) some Dutch banks did make excursions into the field of mixed banking. Lack of experience, however, soon made itself shown. A number of banking 'reorganisations' followed very shortly culminating in 1924 when the *Rotterdamsche Bankvereeniging* lost substantial long-term investments and had to be bailed out by the Netherlands Bank, backed in turn by the government. The matter itself was hushed up until 1927 due to fears of a financial crisis.(8) Chastened by the experience, the Dutch banks voluntarily backed away from long-term links with industry between the Wars. It is nonetheless this distancing which is generally regarded as the reason why the Netherlands was largely spared a banking crisis

TABLE 9.1
COMPARATIVE INDICATORS OF BANK BALANCES IN BELGIUM, HOLLAND, FRANCE AND SWITZERLAND, 1930

	+	liquidity		–	
	Cash, banks, bankers % of assets	Commercial portfolio % of assets	Advances/ loans % of assets	Securities % of assets	Capital + reserves as % of liabilities
All Belgian banks	10.2	19.6	53.4	16.8	20.9
Société Générale + Banque de Brussels	27.9	12.7	31.3	28.1	35.0
Main five Dutch Banks	17.8	22.4	54.0	5.7	23.0
Main six French deposit banks	19.7	49.4	30.2	0.6	7.6
The French banques d'affaires (1929)	22.9	25.7	36.3	15.1	14.7
Main eight Swiss banks (1926)	22.0	20.6	53.9	4.3	14.2

Material taken from G.M. Verrijn Stuart, *Geld, Crediet en Bankwezen*, Vol. 2, 's-Gravenhage, 1956, E. Schwarzenback, The Banking System of Switzerland, in: *Foreign Banking Systems*, H.P. Willis and B.H. Beckhart (eds.), London, 1929, 1075-1143 and Annual Reports of the Société Générale and Banque de Bruxelles.

in the 1930's. It also seems evident that, in retrospect, the Dutch banks were very careful in their loan and overdraft commitments.

In France the situation is complicated in that there were two sets of banks. In terms of asset value, the banking sector was dominated by deposit banks whose long-term commitments were limited to help in the issue of shares and bonds. The *banques d'affaires*, on the other hand, had assets structured in a way to allow them to hold a considerable share portfolio on a long-term basis, as well as possessing significant short-term holdings. It was their practice to counterbalance their long-term assets with very large own resources. Nevertheless, the *banques d'affaires* also held substantial deposits and, in fact, by the end of the inter-war period they were turning increasingly to deposit banking.(9) The dominant feature of the French banking network between the Wars appears to have been a general weakening of its position, especially in respect to industry. This point is repeatedly pressed by Bouvier(10) who draws attention to the adverse effect inflation had on banking assets and particularly to the inability of the banks to tap sufficient new deposits and increase their capital to keep pace with rising prices. Indeed, in real terms the three main banques d'affaires never regained the level of deposits reached in 1913 during the inter-war period.

Belgian banks were much more successful in finding new deposits. Certainly the volume of liquid assets in Belgium was considerably swollen by the government decision to convert into francs the marks which had been introduced into circulation by the occupying German authorities into Belgian francs after the War. Another factor was that during the war large numbers of the Belgian bourgeoisie fled to Britain where they were introduced to and became familiar with the concept of scriptural money.(11) A further explanation, however, must be the succesful drive on the part of the big banks in chasing sufficient deposits to finance their investments. In France the main commercial banks were squeezed on the one hand, by the continued existence of a large number of local/regional banks and on the other, by the growth of the semi-public banking sector. In Belgium this sector was much smaller and the commercial banks surged ahead during the 1920's. There was also a very strong concentration movement.

Information on Swiss banks is more scarce. What does emerge is that the Swiss banks were much more involved in loans (often abroad) and little interested in acquiring large share portfolios. While they helped in share issue, shares were not held on a permanent basis and the banks did not seek to control Swiss industry to any degree.(12) The banks in Switzerland, nonetheless, did run into liquidity problems during the Depression, but these seem to have been ironed out by the banking legislation of November 1934. This strengthened the National Bank's supervisory powers over the private banking network, enabling it among other things to enforce mandatory liquidity ratios, influence the level of interest rates charged by the banks and to veto foreign loans. Public confidence in Swiss banks revived throughout 1935 and 1936 and, indeed, by the time of the devaluation the banks were in good shape.(13)

The other side of the bank-industry equation is, of course, the extent to which industrial companies in Belgium financed themselves via the banks. There was no use the Belgian banks having considerable resources if the demand lacked. In fact, in the immediate postwar period the capital needs of Belgian industry were massive. It needed resources to rebuild its productive capacity on modern lines and also to pay off debts incurred during the war. Many family firms were forced into the capital market for the first time. Later on the extent of the 1926-29 boom in Belgium was such that industry again had no chance of financing operations and mergers, the amount of fresh capital raised by industrial companies between 1927 and 1929 was well over twice the level of undistributed profits. In addition, the amount paid out in dividends and interest payments only represented some 70 percent of new capital issues over the same period. Finance was raised mostly in the form of loans and share capital since the Belgian bond market was very restricted between the wars. Only a few major companies, mainly in the steel sector, were in a position to raise loans abroad. The Belgian mixed banks were quick to seize their chance in terms of loans and investments and by 1931 even the steel sector had fallen into their sphere of influence.

Throughout the 1920's the ascendancy of the Belgian banks in society gained firmer and firmer roots. In 1926 they contributed to the bringing down of a mildly reformist government they considered hostile to their interests. At the same time, they used the opportunity to strengthen their own position in relation to that of the National Bank. This latter development allowed some smaller and less responsible banks to grow unchecked. Yet even the liquidity position of the *Société Générale* group becomes less clear when it brings subsidiary holding companies into the picture, most of which held share portfolios far in excess of own resources.

The upshot of all this was that in the 1920's and early 1930's the Belgian banks, unlike those in other gold bloc countries, were both willing and able to increase greatly their influence over industry and, naturally, their commitments to it. As the world economy slipped into recession, however, this took on increasingly the appearence of a liability.

As the Depression worsened, pressure on the Belgian banks came on two fronts; increasing withdrawals and problems liquifying assets. In fact, many of the speculative investments and loans made by the banks proved to have been unsound. Indeed, as early as 1929 one of the two main banks the *Banque de Bruxelles* had to make hurried sales of shares in order to restore a temporary liquidity shortage. After a number of minor incidents public confidence was rocked by well-published difficulties of the Socialist-oriented *Banque Belge du Travail* and the agricultural-based *Algemene Bankvereeniging*. This latter threatened the financial structure of the influential farmers' organisation, the *Boerenbond*.

The heart of all these problems was that under the conditions of rapidly expanding capacity and increasing production, as had existed in Belgium in particular between 1926 and 1929, there had been a strong temptation for the banks to overcommit their resources in the desire for profit. Not only did this make more likely future liquidity crises, it also added fuel to the fire by encouraging the general movement towards overproduction and overcapacity. A major problem for Belgium (and France to a lesser extent) was the abrupt switch from an undervalued to an overvalued currency. In a sense then the seeds of the 1935 Belgian devaluation lay in the 1926 stabilisation and the boom it generated. It was the combination of the sudden reversal of currency evolution with the particular nature of the banking network which served to weaken dramatically Belgium's grip on the gold standard.

The institution of the mixed bank was unfairly held to be responsible for these banking troubles. This was unjust, since a major source of the difficulties stemmed from the advances made earlier (now immobilised in struggling Belgian industry) rather than purely the investment portfolio. Nevertheless, government measures were begun in August 1934 to separate clearly the functions of pure deposit bank and investment institution i.e. to abolish the mixed bank. These measures provided too little, too late and were unable to prevent a major slump in public confidence together with heavy deposit withdrawals. There are no detailed figures available on the extent of these withdrawals and indeed with the partial exception of the *Société Génerale* there were no banking statistics released at all for the year 1934. Banks, which were hard pressed to cope with the withdrawals, found themselves unable to realise sufficient quantities of their assets.

An added dimension was brought by the dwindling faith in the value of the franc itself. In the case of Belgium, naturally, the known shakiness of the banks gave an added stimulus to capital outflows. Outward flows of capital had taken place before Autumn 1934, but it was after this date that they really began to take on worrying proportions. This flight of capital was mostly financed by withdrawals from the banks. Indeed, some saw it as being actively orchestrated by banks in order to bring about a devaluation which they perceived as their only salvation. In the aftermath of the actual devaluation a parliamentary enquiry was held to look into these allegation, but found them largely groundless. Nonetheless, increasingly the banks did have motives in wanting the devaluation, not for their own speculative purposes, but because it was hoped that this would generate an upturn in the economy currently being felt outside the gold bloc. One can certainly argue that the banks did nothing to discourage the growing export of capital. Janssens writes that they were simply too scared to try blocking the flow.(15) This does not appear to have been the case in, say, the Netherlands or Switzerland, where at times of financial difficulties the commercial banks were requested by the government to block attempts to speculate against the currency. In Belgium, one cannot see the banks as being last-ditch defenders of the gold standard. Another noteworthy point is that the Belgian government (heavily influenced by the big banks) did not institute exchange control until a few days before the devaluation. Admittedly the gold position of the National Bank was not under threat, but the private banks most certainly were. The idea of government guarantees for bank deposits was not discussed either.

The month of February brought a further depreciation of sterling, which wiped out all the past year's deflation. The gold outflow accelerated, as did the withdrawal of deposits from the banks. It is beyond doubt that, in any case, the banking network was nearing the point of collapse by March 1935. After the devaluation towards the end of that month, the *Société Générale* was quick to point out that at the time it still had immediate funds totalling over BF. 1,000 million. The other banks were noticeably silent on this matter. In fact, the finance minister later privately disclosed that as late as 25 March he had had to grant an emergency loan to the *Banque de Bruxelles*, which, if refused, in his opinion would have inevitably led to its closing its doors.(16) The other banks, including the *Société Générale*, would very probably not have survived such a disaster.

There was, of course, never any real question that the big banks would be allowed to fold. The situation of the banks does not explain the long-term causes of the devaluation, but it does explain why it took place when it did. The banking crisis in Belgium served as a useful tool for the government to justify an act properly regarded as dishonest – if not immoral. The government at last had an excuse for which at least some of its members had been looking for many months, and it enabled Belgium to be the first member of the gold bloc to defect.(17) A further example of this is the now famous speech given by Baudhuin in Liége on 15 March. Baudhuin was one of the most well-known Belgian economists of his day. Although privately he had long been convinced of the need for devaluation, he had restrained his public pronouncements for fear of the effect on public confidence should he condemn government policy. Finally deciding he could no longer remain silent, he wrote a pro-devaluation speech and sent the text to the government saying that he would not deliver it if requested not to. No reply came.(18) The capital outflow and its effects on the banks made devaluation politically acceptable, and it was on this basis that the pro-devaluation economists of the 'Louvain School' could be brought in to implement the technicalities that they had prepared in the previous months. Admittedly, the gold position of the National Bank was not under any threat, but the private banks most certainly were. The possibility of a government guarantee for bank deposits was not even discussed until after the devaluation.(20)

Meanwhile, some of the moves to support the banks made life still harder for industry. An attempt to reduce interest rates paid by industry for its loans in early 1935 was quickly torpedoed when it was confidentially revealed by bankers that such measures would precipitate the collapse of the banking system.(21) Clearly, the heavy reliance by Belgian industry on the banks was a complicating factor in the deflationary process. The refusal by the banks to countenance cuts in the interest paid to them virtually sabotaged the continuation of the deflation policy. The progressive wing of the dominant catholic party did not see how further deflation would cease when retail prices fell to the level of 1930. On the other hand, the classical defence against capital exports – a raise in the discount rate – was not feasible either, again because this would have squeezed the banks and thus the rest of industry. In fact, the whole deflationary process during the Depression in Belgium involved negligible monetary deflation. Belgium's failure on the gold standard (a tactic repeatedly employed by the Dutch, for example) in effect meant that Belgium was drifting helplessly, waiting for the coup de grace to be delivered by a further speculative run.

Apart from the case of the banks, from which there came a deafening silence, the Belgian devaluation issue itself ran on very similar lines to that in the Netherlands. One set of arguments equated devaluation with the government renagueing on its debts for the second time in less than ten years. The spectre of rampant inflation was continually raised, greatly impressing the rentier class. A second set of arguments stressed the need for stability and confidence, which it believed could only be obtained by defending the franc. The point was also made that what was really blocking exports was protectionism through tariffs and quotas and that currency depreciation alone would not be enough to penetrate such walls.

The main national industrial grouping, the *Comité Central Industriel*, held an anti-devaluation attitude to the last. It maintained that any short-term advantage to be gained from devaluation would soon be countered by rises in domestic prices and, to this end, pointed to the unsettling experience of the 1926-29 period, when the dreams of prosperity and progress soon turned sour. In fact, really the only industrialist grouping in favour of devaluation was the

Antwerp Chamber of Commerce since the port had been badly hit by the Depression. The governor of the National Bank was a strong critic of any whisper of exchange rate manipulation.

Turning to the political scene, the catholic party firmly refused to contemplate devaluation although its left wing, the christian democrats, grew increasingly uneasy regarding the official policy of enforced deflation. On the socialist side, the traditional old guard was inclined to view devaluation as another example of capitalist exploitation, with the ordinary working man ending up having to shoulder the main burden of economic recession. The more radically inspired planning movement, as represented by Hendrik de Man, almost certainly recognised devaluation as inevitable but was careful not to admit this publicly for electoral reasons. The liberals, naturally, supported the gold standard for reasons of principle.

Just as in the Netherlands, there was a small group of academics supporting devaluation, this one centred on the university of Leuven (Louvain). Included here, in addition to Baudhuin, were, among others, L.H. Dupriez and Robert Triffin. When the devaluation came it was very much based on the work of the so called Louvain School.

One argument which developed in Belgium but did not appear to come out very clearly in the Netherlands was that of the problem of domestic price disparities.(22) According to the classical economic theory of the time, as exemplified by, say, Cassel, there was a tendency to see the international economy as consisting of a rather mechanistic and uniform market. That is, in real terms the value of a given good in country A should be the same as in country B, this equilibrium being brough about by the 'general' price level and/or exchange rate. Classical theory also held that the existence of currency undervaluation was indicated by a trade surplus and gold inflow. For Belgium (and the Netherlands) the trade balance actually improved during the Depression, in value terms imports falling more than exports. On the basis of this a case could be made that the currency was undervalued rather that overvalued! Of course, capital movements were working in the opposite direction by 1933-34 – but who was to say that these were a better relector of monetary positions than the balance of trade? This trade balance point was, however, argued by the Louvain School to be misleading as regards the gold bloc situation. To take the extreme example, one might have expected Belgian exports of standardised goods to have been seriously curtailed after 1931 since markets in this case were highly competetive. In fact, manufacturers, due to heavy fixed costs, chose to maintain production levels and market share even at the cost of sacrificing profits. For this reason, exports held up rather well. Goods with a lower price elasticity of demand would, in the short-run, be still less affected by exchange rate disparities. Thus, though of course export value slumped, sales still continued. The various protectionist measures pushing down the level of imports should also be remembered.

The real problem for the gold bloc countries, it was held, was that there was no 'general' price level, since different prices behaved differently during the course of the Depression. Again taking the example of Belgium, we see in Figure 9.2 that industrial raw material prices (including highly standardised products) fell more than less standardised manufactured goods, whereas nominal wages fell little and, indeed, real wages actually rose.

In terms of international comparison, one had to fall back on the official 'wholesale', 'retail' and 'cost of living' indices, the very comparability of which were highly questionable. Nevertheless, in an article which won considerable interest in devaluation circles, in Belgium and Switzerland at least, Strakosch (23) made a strong case for the devaluation of the gold bloc countries. Basing his case on wholesale and cost of living indices, he argued that the domestic price disparity within the gold bloc was significantly greater than elsewhere. In modern economies, Strakosch went on, it was no longer possible to reduce instantaneously cost items such as wages and rents. As put later by Triffin, devaluation, as well as ending the external price disparity, would also be the neatest way to realign domestic prices on a more secure basis. Assuming the correct degree of devaluation, the most flexible prices would rise, thus eliminating the disparity with the more rigid prices.

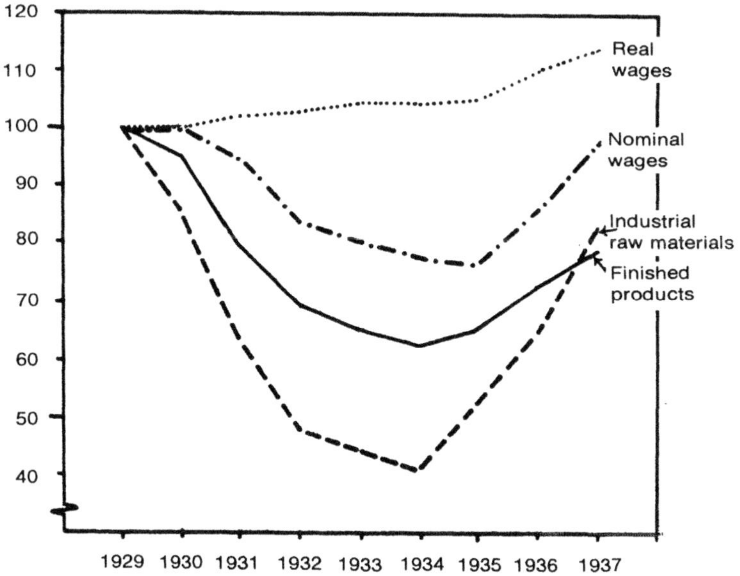

Figure 9.2. Selected Price and Wage Indices for Belgium, 1929-1937.
Source: National Bank Statistics 1929-1940.

SWITZERLAND

In Switzerland, the banks were again a crucial influence in the devaluation/deflation debate, in general terms, as in the Netherlands, pressing for a continuation of the gold standard. The development of Switzerland as an international financial centre during the inter-war period had made them powerful and greatly concerned with their prestige abroad. The banks felt a devaluation of the Swiss currency would come as a shock to their foreign customers (nearly a third of their loans went abroad) and adversely affect Switzerland's place in world finance. As already mentioned, by the end of 1934 the banks were in good shape and in no way a factor working against the current gold parity. Consequently, the government was able to raise the discount rate in order to counteract periodic runs on the Swiss franc.

The banks also played an interesting role in combating speculation against the franc. In June 1935 (a month after the Belgian devaluation) the government made a so-called 'Gentleman's Agreement' with the banks. According to this the banks agreed to abstain from speculation on their part and refuse to assist speculative activities on the part of their customers too. In June 1936 the government went still further. Under the 'Gentleman's Agreement' there had been no legal sanction, but now it passed legislation, making punishable by law any purely speculative act against the Swiss franc. With this step the Swiss came perilously close to a *de facto* abandonment of the gold standard and there was much criticism on this point.

The argument for devaluation was made on two fronts; the external price disparity and the growing level of indebtedness in the industrial and tertiary sectors. The devaluation lobby was, however, a relatively incoherent one. Apart from a few academics, it consisted of disparate export industries (tourism, watches etc) and some professional workers. Interestingly Schulthess, head of the federal economics department, grew increasingly concerned by the poor position of the Swiss export industry. In November 1934 he made public his doubts regarding the possibility of avoiding devaluation and in February 1935 resigned to devote himself to the devaluation cause.

Apart from the lack of cohesion, a further problem for the Swiss devaluation movement was the popular confusion made between itself and the *Ligue pour la Monnaie Franche*. This latter body held that a major depressing effect on the level of economic activity was caused by unpredictable changes in the price level. After a once and for all rise in wholesale prices (to re-establish the index around its pre-depression level) the Ligue argued that the existing price level should be maintained on a permanent basis. In terms of the Depression, the downward pressure on prices would be counteracted by an unbacked national currency which would lose a variable proportion of its value from week to week. This rather eclectic theory was not held on a widespread basis but was certainly enough to confuse somewhat the gold standard issue in Switzerland. The part relating to a rise in wholesale prices often caused it to be popularly linked with devaluation.

Until the final day, the anti-devaluation movement was always the most powerful. It was led by Neyer, the head of federal finances, and enjoyed a majority in the federal council. The anti-devaluationists stressed the need for orthodoxy and tradition and, more importantly, the danger of rising inflation, the damage to Swiss investment abroad and the loss of confidence in the banking and insurance sectors which would necessarily result from any abandonment of the gold standard. The anti-devaluation stance of the ruling liberal party was reluctantly shared by the socialist party. After a long period of vacillation, the socialist party finally came out against devaluation in June 1936, arguing that such a move would simply comprise camouflaged inflation which would serve to erode the real purchasing power of the working class. The socialist party was more interested in fighting the Depression via a policy of structural reforms (planning etc).

Interestingly, this programme was put to the public in June 1935 in the form of a national referendum. In order to marshal opinion against this socialist proposal, the government tactic was to claim these measures could only be realised if the current gold parity was abandoned, and thus sought to turn the issue into one of devaluation or not. The socialists in their turn denied that devaluation was on the cards. The success of the government electoral ploy is impossible to judge, although the socialist proposal was defeated by 566.000 votes to 426.000.

Nevertheless, by the summer of 1936 deflation had become increasingly unpopular. The government consequently changed tack somewhat, publicly renouncing 'blanket' deflation and instead pressing for 'differential' deflation. This involved turning attention to sectors in the economy which had been relatively spared by the official deflation policy. Further cracks in the solid front against devaluation began to appear. In July 1936 the union movement, whose study department included Max Weber, sent a secret memo to the federal palace, arguing that devaluation was inevitable and should now be effected in the best possible conditions. Although the federal council was now beginning to waver,(24) the heads of the finance and economics departments were both publicly supporting the gold standard in September 1936.

In the end, of course, the Swiss franc was brought down by *deus ex machina*. The fall of the French franc brought the federal council together the next day for rapid consultation. The council's undecidedness was illustrated by the fact that the first official declaration announced a continuation on the gold standard – only to be reversed in the afternoon.

FRANCE

This brings us naturally to the case of France. Here there were even more forces working against the cause of devaluation than in the rest of the gold bloc. In the first place, France was a large economy and less dependent on exports. It also had a fairly extensive imperial market to fall back on, although ultimately this was never sufficient to compensate for the loss of export markets elsewhere. The first French reaction to its economic downturn was to defend its domestic market, and soon a whole battery of protective mechanisms was in place. French industry was in a position to try holding up selling prices by restricting supply.(25) Producers never saw a contradiction in their support for economic liberalism on the one hand and cartellisation on the other, since they believed such measures as the latter simply 'regularised' competitive markets. Indeed, a sizeable part of heavy French industry had an added cushion to the extent it was working on public contracts.

In addition to these factors, there was, of course, a large middle class (and a substantial number of workers who aspired to this station) whose savings had been ravaged during the inflation of the 1920's. This made devaluation a politically unpopular issue. Lastly, there was a large degree of insularity which involved an ignorance and indifference towards what was happening in other economies.

Successive governments spent several years paying lip service to the need for deflation without actually doing very much about it. Finally, however, in 1935 the Laval administration began to grasp the nettle. Working with special powers, it passed over 500 decrees within six months as it set about deflation *á outrance*

There was overwhelming support in France for adherence to the gold standard (if not for the deflation it entailed). Devaluation was opposed by virtually every interested group in the country, including export organisations. In a 1935 survey, only 10 out of 1,156 chambers of commerce supported devaluation. The day following the ultimate 'catastrophe', the *Journée Industrielle* ran an article expressing incomprehension as to why the French government had chosen to abandon its fixed gold parity. Officially, industrialists argued that a reduction of prices and costs was necessary as a way of squeezing out inefficient producers. This belief, nevertheless, did not stop hard-pressed sectors of the economy from calling for protection from the government and from forming domestic cartels.

One notable voice in the wilderness was that of the radical, Paul Reynaud. From 1932 onwards he began to raise awkward questions regarding the deflation/devaluation issue. By 1934 he was openly calling for devaluation, stressing the external price disparity and the difference in economic fortunes inside and outside the gold bloc. Leon Blum, the socialist leader, took a more ambiguous position. In November 1934 he guardedly declared: "Il est difficile á la France de tenir une position isolée (...) Voilá longtemps qu'au lieu d'écarter (dévaluation) avec indignation et horreur, les gouvernements auraient dû l'étudier." He then went on to dismiss devaluation as a "mal capitaliste" and to advocate a programme of raising wages, increasing government expenditure and the like. The socialists' partners in the popular front, the communists and the radicals categorically opposed devaluation, but for different reasons, the communists saw it as a means of exploiting the working classes (by reducing real wages) and, moreover, believed it vital to unify popular support in France against fascism. The radicals on the other hand, were firm supporters of the working of the international gold standard.(26) It was in this context that the 'neither deflation nor devaluation' electoral stance of the popular front developed. Nonetheless, the popular front's relationary package was clearly not a practical proposition without devaluation and, indeed, some later commentators considered it impractical without the introduction of exchange control.(27)

The accession to power of the Blum administration unleashed a massive capital exodus, though there was still no question of exhausting gold reserves. The socialist leader, struggling to hold together a political consensus, recognised that exchange control was not a practical option. Instead he had decided on devaluation soon after assuming power but was prevented from immediately announcing his attention by two factors. Firstly, the unexpected wave of strikes and factory occupations that followed the election of the popular front gained prior attention. Secondly, there remained the problem of swaying public opinion. As early as June 1936 Blum began negotiations with the U.K. and the U.S. regarding a joint statement on exchange rate policy. The resulting so-called Tripartite Agreement was announced at the same time as the French currency realignment. The signatories agreed to renounce competitive change depreciation and called for the relaxation of trade and exchange restrictions. To a large extent the Tripartite Agreement was a way to get Blum off the hook, though, on the other hand, it may have had the effect of preventing the French from devaluating more. Blum presented the devaluation as an international act of great importance, although public opinion remained unconvinced. The devaluation triggered a perceptible economic upturn, but Blum did not know it at the time due to lack of refined statistics. It was, however, soon choked off by the subsequent introduction of the 40 hour week and the preference of the French at the time to invest abroad rather than at home.

France, Belgium, the Netherlands and Switzerland were different countries, each with their own circumstances. Their basic differences should not be forgotten in a search for similarities. Nevertheless, there were a striking number of common factors in their experiences during the years 1931-36.

Firstly, there was a degree of general economic illiteracy. The same people who had been so slow to recognise the effects of inflation (or 'inflammation' as one leading Belgian advisor called it), were also unable to distinguish properly between inflation and devaluation. Even many exporters, who might have been expected to have had a practical grasp of the meaning of overvaluation, simply regarded the existing exchange rates as given.(28)

This problem was compounded by a very poor statistical back-up. For example, the various price indices produced were, even at the time, recognised by many specialists as being highly inadequate. This necessitated falling back on non-quantifiable perceptions when it came to implementing the various devaluations. Switzerland, for instance, (where there was not even an industrial production index) abandoned calculations based on wholesale price indices as worse than useless. The cost of living index was judged more useful, but even then the choice relating to the degree of devaluation was heavily influenced by the economics department's experience in subsidising exports. Even the famed declaration *á froid* in Belgium, based on a comparison between Belgium and the U.K. cost of living indices in 1928, had to leave a rough and ready margin to allow for the recognised undervaluation of the Belgian franc in that particular base year.

Naturally, pleas for devaluation based on contrasts between gold bloc countries and non-gold bloc countries ran up against a comparability problem. Many economic indices were simply not truly compatible. Furthermore, even in the smaller gold bloc countries there was a surprising insularity and ruling administrations were quick to stress the differences rather than the similarities between their countries and, say, the U.K. or Denmark.

Another problem for those in favour of devaluation was that their arguments held something of a self-fulfilling nature. The very fact that certain groups in a country were considering devaluation was sufficient to undermine confidence in the currency and trigger capital exports. Responsible advocates of devaluation were thus often forced into a low-profile attitude where they could easily be ignored. This, of course, partly accounts for the conspiracy of silence that prevailed in the whole gold standard issue. Devaluation was simply not up for discussion.

Having decided to stick to gold, the bourgeois governments of the four countries studied here at the same time refused to face the logical alternative – deflation. This was primarily due to political factors. If an electorally sizeable sector (e.g. agriculture) made enough noise, it gained protection. For somewhat different reasons the Belgians were forced to pump money into the banking sector, indeed, in general there was no actual money deflation. Often the gold bloc countries tried reflationary and deflationary measures at the same time, e.g. France during the Flandin administration.

Opposition to the continuation of the current gold parity came usually from isolated academics and sometimes from export groups. The left-wing political opposition parties, who might have been expected to have supported devaluation, were as a whole equally unable to grasp the devaluation/deflation nettle. In all cases they seemed genuinely split on the issue and, to an extent, they were more interested in wholesale structural reforms on society. Above all, they sensed that devaluation was not a winning electoral plank. As with so many other pressure groups internally split on an issue, they preferred to ignore it.

Finally, all four countries attempted to present devaluation as something that had been thrust upon them by circumstances beyond their control. In Belgium the banking crisis provided a justification. Furthermore, the fact that a new government was formed to implement the devaluation made it impossible for both administrations to blame each other at the time for being ultimately responsible for the decision. Blum apologists tried the same tactics, claiming his government had inherited a 'devaluation situation', though there was little plausibility in this since Blum had waited two months before devaluing. The Blum administration also tried to use the Tripartite Agreement as an external factor militating in favour of devaluation. The Dutch and Swiss could naturally follow in the shadow of the French, with a suitable show of reluctance, one might perhaps add.

One final word about the respective currency arrangements after the respective realignments. In Belgium the anti-devaluationists had something of a rearguard victory. After devaluation the Belgian franc was statutorily fixed back onto gold. This was against the advice of Dupriez et al. and caused the Belgians problems when sterling began to depreciate again in the late 1930's. The Belgian motive for re-joining gold was the old one of the need for confidence-building, but after 1936 Belgium's continued fixed link with gold put it in an extremely isolated position. The others went in for a sort of managed floating. This entailed the central bank being given informal gold parameters to work with, although in the case of the French these parameters proved easily adaptable to further currency depreciations.

The passing of the gold bloc was not mourned – since it had hardly ever existed in the first place. With its eventual collapse, the last tentative grip on the old international gold standard was lost. In a sense, its end was a positive factor, since it cleared the way for more fundamental reforms to come with the Bretton Woods Agreements. The end of the gold standard launched a search for a new and lasting international monetary system. The search continues.

Notes

1. For the sake of convenience, Luxembourg will be treated, economically speaking, as comprising part of Belgium. There was already an economic union between the two countries.
2. R.S. Sayers, The Return to Gold, S. Pollard (ed.), *The Gold Standard and Employment Policies Between the Wars*, London, 1970, 9, argues that the French and Belgians deliberately undervalued their currencies. This was certainly not the case for Belgium and too sweeping as regards France. For the French stabilisation see G.C. Schmid, The Politics of Currency Stabilisation, *Journal of European Economic History 1974*, Vol.3, No.2, 359. For Belgium see R.L. Hogg, *Structural Rigidities and Policy Inertia in Interwar Belgium* , Unpublished Ph.D. thesis, Manchester, 1982, Chapter 1.
3. R. Ruffieux, *La Suisse de l'entre deux guerres*, Lausanne, 1974, 122.
4. C.P. Kindleberger, *The World in Depression*, London, 1977, 246.
5. The Ouchy Agreement was never implemented since it was torpedoed by the British invoking the most-favoured-nation clause.
6. P.W. Klein, Depression and Policy in the Thirties, *Acta Historia Neerlandicae*, Vol.VIII esp. p.147.
7. B.R. Mitchell, *European Historical Statistics,* London, 1980, 174-8.
8. See Joh. de Vries contribution on inter-war Holland in J.H. van Stuijvenberg (ed.) *De Economische Geschiedenis van Nederland*, Groningen, 1977, 280.

9. J. Bouvier, Les Grandes Epreuves de l'Etat, F. Braudel and E. Larousse (eds.) *Histoire Economique et Sociale de la France*, Vol.4/2, Paris, 1980, 720.
10. For example see J. Bouvier, *Un Siécle de Banque Française*, Paris, 1973, 250.
11. H. van der Wee and K. Tavernier, *La Banque Nationale de Belgique*, Bruxelles, 1975, 65.
12. E. Schwarzenbach, in H.P. Willis and B.H. Beckhart (eds.) *The Banking Systems*, London, 1929, 1089.
13. P. Renou, *La Dévaluation du Franc Suisse*, Bordeaux, 1939, 219.
14. R. Triffin, La Théorie de la Surévaluation Monétaire et la Dévaluation Belge, *Bulletin de l'Institut de Recherches Economiques de Louvain,*, 1937-38, 19.
15. V. Janssens, *De Belgische Frank. Anderhalve Eeuw Geldgeschiedenis*, Antwerpen/Amsterdam, 1975, 250.
16. "Le juge d'instruction m'ayant demandé si j'aurais pû arrêter cette opération, je lui ai répondu que oui en principe mais que pareille décision aurait instantanément conduit á la fermeture des guichets de la Banque de Bruxelles et par contrecoup évident de toutes les autres." Archives Royales, Gérard Papers, Gérard to Finance Minister Soudan, 8.1.1937.
17. It is thus argued that the banking crisis was the main factor in splitting Belgium from the gold block. Einzig viewed the Belgian 1935 devaluation as one of the turning points in currency experience between the wars. P. Einzig, *World Finance 1935-37*, London, 1937.
18. See Van der Wee and Tavernier, *La Banque Nationale*, 276.
19. See evidence of E. Franqui to the Commission d'Enquête Parlementaire 17.3.1936. See also M.R. Thielemans, *La Grande Crise et le Gouvernement des Banquiers*, s.l., 1980, 23, from which it appears that Francqui privately confided in November 1934 that he felt devaluation was inevitable.
20. As Van Zeeland, the then vice-governor of the National Bank, reported to Gutt the Finance Minister, "Certains taux d'intérêt sont trop élevés, grèvent l'industrie d'une charge trop lourde. Mais faites attention. Ne touchez pas en ce moment l'édifice bancaire. Il est trop fragile." See C. Gutt, *Pourquoi le Franc Belge Est Tombé*, Bruxelles, 1935, 70.
21. See Triffin, La Théorie, 19.
22. Sir H. Strakosch, The Road to Recovery, *The Economist* (supplement), 5.1.1935.
23. Ruffieux, *La Suisse*, 285.
24. This point of 'economic malthusianism' is strongly put by A. Sauvy, *Histoire Economique de la France entre les Deux Guerres*, Paris, 1967, but see the recent work of Levy-Leboyer.
25. G. Lefranc, *Histoire du Front Populaire*, Paris, 1965, 94.
26. See for example H.W. Arndt, *Economic Lessons of the 1930's*, London, 1943, 149.
27. This was of course not limited to the gold bloc. There was a similar incomprehension relating to exchange rate matters in the U.K. when the British went back onto gold in 1925. See W. Adams Brown, The Conflict of Opinion and Economic Interest in England, Pollard (ed.) *The Gold Standard*, 44.

Index of historical persons

GPSR Compliance

The European Union's (EU) General Product Safety Regulation (GPSR) is a set of rules that requires consumer products to be safe and our obligations to ensure this.

If you have any concerns about our products, you can contact us on ProductSafety@springernature.com

In case Publisher is established outside the EU, the EU authorized representative is:

Springer Nature Customer Service Center GmbH
Europaplatz 3
69115 Heidelberg, Germany

Batch number: 10844675

Printed by Printforce, the Netherlands